The

WITHDRAWN

Theodore Roosevelt

Naturalist *in the* Arena

Edited by Char Miller *and* Clay S. Jenkinson

University of Nebraska Press | *Lincoln*

"'I So Declare It': Roosevelt's Love Affair with Birds," by
Duane G. Jundt, was previously published as "Birdwatcher-
in-Chief: Theodore Roosevelt and America's Birds," *Theodore
Roosevelt Association Journal* 38, no. 1 (Winter-Spring-
Summer 2017): 6–13.

Library of Congress Cataloging-in-Publication Data
Names: Miller, Char, 1951– editor. | Jenkinson, Clay, editor.
Title: Theodore Roosevelt, naturalist in the arena / edited by
Char Miller and Clay S. Jenkinson.
Description: Lincoln: University of Nebraska Press, [2020] |
Includes bibliographical references and index.
Identifiers: LCCN 2019030987
ISBN 9781496213143 (paperback: alk. paper)
ISBN 9781496219831 (epub)
ISBN 9781496219848 (mobi)
ISBN 9781496219855 (pdf)
Subjects: LCSH: Roosevelt, Theodore, 1858–1919. |
Naturalists—United States—Biography. | Presidents—
United States—Biography. | Conservationists—United
States—Biography.
Classification: LCC E757 .T388 2020 |
DDC 973.91/1092 [B]—dc23
LC record available at https://lccn.loc.gov/2019030987

Set in Garamond Premier Pro by Mikala R. Kolander.

Contents

Illustrations

Acknowledgments

Theodore Roosevelt, who knew a thing or two about collaboration, would have understood why we are so grateful to our collaborators in this new study of his enduring work as a naturalist and conservationist. This project, which emerged from a 2017 Theodore Roosevelt Center–sponsored humanities symposium on "Roosevelt: Naturalist in the Arena," grew exponentially as each essay was significantly revised and several new contributors were added to deepen and extend the book's reach. Their collective engagement and good humor kept us all on task—yet another reason for thanks.

Our colleagues at the University of Nebraska Press shared our enthusiasm for this anthology; we are grateful to senior acquisitions editor Bridget Barry, assistant editor Emily Wendell, and many others in production and marketing. A special shout-out to the two anonymous outside reviewers for helping us rethink the book's framing and arguments.

We are especially indebted to the faculty, staff, and students of Dickinson State University in North Dakota for their commitment to the exploration of Theodore Roosevelt, who lived in the badlands of Dakota between 1883 and 1886. Home to the Theodore Roosevelt Center, the DSU community, particularly President Thomas Mitzel, has been unwavering in its support of the center's primary mission: to digitize, disseminate, and interpret all the papers of the twenty-sixth president of the United States, Theodore Roosevelt. This anthology is happily dedicated to the TRC staff and above all to Sharon Kilzer, the center's gifted project manager.

Introduction

CHAR MILLER & CLAY S. JENKINSON

"Like all Americans, I like big things," Theodore Roosevelt told Fourth of July celebrants in Dickinson, North Dakota, in 1886, offering a list that included "big parades, big forests and mountains, big wheat fields, railroads—and herds of cattle too; big factories, steamboats and everything else." But occasionally it was something small that caught and held Roosevelt's attention: such moments could prove as revealing as those that loomed large.

These differing scales played out in intriguing ways when, in 1903, Roosevelt embarked on what was then the most ambitious presidential tour of the United States ever undertaken. In a special seven-car train he traveled fourteen thousand miles, visited twenty-five states, gave 262 speeches, including five major policy addresses, before boisterous crowds, and collected a wide range of gifts from cities, elected officials, trade unions, and average citizens—including a live badger named Josiah, offered to him by a farm girl from Sharon Springs, Kansas. This epic journey was part vacation, part campaign swing fifteen months before the 1904 presidential election, part "royal progress," and part conservation tour. Along the way the president spent two weeks in Yellowstone National Park with his naturalist friend John Burroughs, saw the Grand Canyon for the first time, stood on the shores of the Pacific Ocean for the first time, walked in awe among the redwoods and giant sequoias, and camped for three perfect days in Yosemite National Park with the naturalist and preservationist John Muir.

On this grand tour Roosevelt had also wanted to hunt large game, notably mountain lions in Yellowstone National Park. To that end he corresponded quietly with park superintendent Major John Pitcher about his intentions and made contact with a western guide who might be able to supply TR with hunting dogs. It was the savvy secretary of war Elihu Root (1845–1937) who talked the president out of hunting—not yet illegal—in the nation's first national park. The optics, said Root, would be problematic. A disappointed but stoic Roosevelt wrote, "I will not fire a gun in the Park; then I shall have no explanations to make."[1]

So it is fitting that the ever-enthusiastic president could not wait to talk about the only animal that he bagged in the park, even if was a tiny quadruped, a meadow vole.[2] Its diminutive size did not disappoint the bespectacled Roosevelt, who, seeing it scurrying in the snow, leaped out of his sleigh and captured it in his hat. Roosevelt reckoned, as soon as he had spotted the little creature, that it might be unknown to science. "He wanted it for Dr. Merriam," Burroughs later wrote, "on the chance that it might be a new species. . . . It turned out not to be a new species, as it should have been, but a species new to the Park."[3] Afterwards, while the rest of the party went fishing, TR remained in camp to skin and eviscerate the vole and preserve the pelt with salt, since he had no arsenic in his travel kit. According to biologist and nature writer Michael R. Canfield, Roosevelt emptied "a salt shaker for preservation in the name of science,"[4] with Burroughs reporting that "it was done as neatly as a professional taxidermist would have done it."[5] It is no surprise that Roosevelt was so skilled: as a youth he had taught himself taxidermy and through his early twenties had prepared himself to become a professional naturalist. When he spotted that vole, his instinct and training kicked in. Even as president this most acute politician still thought and acted as a naturalist.

It was as a committed naturalist, too, that he sent a detailed description of the meadow vole to his close friend C. Hart Merriam (1855–1942), who headed up the Division of Biological Survey in the U.S. Department of Agriculture; in 1905 President Roosevelt would grant the agency status as a bureau. "I send you a small tribute in the shape of a skin," he wrote Merriam, "with the attached skull, of a *microtus*, a male, taken out of the lower geyser basin, National Park, Wyoming, April 18, 1903. Its length, head and body, was 4.5 inches; tail to tip, 1.3 inches, of which .2 were the final hairs. The hind foot was .7 of an inch long. I had nothing to put on the skin but salt." Then, with professional caution, Roosevelt added, "I believe it is of no value to you, but send it on the off chance."[6] Merriam graciously thanked TR for the specimen, informed him that he had previously found the vole in Idaho, and acknowledged, no doubt to soften the blow, that the vole had never previously been spotted in Yellowstone National Park.

Roosevelt would have been thrilled to know that this vole is still housed in the collections of the Mammals Division of the National Museum of Natural History, Smithsonian Institution, as #126419, *Microtus montanus nanus*—a small mark of his enduring reputation as a naturalist. This anecdote suggests how integral this kind of work was to Roosevelt's sense of himself. Indeed it was almost as if he had been born to this form of scientific inquiry. In an oft-told story, it was a dead harbor seal that apparently first caught this budding naturalist's eye. When a boy, "Teedie" happened upon its carcass on display on lower Broadway in New York City, he was transfixed and intrigued. He measured it and eventually obtained the skull for what would become the self-styled Roosevelt Museum of Natural History. Roosevelt's natural curiosity, boyish enthusiasm, and love of the outdoors persisted through his youth and adolescence. These qualities also infused his approach to life as a rancher and explorer, police commissioner and governor, vice president and president. Conservation and natural history were parts of a whole for this driven, charismatic public servant. Whether child or adult, Roosevelt approached the natural world with a kind of clear-eyed joy and passionate engagement: "It is an incalculable added pleasure, to any one's sum of happiness if he or she grows to know, even slightly and imperfectly, how to read and enjoy the wonder-book of nature."[7]

Learning how to read Roosevelt is central to *Theodore Roosevelt, Naturalist in the Arena*. Drawing on a weave of interdisciplinary methodologies—biographical, ecological and environmental, literary and political—the anthology probes different facets of this strenuous man's manifold encounters with the great outdoors. It also establishes a critical context for understanding Roosevelt's intellectual and affective response to the natural world, at home and abroad. Plumbing the dimensions of his varied and evolving responses is made easier by TR's considerable abilities as a writer and his astonishing productivity. He knew how to think about what he witnessed, to frame his words and structure his prose to capture its essence, and to write fast. These qualities were manifest in his many books (forty or so), the hundreds of articles, essays, and reviews he crafted over his life, and the endless stream of correspondence that from childhood to death flowed from his hand—one staggering estimate puts the number of letters at more than 150,000! These missives alone fill box after box in his papers in the U.S. Library of Congress and innumerable repositories around the globe. Then there are the countless speeches. Some were extemporaneous (or so they sounded). Others were carefully mapped out (until he went off message). Some were short (or were supposed to be). Others were intended to be major in length (and could ramble on). Some were thankfully bulky—one, a thick sheaf of fifty pages that he had double-folded and tucked into his jacket, helped saved his life in 1912, slowing an assassin's bullet fired during a campaign event in Milwaukee. All these many words, and the ideas and images they contained, form the bulk of the voluminous record that Roosevelt left behind, amounting to one of the largest of any American public figure or private individual.

By digging deep into this mass of primary and secondary sources, the contributors to *Naturalist in the Arena* have been able to reanalyze some key elements of Roosevelt historiography. The first section, "Field Notes," sets the stage by assessing Roosevelt's formative, serious, and underappreciated work as a scientist and curator, observer and recorder. Darrin Lunde, himself a professional naturalist, offers a first-person meditation on the nature of natural history and the scientific ethos that governs why its practitioners kill, describe, catalog, and preserve specimens. In tracing TR's collecting expeditions in the American West, Africa, and South America, and comparing them to his own fieldwork, Lunde sees a fellow traveler carefully plying his craft. "To really understand Roosevelt the naturalist," Lunde concludes, "we need to locate him in the world that he revered—a world that wholeheartedly embraced guns, hunting, and taxidermy as vitally important tools in the naturalists' craft." As with so many perceptions of Roosevelt, it was his pursuit of large animals that caught the attention of his contemporaries and subsequent commentators. But birds, historian Duane Jundt argues, were his first love. What initially drew Roosevelt to them were their songs, perhaps reflecting the fact that, until he got his first pair of glasses at twelve years old, he could barely see. However melodic their calls—and the meadowlark was particularly compelling to him—this was only part of their appeal. A self-aware Roosevelt recognized even at an early age that his marked ability to listen and identify was bound up with the time and place of first hearing. His affinity depended on memory and on the interplay between call and response, singer and listener: "it is hard to tell just how much of the attraction in any bird-note lies in the music itself," Roosevelt once wrote, "and how much in the associations."[8]

The shrewdness found in his written impressions of the natural world gained physical expression every time Roosevelt stepped outside. *Bolted* may have been the more apt verb, for Roosevelt was an inveterate and quick-paced tramper, as any number of friends and colleagues discovered to their chagrin. Even dignitaries who showed up to the White House dressed to the nines for a formal audience with the president learned that Roosevelt did not stand on ceremony. He preferred getting acquainted with people in the rough and tumble, Melanie Choukas-Bradley relates, and there was no place better suited to test their stamina—and thus their fitness, in every sense of that word—than Rock Creek Park in Washington DC. "This surprisingly challenging landscape afforded an energetic president a ready outlet for rock scrambling, horseback riding, swimming, wading, birding, and other naturalist pursuits near 1600 Pennsylvania Avenue," she notes. Particularly daunting were the cross-country jaunts: "Often, especially in the winters and early springs," Roosevelt later wrote, "we would arrange for a point to point walk, not turning aside for anything—for instance, swimming Rock Creek or even the Potomac if it came in our way."[9] A frequent companion on these treks, French ambassador Jules Jusserand (1855–1932), described their arduousness as an outgrowth of Roosevelt's indefatigable energy: "What the President called a walk was a run: no stop, no breathing time, no slacking of speed, but a continuous race, careless of mud, thorns and the rest." Hazards only added spice to these rough jaunts: "A walk with no danger would have seemed to the President like food without salt."[10]

Roosevelt's fervent embrace of Rock Creek Park, this small, "wild playground," led him to fight for its protection with the same ardor that defined his actions on behalf of vast wildernesses in the western United States. He was just as keen to tell stories about these varied landscapes and his encounters with them. The best of them are found not in his *Autobiography* (1913), a pretty workman-like project about his political career, but are scattered across his correspondence, journals, essays, and ephemera. Balancing his scientific insistence on detail and precision with his unadorned prose, he could be objective and opinionated in the same paragraph. Roosevelt's unusual blend of an "open and agile" style, sharp analysis, and considered argument, observe literary scholars Thomas Bailey and Katherine Joslin, animated his private musings and public discourse. As evidence of his ability to pull from various genres to inform his prose, they quote Roosevelt's eagerness to develop a new form of writing, in which "hunting should go hand in hand with the love of natural history, as well as with descriptive and narrative power."[11] Whatever his presumed audience, TR hoped to engage his readers in his lifelong, imaginative quest "to turn experience into language and language into art."

Collectively these chapters remind us that natural history was not a hobby for Roosevelt—it was absolutely central to the meaning of his life and activism. Indeed while in college he seriously considered becoming a professional naturalist; even though his life took a different turn, TR never strayed far from this first, engrossing passion. That engagement may have also influenced whom he counted as friends, colleagues, and collaborators. That Roosevelt drew on the ideas and energies of others does not diminish his many accomplishments, but actually ramifies their import. That vital reciprocity plays out in this volume's second section, "Outside Influences." George Bird Grinnell, Gifford Pinchot, John Muir, and William T. Hornaday were among the many conservationists in close contact with Roosevelt. Their letters and memos filled his inbox—correspondence that could morph into national policy. A lucky subset hiked, hunted, or camped with him, activities from which could emerge new political commitments. These men—Roosevelt's closest advisers and boon companions were almost exclusively male—were among the contemporaries who helped develop a progressive argument for the conservation of natural resources.

Start with George Bird Grinnell (1849–1938), who, as historian John Reiger makes clear, had a profound influence on the younger Roosevelt. It was Grinnell, after all, who caught TR off guard with a critical review of his *Hunting Trips of a Ranchman* (1885). Growing out of Roosevelt's adventures in the North Dakota badlands, this sprawling text earned Grinnell's praise for its "freshness." But it contained errors, Grinnell thought, that were the result of the younger man's limited experience in the West and his as-yet inability to "sift the wheat from the chaff and distinguish the true from the false." Initiating a pattern that would persist throughout his life, Roosevelt showed up unannounced at Grinnell's editorial offices. Typical, too, was his willingness to engage with his critic and seek his guidance. In this instance the two men launched into a rapid-fire conversation that moved from literary criticism to political activism. In short order, they established the Boone and Crockett Club (1887): this new, national conservation organization, comprising hunters committed to the protection and preservation of large-game habitat across the continent, helped promote the conservationist agenda so associated with Roosevelt's subsequent tenure as president. Among its members who did much to advance the related commitments of the club and the Roosevelt administration, was the nation's chief forester, Gifford Pinchot (1865–1946). In his portrait of TR and Pinchot's unusual partnership, Char Miller delves into the interconnection between recreation and work. For them the two were parts of a whole—they boxed, wrestled, and hiked together with the same level of energy that characterized their dovetailing political activism on behalf of conservation. It is safe to say that no president of the United States has had a closer relationship with the chief of the Forest Service, and vice versa: an intensely personal friendship that had its boundaries but was also boundless. In this they made history.

So, too, did Roosevelt and Sierra Club founder John Muir (1838–1914) during their celebrated 1903 camping trip in Yosemite National Park. Underscoring the unusual nature of their meeting—rarely if ever has a president gone off in the woods for three days with a person he had just met—is the manner in which Barb Rosenstock narrates this groundbreaking encounter. A subtext to her award-winning children's book of the two men's fabled tour is the twenty-first-century worry that Richard Louv has highlighted in the title to his best-selling *Last Child in the Woods*. In it he argues that the "child in nature is an endangered species," and that correspondingly "the health of children and the health of the Earth are inseparable." Rosenstock shares Louv's conviction that adults must help "heal the broken bond between youth and nature." By captivating her youthful readers with Muir and Roosevelt's deep affinity for the natural world, which just might entice some of them outdoors, they, too, might recognize that they could join together to "save the planet for future generations."[12]

Yet Rosenstock also provides an artful lesson in how historians reconstruct the past. She probes the origins of Roosevelt and Muir's meeting in Yosemite; gathers the extant evidence and assesses these sources' credibility; and explores how a writer, regardless of genre and target audience, uses these documents and remembrances, these texts and their context, to develop her storyline, construct a narrative, and build a compelling interpretation. Clay S. Jenkinson is as alert to these authorial concerns as they relate to his recasting of Roosevelt's connection with yet another ally, William T. Hornaday (1854–1937). Strikingly Jenkinson opens his chapter with the two men inhabiting roughly the same region at the same time—in 1886, Hornaday was in Miles City, Montana, while Roosevelt was in the Dakota badlands. Each unaware of the other, they reached similar kinds of conclusions about the brutal extermination of the once-thunderous herds of bison that had roamed the northern plains, the most important of which was the felt need to protect what remained of the animals and the range they had inhabited. Yet, despite their similar "conversion experiences," Hornaday and Roosevelt did not meet out west. Instead it was Roosevelt who sought out Hornaday two years later, tracking him down in his curtained-off workspace at the National Museum of Natural History at the Smithsonian. Hornaday had been touting his innovative efforts to construct a lifelike display of bison on the Plains; Roosevelt wanted to know more about the project, so he began peppering the taxidermist with questions, ignoring the cloth screen that Hornaday had erected in hopes of forestalling exactly this kind of interruption. From this original, if initially one-sided conversation grew an effective collaboration to protect and preserve the American bison.

Whether they worked on behalf of the Boone and Crockett Club, the U.S. Forest Service, the Sierra Club, or the American Bison Society—or any of their many analogues that emerged amid the fertile Progressive Era—Roosevelt and his peers assiduously and collaboratively constructed a powerful conservation movement that over time would set aside forests, parks, and refuges to protect habitat and the species that inhabited them; regulate and control the hitherto-unchecked exploitation of the nation's natural resources; and bring about a more potent and democratic nation-state. Collectively these Progressive Era naturalists, scientists, writers, bureaucrats, and politicians invented the world we have inherited.

This grand legacy, and Roosevelt's forceful role in its development, bears as well some troubling domestic and global ramifications. At home, a significant portion of the 150 million acres of national forests that he designated while president—the most by any chief executive—came at the expense of Native American tribes. By the power of his pen and under the authority granted to him by the Dawes Act of 1887, Roosevelt signed off on the transfer of an estimated eighty-six million acres of ancestral and treaty lands to the nascent national forest system. That meant that the Forest Service, another of Roosevelt's landmark achievements, which was established in 1905 to manage these and other forests and grasslands, and whose first chief was Gifford Pinchot, grew at the expense of the rights held by and resources available to the nation's embattled Indigenous peoples.[13]

That for Roosevelt conservation was often embedded with a eugenic impulse and an imperial mien is not mere happenstance. That is one of the takeaway messages of the third section of *Naturalist in the Arena*. In "Natural Politics," historians Elliott West and Ian Tyrrell offer a series of sharp observations about the twenty-sixth president's uncritical reading of social Darwinism and his occasional embrace of its divisive social, racial, and ethnic consequences. Roosevelt, for example, fused his call for the conservation of resources—natural and human, in the United States and internationally—with a deep-seated conviction that some people were more fit than others to control the world and define its future. "Society has no business to permit degenerates to reproduce," Roosevelt asserted in a 1913 letter, "Some day we will realize that the prime duty, the inescapable duty of the *good* citizen of the right type is to leave his or her blood behind him in the world; and that we have no business to permit the perpetuation of citizens of the wrong type."[14] Historian Douglas Brinkley dubs Roosevelt the "premier champion of Anglo-American settlement of North America," and by his sweeping declaration that "Native tribes, Spanish settlers, even French Canadians . . . [were] riffraff who needed to be cleared away like so many weeds,"[15] he imagined his beloved western frontier empty of those who did not match his ideal. Elliott West deftly upends Roosevelt's prejudice in his thorough exploration of the shifting character of the nation-state that Roosevelt grew up in and would ultimately lead. Among other things, he demonstrates that the percentage of foreign-born populations was considerably larger in the frontier West than in the urbanized East—precisely the citified, immigrant-filled region Roosevelt and others routinely used as a foil to celebrate the "purity" of the West.

TR was no more inviting or inclusive in his perceptions of the value of certain nations, nationalities, and peoples. The social and political conclusions that emerged from his overseas travels, particularly those journeys undertaken in the final decade or so of his life, reveal some of the same tensions present in his studies of the American scene. Roosevelt's home ground, Ian Tyrrell argues, framed what the former president saw in Africa and South America, shaping how he interpreted their present and future prospects. Overseas this American visitor cheered on an expanding settler-colonialism much as he had domestically, believing it to be the best and perhaps only path to civilizing the uncivilized. While abroad, and drawing on "his idealized memories and experience of the American West," the former president routinely voiced his anxiety about national vitality or race suicide. Yet in Argentina he was pleasantly surprised to find "no symptoms of that artificially self-produced dwindling of population which is by far the most threatening symptom in the social life of the United States, Canada, and the Australian commonwealths."[16] This perception leads Tyrrell to conclude that the "question for Roosevelt was not how to preserve the purity of blood lines; rather he advocated an evolutionary adaptation of the race in the struggle for survival that human civilization—as much as "nature"—required."

How then should Roosevelt be remembered in the twenty-first century? What are we to make of this man who died in 1919 and would be delighted to know that he remains a subject of considerable conversation and debate one hundred years after he left the arena? Clay Jenkinson explores some of these complicated and complicating possibilities in the final chapter. While it is true that Roosevelt often pondered his legacy, and that his family, friends, and contemporaries wrestled with the same issue, it was not obvious to any of them what would suffice. "Even if Roosevelt had whole-heartedly supported the idea of a grand monument in his honor," and he did not, Jenkinson notes, "it would be hard to know quite how to reduce his hyperactive, hyperkinetic life to a thing of water, concrete, and bronze." Could any combination of static materials embody the "essence of a man of such wide, varied, and outsized achievement"? Whatever decision Roosevelt's puzzled peers might have made, Jenkinson comments, would have run up against a "fundamental paradox"—the erection of "an immobile monument to a man whose life was synonymous with action."

Because this president, a well-trained naturalist and dedicated conservationist, acted as powerfully as he did in defense of the land itself, perhaps the physical environment is where Americans can best encounter and remember Roosevelt's import. For those seeking a vast marker, the 1.2-million-acre Grand Canyon National Park, an early iteration of which Roosevelt had designated as a national monument in 1908, seems up to the monumental task of venerating this man who loved all things big. So do the memorable words he uttered while standing on the canyon's south rim, during a whistle-stop visit in May 1903:

> I hope you will not have a building of any kind, not a summer cottage, a hotel, or anything else, to mar the wonderful grandeur, the sublimity, the great loneliness and beauty of the canyon.
>
> Leave it as it is. You can not improve on it. The ages have been at work on it, and man can only mar it. What you can do is to keep it for your children, your children's children, and for all who come after you, as one of the great sights which every American if he can travel at all should see.[17]

Roosevelt never said anything as visionary about a smaller, less well-known candidate for top honors, a modest eighty-eight-acre island that now bears his name and is located close to the Virginia side of the Potomac River. It is not even clear that he ever visited what is now called Roosevelt Island.[18] In this he is not alone. Part of the secluded site's charm is how few people walk along its trails, shaded by elm, cherry, dogwood, and mulberry, or stop and listen to the sonorous songs of white-throated sparrows, Carolina chickadees, Baltimore orioles, or the occasional eastern meadowlark. This discreet space stands in stark contrast to the massive marble monuments for Presidents Washington, Jefferson, and Lincoln. Yet no less a figure than President Lyndon Johnson recognized the tranquil appeal of "this little wild island in the center of a historic river," a pivotal location that Theodore Roosevelt surely would have appreciated. He would have been grateful too for Johnson's suggestion that Americans should repair to this sylvan isle whose very nature would draw their attention to Roosevelt's "generous, passionate spirit" and his far-reaching legacy: "He fought the trusts, he fought the selfish interests, he fought those who plundered this land. The Nation changed because of what he said, and because he put his words into action."[19]

Notes

1. Quoted in Douglas Brinkley, *The Wilderness Warrior: Theodore Roosevelt and the Crusade for America* (New York: HarperCollins Publishers, 2009), 510.

2. John Burroughs, *Camping & Tramping with Roosevelt* (Boston: Houghton Mifflin Company, 1907), 67.

3. Burroughs, *Camping & Tramping with Roosevelt*, 66–67.

4. Michael R. Canfield, *Theodore Roosevelt in the Field* (Chicago: University of Chicago Press, 2015), 243.

5. Burroughs, *Camping & Tramping with Roosevelt*, 66.

6. Etling E. Morison, *The Letters of Theodore Roosevelt* (Cambridge MA: Harvard University Press, 1951), 3:461–63.

7. Theodore Roosevelt, *Outdoor Pastimes of an American Hunter* (New York: Charles Scribner's Sons, 1908), 339.

8. Roosevelt, *Outdoor Pastimes of an American Hunter*, 339.

9. Theodore Roosevelt, *The Autobiography of Theodore Roosevelt* (New York: Charles Scribner's Sons, 1913), 30.

10. Jules Jean Jusserand, *What Me Befell: The Reminiscences of J. J. Jusserand* (Boston: Houghton Mifflin Company, 1933), 332–33.

11. Roosevelt, *Outdoor Pastimes of an American Hunter*, 330.

12. Richard Louv, *Last Child in the Woods: Saving Our Children from Nature-Deficit Disorder* (Chapel Hill NC: Algonquin Books, 2008), 135.

13. Theodore Catton, *American Indians and National Forests* (Tucson: University of Arizona Press, 2016), 35–53; an earlier and parallel study of how the Park Service bene-

fited from and extended this exploitation is Mark David Spence, *Dispossessing the Wilderness: Indian Removal and the Making of the National Parks* (New York: Oxford University Press, 1999).

14. Theodore Roosevelt to Charles B. Davenport, January 3, 1913, Image 1242, American Philosophical Library, https://www.dnalc.org/view/11219-t-Roosevelt-letter-to-C-Davenport-about-degenerates-reproducing-.html.

15. Brinkley, *The Wilderness Warrior*, 243.

16. Theodore Roosevelt, *A Book-Lover's Holidays in the Open* (New York: Charles Scribner's Sons, 1916), 103.

17. Theodore Roosevelt, Proclamation 794: Grand Canyon National Monument, January 11, 1908, National Archives, https://catalog.archives.gov/id/28894539; *Address of President Roosevelt at Grand Canyon, Arizona, May 6, 1903*, Theodore Roosevelt Papers, Library of Congress Manuscript Division, http://www.theodorerooseveltcenter.org/Research/Digital-Library/Record?libID=o289796, Theodore Roosevelt Digital Library, Dickinson State University.

18. Jusserand recounts that occasionally the president led the venturesome group "to the Potomac islands, now beautiful gardens full of flowers, but then mud shoals, with thick cane-breaks so high we had to follow in close formation not to lose track of our leader," but he offers little other identifying information. Jusserand, *What Me Befell*, 333–34. See Melanie Choukas-Bradley's chapter in this volume, in which she offers compelling evidence that the islands Jusserand refers to are within reach of the northern bank of the Potomac, that is, on the opposite shore from Virginia.

19. Lyndon Johnson, "Remarks on the Dedication of the Theodore Roosevelt Memorial in Washington," October 27, 1967, http://www.presidency.ucsb.edu/ws/index.php?pid=28506.

Theodore Roosevelt, Naturalist *in the* Arena

PART 1

Field Notes

I

Beauty and Tragedy in the Wilderness

The Naturalism of Theodore Roosevelt

DARRIN LUNDE

Theodore Roosevelt was a New Yorker—a *Knickerbocker*—born on Manhattan Island in 1858, and raised in a stylish townhouse on East 20th Street. Commerce thrived in the northern city through the years of the Civil War, and although his neighborhood bustled with merchants and Union soldiers, little Theodore was more inclined to focus on the ants marching along the slate sidewalk under his feet. Like most children, he had an innate affinity for nature and, although horse-drawn carriages rumbled over the cobblestone street mere footsteps from his home, Theodore honed his hearing to pick out the faintest birdsongs over the din. In the neighborhood of his youth, civilization overpowered nature; yet it was in the heart of New York City that Theodore Roosevelt first made up his mind to become a naturalist.

Roosevelt recalled one transformative incident in particular. He was just seven years old and walking down Broadway past a familiar marketplace when something caught his eye. Amid the usual push-carts of fruits and vegetables lay the large, dull mass of some kind of animal—it was a seal, dead less than a day. Stretched out on a board in the market, the seal may have been put out to draw paying customers, but it proved most effective in attracting young Theodore. Nose to nose with an exotic specimen from the wilds of nature, he was fascinated with the beast. Best of all it was something he could study in detail and touch. He could run his fingers through its lush pelage, or tap his fingernail on the seal's gleaming white teeth. Day after day Roosevelt returned to the market to study the seal. He wanted to possess it, so that he could take it home to put on display. Theodore eventually got his wish when he acquired the seal's skull, which he used to found his own museum—the "Roosevelt Museum of Natural History."[1]

When I first learned the story of Theodore's museum, it really stirred my interest because I had got my start as a naturalist in much the same way. Like Roosevelt I grew up in New York City, where nature always seemed so small and insignificant, and like Roosevelt I had a formative experience with an "exotic" specimen that prompted me to start my own youthful museum—the "Lunde Museum of Natural History."

I was seven or eight years old and on my first trip to the country just a few hours northwest of the city. It was a hot summer day, and I was free to explore an overgrown meadow on my own. The grass was as high as I stood tall (nobody worried about ticks back then) and I pulled wildflowers loose from their stalks as I walked. Grasshoppers sprung before me, leading me to the shores of an old farm pond hidden in the tall grass. Dragonflies hovered over the water. Pollywogs swarmed in the shallows. Frogs plunged into the water at my feet. I was captivated. I had no idea that such a place could really exist, a place where you could be enveloped in nature.

Walking the shores of that frog pond, I sensed that everything seemed alive until I stumbled upon the skeleton of a deer half buried in the ground, like a fossil. Cracked and sun-bleached, the bones held a special power over me, for of all the animals swirling around me the skeleton was the only one I could hold in my hands and study. All the other animals would soon be nothing more than memories because far off in the distance I could already hear my parents calling. It was time to go home. My dreamy immersion in nature would soon come to an end—no more frog pond, no flowery meadow, no freedom to wander, and no chance to explore.

The car horn honked and I crouched down to get a closer look at that deer skeleton. It was nearly perfectly clean. Picking up the skull I marveled at its intricacies—the delicacy of its teeth and the mystery of the swirls of paper-thin bone inside its nose. That skull was as fascinating as it was beautiful and, just as soon as I held it in my hands, I was overcome by a powerful urge to carry it home.

Like young Roosevelt's seal skull, my deer skull provided me with a link back to the wonders of nature; like young Roosevelt's museum, my youthful museum was the start of my own lifelong dedication to natural history collections. Before my first trip to the country I had found it hard to believe that wild animals and wilderness really existed. Growing up in a semi-urban environment, I had no idea there were actually places where you might see wildlife living free, places where you could wander alone in solitude. Until, that is, I discovered that pond in the grassy meadow. It was because of my formative encounters at that specific location that I became obsessed with the world of nature. Yet it was an obsession that had to be realized in a most unusual way—through preserved specimens. My life was in the city, but I adapted by accumulating natural history specimens in my home.

Theodore Roosevelt was much the same. Prior to his discovery of the seal on Broadway, Roosevelt had mostly only read about natural history. He was a rather sickly boy who suffered all kinds of ailments, but most of all he struggled with asthma. Doctors did not know how to treat the disease, and it was never really certain whether he would survive to adulthood. Trapped inside all day, he found respite in his father's library, which he described as having a certain "gloomy respectability." Here Roosevelt immersed himself in books about animals and outdoor adventure, and any books that combined the two proved especially attractive.

Some of his favorite books were the stories of Captain Mayne Reid, which were full of descriptions of young boys who went on vigorous adventures in the wilderness. One of Reid's books in particular must have been especially inspiring to young Roosevelt, because it presaged much of his naturalist's career. *The Boy Hunters* details the exploits of three brothers sent off by their father on an expedition to shoot a white buffalo for a great museum in Europe. The book describes how they kept all kinds of natural history treasures

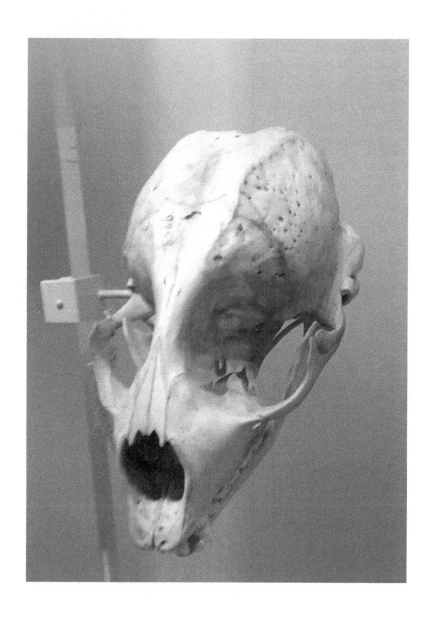

1. Seal skull collected by Theodore Roosevelt. Darrin Lunde collection.

in their home: "Horns of the stag and elk were fastened to the hewn logs . . . In addition to these were skins of rare birds and quadrupeds, artistically preserved by stuffing, and placed on pedestals around the wooden walls. There were glass cases, too, containing moths, butterflies, and other insects, impaled upon pins, and arranged in systematic order. In short, this hall resembled a little museum."[2] Decades later Roosevelt admitted that it was his encounter with the dead seal on Broadway and his readings of the Mayne Reid adventures that fired his lifelong interests as a naturalist.[3]

As for myself, the north shore of Staten Island in the 1970s may not have been as urban as the other boroughs of New York City—the Bronx, Queens, or Brooklyn—but I grew up knowing that I was a New Yorker. My neighborhood was a weird combination of graffiti-tagged buildings, weedy lots glistening with bits of broken glass, and old wooden houses in the shadow of the Bayonne Bridge. To the west of my childhood home, toward the Kill van Kull, there was an oil refinery—a jungle of pipes nestled in a cordillera of petroleum tanks that occasionally caught fire, keeping half the island from school on account of the toxic fumes. To the south was Fresh Kills—the word *kill* being the Dutch word for stream—where the largest garbage dump in the world was then located. Every piece of trash from New York City was barged upstream into Fresh Kills. Depending on which way the wind was blowing, I could wake up in the morning smelling petrochemicals or garbage.

I grew up knowing that my family—at least the old New York Dutch side of the family—had lived on the north shore of Staten Island for hundreds of years, going all the way back to the first settling of the island in the late 1600s. I learned how the names of many of the north-south streets were those of distant relatives, the streets having been laid out to demarcate the boundaries of neighboring family farms. I often imagined what it must have been like when, beneath all the asphalt and concrete, the land was rural, even wild.

The Roosevelts had deep roots in New York, too, and were among the wealthiest families in the city. When the American Museum of Natural History (AMNH) was founded in 1869, Theodore's father—

Theodore Sr.—was one of its first trustees. The museum's charter was signed in Theodore's front parlor when he was just ten years old, and the younger Roosevelt was present for the unpacking of the first specimens shipped to the new museum.

Young Roosevelt knew that, in addition to public exhibits, museums kept vast collections of scientific specimens behind the scenes. Unlike the specimens on exhibit, which are typically positioned in dramatic poses, scientific specimens are prepared to fit in tidy cabinet drawers, one after the other. Most importantly, study specimens are individually tagged with data summarizing such things as where and when the specimen was killed, measurements, and its scientific name. Our most basic knowledge of the diversity of life on earth comes from the study of these kinds of research specimens, while the specimens on exhibit help the public understand that diversity.

Roosevelt was interested in both kinds of collections, and he worked constantly to build up his museum. He took taxidermy lessons when he was about twelve years old, mounting a number of bird specimens still on exhibit in the AMNH. He became proficient with firearms and used them to collect bird specimens. Like a good museum curator, he labeled each specimen with his own, specially printed "Roosevelt Museum" tags, and he kept meticulous catalogues of all his specimens. By the time he was in college, Roosevelt had grown his research collection to 224 mammals, 931 birds, 50 reptiles, 130 amphibians, and 160 fish—an impressive 1,495 specimens in total. The seal on Broadway had clearly made a lasting impression on Roosevelt, forever grounding his thought process in the truths that can be gleaned from the careful study of nature through both observations of living animals in the field and the study of preserved specimens in museums.[4]

Although I did not have the benefit of a taxidermy instructor (I taught myself through experimentation and, later, from mail-order kits), preserving animal specimens is not nearly as difficult as it might seem. Much of it is intuitive once you overcome any initial squeamishness. I cannot really even remember my earliest forays into the craft because I began so young and informally. I had

2. Darrin Lunde as a young taxidermist. Darrin Lunde collection.

always saved treasures from nature—dried insects, pressed plants, and old bones—but things took a serious turn when I started picking up dead birds and mammals. Opossums were frequent road-kill on Staten Island back then. Vacant lots were being developed for housing and these fascinating animals were flushed from their homes and squished on the streets along with squirrels and the occasional raccoon.

I often found animals too late, the carcasses already festering with maggots and unsuitable for taxidermy, but, even so, getting a nice skull was simply a matter of cutting off the head, peeling off the skin, and stripping away the flesh. I also experimented with preserving smaller specimens whole in jars of rubbing alcohol. When properly done, such fluid-preserved specimens should be injected to ensure that the insides of the critter are well preserved, but hypodermic needles are not so easy for a ten-year-old to obtain. Instead I cut a little slit in each animal—many of them mice that I caught with traps—so that the alcohol could flow inside. I remember eating a lot of Hellman's Real Mayonnaise in those days, not because I had any particular craving but because those were the very best jars for alcohol-preserved specimens—wide-mouthed and big enough to hold a dead bullfrog.

People assumed I was a psychopath—a youngster well on his way to becoming the next serial killer! My true interests, though, were entirely focused on zoology, never straying into anything remotely akin to macabre fascination. If anything, I always found specimen preparation tedious, perhaps sometimes even a little disgusting, but the thought of a beautifully finished specimen always kept me going. Like Roosevelt, I was much less interested in the process of preserving animal specimens than in forming a microcosm of nature for study. I was determined to possess some semblance of nature through the creation of my own natural history museum.

Museum naturalists have always been an odd bunch—never very numerous or well understood—but after graduating from Cornell University, I was fortunate enough to move directly into a position at the American Museum of Natural History in New York City. Mammals are my specialty, and my twenty years of full-time service at the AMNH come back to me as a series of journeys to the remotest parts of South America, Africa, and Southeast Asia. These were not tours but rather scientific collecting expeditions to remote and largely unexplored forests far from any tourist attractions. A typical expedition would last weeks, if not months, as our small scientific team bushwhacked from one suitable campsite to another, all the while collecting specimens.

As part of my scientific equipment I often toted a shotgun for shooting animals out of the trees and I hauled traps to set in the forest for all different kinds of mice and shrews. In the evenings I strung nets to capture bats and would wander the forest trails with a headlight, shooting still more specimens through the dark of the night. Part scientist and part explorer, my purpose was to collect zoological specimens by the hundreds—and by *collect* I mean *kill and preserve*, a fact easily forgotten today.

After the American Museum of Natural History, I moved on to the Smithsonian's National Museum of Natural History in Wash-

3. Darrin Lunde collecting scientific specimen in Central African Republic, 1996, for the American Museum of Natural History. Darrin Lunde collection.

ington DC, where scientists are still going off on expeditions to collect and preserve scientific specimens for study today. Despite all we do know about animals, the natural world remains only partially explored. New species are still being discovered, along with new information that can only be gathered from specimens. It is a science that, despite all the technological advances of the past century, is still very much like it was in Roosevelt's time. If we are to truly understand Roosevelt's complex life as a naturalist, we need to locate him in this same naturalist's world. This is why I decided to write a book about Roosevelt the naturalist—to tell his story from my own perspective as a kindred spirit.

By the time he was a teenager, Roosevelt's passion for natural history had turned into an all-out obsession with birds. He knew all the birds of the eastern United States by sight and sound. John James Audubon had already set the tone for collecting that carried into Theodore's day, but it was Audubon's student—Spencer Baird (1823–87)—who really transformed ornithologists into hardcore field collectors. Like so many museum naturalists, he had gotten his start by building up his own natural history museum as a young boy, amassing hundreds of specimens before formally beginning his studies.

As the first curator of the Smithsonian's nascent natural history museum, Baird was so determined to build up a study collection that he sent a railroad car full of specimens that he had personally collected down to Washington DC in order to enhance the Smithsonian's collection. Not satisfied with the numbers of animals he could collect on his own, he enlisted a cadre of collectors to grow the Smithsonian's collections to more than 150,000 specimens in its first decade alone. Baird made a special effort to recruit soldiers and army medics for collectors because they were often stationed in far western forts, where they had ready access to little-known animals on the American frontier. Roosevelt idolized these adventurous zoological collectors, declaring that he wanted to become a naturalist like John James Audubon or Spencer Baird.[5]

Roosevelt got his first chance to play the role of a museum collector when his family took an extended vacation through Egypt and the Middle East when he was just was fourteen years old. Almost every day he collected specimens, at first buying them in markets, but when the family rented a touring boat to take them on a weeks-long journey up the Nile, he learned how to use his shotgun effectively to ride off on a donkey in search of birds—and an occasional bat—along the Nile's crocodile-infested shores. He never collected more birds than he could prepare as specimens, and much of his time was spent hunched at a table taking notes and measurements of his specimens before stuffing them. His sister complained that whenever he appeared she invariably heard the words *bird* and *skin*. His brother Elliott resented having to share a room with someone who left the guts of animals in the washbasin. Roosevelt merely shrugged off his lack of cleanliness as part of being a bird collector, stating, "I suppose that all growing boys tend to be grubby; but the ornithological small boy, or indeed the boy with the taste for natural history of any kind, is generally the very grubbiest of all."[6]

In 1876 Roosevelt went off to Harvard, "devoted to out-of-doors natural history" and determined to "become a scientific man of the Audubon, or Wilson, of Baird, or Coues type—a man like Hart Merriam, or Frank Chapman, or Hornaday, to-day."[7] All of these men had made their careers collecting specimens for natural history museums. Growing up, Theodore had always assumed he would be obliged to enter the world of business, like every other male in his family. Shortly after entering Harvard, however, he had a serious conversation with his father—the man whom Theodore revered above all others—and was pleasantly surprised to learn that he was supportive of his scientific ambitions. He said that if Theodore wished to become a scientific man, he could do so, but that he must be absolutely sure that he "really intensely desired to do scientific work" and that, if he went into science, he must make it "a serious career." Roosevelt Sr. went on to explain that he had enough money to enable him to take up such a career but that he "must not dream of taking it up as a dilettante."[8]

As a freshman at Harvard, Roosevelt was certain of his future as a

4. Image of one of Roosevelt's bat study skins. Photo by Megan Krol, 2018. Darrin Lunde collection.

natural scientist. For the spring break of his freshman year, he planned an expedition to collect birds in the Adirondacks. He wrote home: "By the way, as the time when the birds are beginning to come back is approaching, I wish you would send me my gun, with all the cartridges you can find."[9] Roosevelt had been to the Adirondacks with his family for summer vacations three times before, but this time he was planning his expedition to coincide with the peak of the breeding season, when all the birds were in full plumage and song. As soon as the spring semester was over Roosevelt was up north observing birds, writing detailed notes on the breeding behavior and collecting representative specimens for science.

Roosevelt had become an expert at observing and collecting birds, but the very best naturalists made their reputations by writing research papers that presented new information, of which he had none. All Theodore had were two boyhood notebooks from his family vacations: "Journal of a Trip to the Adirondacks" and his more substantial "Notes on the Fauna of the Adirondack Mountains." These were filled with anecdotal accounts of animals he observed on these trips, but in making a spring expedition he was hoping to collect enough additional data to transform his notes into something he could publish.

Roosevelt returned to his family's summer retreat at Oyster Bay, Long Island, and in mid-July 1877, he published his first ornithological work, *The Summer Birds of the Adirondacks in Franklin County, N.Y.* To his delight, C. Hart Merriam—one of Roosevelt's naturalist heroes—gave his publication a favorable review, mentioning that it covered ninety-seven species and that "it bears prima facie evidence of reliability," providing "exactly what most needed, i.e., exact and thoroughly reliable information."[10] Encouraged, he followed up with a second publication—*Notes on Some of the Birds of Oyster Bay*—yet intellectually Roosevelt remained somewhat adrift. None of his professors seemed to notice or care much about his passion for outdoor natural history. Without the mentorship so vital to a burgeoning scientist's development, at times it seemed he was carrying on his studies solely to please his father. More distressing, his father had fallen ill, and when he died in February 1878, Roosevelt was devastated.

As he did whenever he reached a traumatic turning point in his life, Roosevelt dealt with his grief by taking strenuous trips into the wilderness, this time going all the way up to the deep woods of northern Maine, where he trekked for miles in search of game to hunt. He befriended his guide, Bill Sewall, who became something of a father figure to him while he still mourned. His grief finally subsided when he found an entirely new outlet for his emotional energy back at Harvard, when he was introduced to the beautiful Alice Lee, the woman who would soon be his first wife.

While courting Alice, Roosevelt finally accepted the fact that the faunal naturalism that so engrossed him was going out of style. Harvard was just one of many schools abandoning the old-style natural history curriculum in favor of laboratory-based science, and as Roosevelt's relationship with Alice blossomed, he slowly moved away from the idea of becoming a professional naturalist. Later in life he insisted that the ultimate blame for his decision rested with Harvard, which "utterly ignored the possibilities of the faunal naturalist, the outdoor naturalist and observer of nature. They treated biology as purely a science of the laboratory and the microscope, a science whose adherents were to spend their time in the study of minute forms of marine life, or else in section-cutting and the study of the tissues of the higher organisms under the microscope." He went on to lament: "There was a total failure to understand the great variety of kinds of work that could be done by naturalists, including what could be done by the outdoor naturalists." He continued: "My taste was specialized in a totally different direction, and I had no more desire or ability to be a microscopist and section-cutter than to be a mathematician. Accordingly I abandoned all thought of becoming a scientist."[11]

Instead Theodore focused his devotion on Alice. As if to prove to her that he was through studying birds and mammals, he dissolved his boyhood museum. Painstakingly accumulated over the course of a decade, his collection included hundreds of scientific specimens representing thousands of hours of dedicated work. Most of his specimens were sent to the Smithsonian Institution. A few years later he donated what remained (about twenty specimens) to the American Museum of Natural History. At the time Theodore Roosevelt was just another amateur naturalist—one of many thousands who routinely donated their specimens to these museums. Nobody could have predicted that these specimens would one day gain a degree of cultural value, thanks to their famous collector. They were simply valuable specimens from a serious naturalist—nearly all of these specimens remain in the Smithsonian Institution and the American Museum today.

Roosevelt went on to study law at Columbia and soon after got interested in politics. He became a reformer and a man of letters—a politician—yet the naturalist in him never really died. He found a surrogate for specimen collecting in the form of big-game hunting. He wished to become an expert on North America's largest mammals. Hunting these species gave him a context for interacting with them directly in the wild. More importantly his hunts ensured that he would have a sufficient number of readers when it came time to publish. Not many people were interested in reading about the secret lives of pronghorn and elk, but by presenting his observations in the context of an exciting hunt he was able to reach a wider audience. For his first big-game hunt he went west to shoot a buffalo. He wanted to experience something of the untamed West before its inevitable transformation. Although the bison herds had already been severely shot out, Roosevelt was drawn to bagging a bison as the quintessential symbol of the old West. It was his ticket to membership among bona fide western hunters. His hunting guide and hosts regarded him with considerable skepticism at first, but his sheer determination eventually won them over, so much so that they wanted to see him get his bison as much as he wanted to get it himself. He did, after a long hard hunt.

In the West Roosevelt rekindled his passion for nature. He was so captivated with the land that he invested a sizable portion of his wealth into raising cattle in the North Dakota badlands. His plan was to divide his time between New York state politics and western ranching and hunting. It was not too long after settling into his new life that Alice, his first wife, died from complications during childbirth. Devastated, Roosevelt left the care of his newborn to his older sister and once again retreated deep into the western wilderness to mourn.

While out west Roosevelt wanted to study animals while playing the role of a predator, all the while recording his observations on the hidden lives of his prey. *Hunting Trips of a Ranchman* (1885) was the initial result, and it set him on course to become the ardent conservationist we revere today.

One of the first to review the book was George Bird Grinnell (1849–1938), the respected editor of *Forest and Stream* magazine. Like Roosevelt he started out with his own boyhood museum, but unlike Roosevelt he went on to earn a doctoral degree while studying at the Yale Peabody Museum. Grinnell had already spent a decade in the American West when Roosevelt first came on the scene, and it was Grinnell who helped Roosevelt solidify some of the conservation ideas he had been contemplating. As the founder of the Audubon Society, Grinnell wanted to found a similar society for the conservation of mammals. Roosevelt came through with the idea of founding the Boone and Crockett Club in 1887—a conservation organization dedicated to the idea that our natural resources were not inexhaustible, but that they could be saved through wise management.

The tenets of the Boone and Crockett Club summarize the ethic to which Roosevelt would adhere for the rest of his life: (1) to promote manly sport with the rifle; (2) to promote travel and exploration in the wilderness; (3) to work for the preservation of large game; (4) to promote inquiry into the natural history of wild animals; and (5) to promote the interchange of ideas on hunting, travel, and exploration.

Soon after the death of Alice, Roosevelt married Edith Carow, a childhood sweetheart he had known almost all his life. Through the prime of his working life, Roosevelt amassed an impressive political career. He made his first political forays as New York state assemblyman (1881–84), then served on the U.S. Civil Service Commission (1889–95) and as police commissioner of NYC (1895–97). He

5. A studio photograph of Theodore Roosevelt as he liked to see himself. Theodore Roosevelt Collection, Houghton Library, Harvard University.

would become the assistant secretary of the Navy (1897–98), from which post, in the aftermath of the Spanish American War, he would win election as governor of New York State (1899–1900). Roosevelt was chagrinned when he became vice president of the United States in 1901 under President William McKinley, thinking he would be bored in the job. That changed when McKinley was assassinated: Roosevelt served out the remainder of McKinley's career and won reelection nearly four years later.

As president of the United States, Roosevelt spent comparatively little time outdoors, though his favorite local haunt was Rock Creek Park. Instead he focused his energies on his conservation agenda, and we should be thankful that he did because he was responsible for establishing five national parks, 51 wildlife refuges, 150 national forests, and 18 national monuments, totaling some 230 million acres of protected land. Oftentimes this is where the story of Roosevelt's life as a naturalist and conservationist comes to an end, but it was in the years immediately following his time in the White House that Roosevelt finally realized his lifelong dream of becoming exactly the kind of museum naturalist he had aspired to be since discovering the seal on Broadway.

After leaving the White House in 1909, Roosevelt was free to do anything he wanted, and it is significant that he chose to lead a nearly year-long scientific collecting expedition in Africa for the Smithsonian Institution. Although it is sometimes referred to as "Roosevelt's safari," what Roosevelt had in mind was something far more ambitious than this moniker suggests. Roosevelt had seen how the advent of transcontinental railroads changed the American West, transforming it from a wilderness teeming with wildlife to a human-shaped landscape of ranchlands, towns, and cities. The same kind of transformation was already underway in East Africa, and Roosevelt wanted to study the life histories of wildlife before the inevitable encroachment of humanity. He wanted to see vast herds of big game and to bring along a team of scientists to collect valuable scientific specimens, whether they were impressive game species, like kudu or eland, or little-known bats and mice. What Roosevelt had in mind, and what he planned and executed, was the largest and most intensive scientific collecting expedition ever launched. He was, at last, finally living his childhood dream of becoming an intrepid museum naturalist.

Working his way through Kenya, Uganda, and Sudan, Roosevelt was joined by a team of naturalists intent on systematically collecting thousands of specimens of mostly birds, mammals, and plants. He added an impressive number of specimens to the Smithsonian's archives while in Africa. Although the expedition is often unfairly dismissed as merely a hunting trip, Roosevelt collected big-game animals with the same scientific rigor as a mammalogist, preserving the skin and skeletal material of almost every animal he shot. In total Theodore collected 296 big-game animals while his son Kermit took 216, for a total of 512 large animal specimens—just about ten percent of the roughly five thousand mammal specimens taken, most of which were tiny shrews, bats, and mice. Today the results of the Smithsonian-Roosevelt Expedition still stand as the single most important scientific record of the East African fauna, a collection that contemporary conservation scientists continue to utilize in their research.

As a naturalist Theodore Roosevelt is most often remembered for protecting millions of acres of wilderness, but he was also committed to something more—preserving a memory of the natural world before the onslaught of industrial civilization. Throughout his life Theodore Roosevelt strived to get out into nature to experience its beauty, but he was unusual in also wanting to understand something of the harsh life and death struggles of the wild. He wanted to understand nature as it truly existed, and was just as strong an advocate for making detailed observations of behaviors as he was for collecting scientific specimens for future study. He felt it was misguided to turn away from the natural history of the Audubon and Baird tradition, and with his leadership of the Smithsonian African Expedition, he hoped to make this point clear. Indeed Roosevelt's high-profile expedition was a big part of the nation's renewed interest in zoological exploration. Many hundreds of museum collecting expeditions were launched in the decades following Roosevelt's example, and natural history museums across the country experienced their most rapid growth through this time.

As more time goes by, and as our views on what constitutes a true naturalist change, it is important to have some insight into the world of the museum naturalists of Roosevelt's time. To really understand Roosevelt the naturalist, we need to locate him in the naturalists' world that he revered—a world that wholeheartedly embraced guns, hunting, and taxidermy as vitally important tools in the naturalists' craft. He had a direct, and often bloody, involvement with nature, but he loved the visceral knowledge that came from his wild adventures. He understood that in the pursuit of knowledge "soundness of head" was more important than mere "softness of heart." From his abundant firsthand experiences with nature, he knew that the true lives of animals in the wild were of necessity harsh. This enabled him to engage in his scientific pursuits without guilt: "Death by violence, death by cold, death by starvation—these are the normal endings of the stately and beautiful creatures of the wilderness."[12]

Notes

1. Theodore Roosevelt, *Theodore Roosevelt: An Autobiography* (New York: Charles Scribner's Sons, 1913), 14.

2. Thomas Mayne Reid, *The Boy Hunters; or Adventures in Search of a White Buffalo* (1855; repr., Chicago: M. A. Donohue & Co., n.d.), 10–11.

3. Roosevelt, *Theodore Roosevelt: An Autobiography*, 14–15.

4. *Catalog of Zoölogical Specimens*, Theodore Roosevelt Birthplace National Historic Site, https://www.theodorerooseveltcenter.org/Research/Digital-Library/Record?libID =0284955, Theodore Roosevelt Digital Library, Dickinson State University.

5. Roosevelt, *Theodore Roosevelt: An Autobiography*, 23.

6. Roosevelt, *Theodore Roosevelt: An Autobiography*, 20.

7. Roosevelt, *Theodore Roosevelt: An Autobiography*, 23.

8. Roosevelt, *Theodore Roosevelt: An Autobiography*, 24.

9. Elting E. Morison, ed., *The Letters of Theodore Roosevelt* (Cambridge MA: Harvard University Press, 1951), 1:26.

10. Paul Russell Cutright, *Theodore Roosevelt: The Naturalist* (New York: Harper & Brothers, 1956), 18.

11. Roosevelt, *Theodore Roosevelt: An Autobiography*, 24–25.

12. Theodore Roosevelt, *African Game Trails*, edited by Peter Capstick. (New York: St. Martin's Press, 1988; originally published New York: Charles Scribner's Sons, 1910), 239.

2

Theodore Roosevelt

"The Outdoor Man Who Writes"

THOMAS CULLEN BAILEY & KATHERINE JOSLIN

Theodore Roosevelt began writing letters and journals as soon as he learned to put pen to paper—and he did not put the pen down until the very day before he died in January 1919. He was prolific, writing dozens of books, hundreds of articles, editorials, essays, and thousands of letters. He wrote in many genres, was adept at gathering his essays into books, and considered himself a man of letters, a professional writer who during many years of his life made much of his money to support his large family by selling his written words to the leading magazines and book publishers of the day.

Very little of that writing would be considered to be pure nature writing, if one defines "pure" as the sort of essays and books written by Henry David Thoreau, John Burroughs, and John Muir about America and, in England, by such writers as Gilbert White. Roosevelt's protean mind was not limited in such a way, and his goals in writing were such that he could move easily from hunting literature into nature writing; from writing narrative histories of the West into long passages describing landscape; from writing about exploring the Brazilian wilderness into passages, sometimes lyrical, sometimes exactingly scientific, about the beauties and noteworthy phenomena of the natural world through which the troubled and endangered explorers were hoping to safely pass. He considered an open and agile style his central strength as a writer, and all his life demonstrated his marked ability to think about more than one thing at the same time. For him nature encompassed human endeavor, enclosed it, sustained it, so that, when he chose, he could stop writing history, for instance, and describe natural beauties and curiosities, in a perfectly spontaneous way.

Reviewers of his *Outdoor Pastimes of an American Hunter* (1905) caught these strengths. "It would be hard to put one's finger on another writer on sport who is so keen an observer as President Roosevelt," wrote the reviewer in the *Independent*.[1] His sentences moved the reviewer in *Public Opinion* to observe: "It is written by a man who is a delightful 'raconteur,' and who has an intense conviction of the virile reality of his own life and of the deep integrity of the life around him."[2]

Roosevelt dedicated this particular book to "Oom John," his affectionate term for "Uncle" John Burroughs: "Every lover of outdoor life must feel a sense of affectionate obligation to you." Clearly the president yearned to do for the hunting tale what Burroughs had done for nature writing. Books on hunting, he quipped, had been written by the rich and the dull: "They are not literature, any more than treatises on farriery and cooking are literature." Itineraries and records of kills are as thrilling to read as Baedeker travel guides, he joked drily. But an "out-door faunal naturalist," who lived for a year in the wild and studied the creatures around him, might well craft a book that "would make a contribution of permanent value to our nature literature."[3] Roosevelt longed to write such a book and worked to create a literary genre almost of his own making: "Hunting should go hand in hand with the love of natural history, as well as with descriptive and narrative power."[4] In the *New York Times*, Scribner's first ad read "Outdoor Pastimes of an American Homer," a typo that delighted the president.

Roosevelt's life as the outdoor man who writes began as he left Harvard in 1880 and crafted an experimental hunting narrative, "Sou' Sou' Southerly."[5] A look at this piece will reveal his many talents in writing, including nature writing, while it can be seen to contain and predict the multifarious nature of the writer to come. Indeed this essay defines a method, mode, and mood that would flower fully in 1914, in *Through the Brazilian Wilderness*.

In tarpaulin jackets, hip boots, and sou'westerly hats, Theodore, twenty-two, and Elliott Roosevelt, eighteen, set out to hunt ducks along Long Island Sound on a blustery day in the late fall of 1880. The young men eyed the gray snow clouds overhead as they chipped through shore ice, rowed out to a twenty-one-foot jib-and-mainsail boat, and eased it into the harbor. In the far-off distance they heard the mocking cry of the long-tailed duck, known locally as "old-squaw" or "Sou' Sou' Southerly" in mimicry of their song. That "not unmusical clangor" served as the title of Theodore Roosevelt's first hunting story, an imaginative effort to turn experience into language and language into art.

"When, with November, the cold weather had fairly set in, then the old squaws come down from the north in full force," he begins, "great flocks of many hundreds, or even thousands can be seen in the open mid-waters of the sound, but they do not come into the harbours till some day when a heavy northeaster begins to blow." The "northeaster," a cyclonic storm blown ashore by northeasterly winds, sets the scene for the young hunters, who risk the perils of the icy storm for a day of shooting. A "splendid, checker-back loon" appears in a shallow cove and dives instinctively to outsmart the hunters. The luck of the morning favors the young men, who deliver a "load of swan-shot" into its neck. The loon turns belly up in the water.

Sou' sou' southerlies lure the young men into narrow channels and along rocky shoals, perilous places for their sailing craft. The boat's bottom grates against sunken rocks and the "bare ribs of the wreck of an old coasting schooner" come into view, ominous signs of what may lie in wait. The ducks, in Roosevelt's vivid, fastidious, and carefully observed prose, float "quietly on the surface, quacking, and pluming themselves, the white on their heads and wings showing well against the glossy black of their bodies." In the deceptive calm, the hunters shoot barrel after barrel into the flock, counting with satisfaction "half a dozen floating dead and three or four cripples struggling wildly." Distracted and triumphant, the brothers begin to lose control, as the boat jolts against a sunken ledge, frees itself, and glides into open waters. The narrator begins to resemble in a predictive way the mature, protean Roosevelt, who will always describe the natural world with such detached care.

Nature menaced. "The steel gray waves showed here and there faint white tops, and our little boat keeled way over as she rushed through them, under the sharp gusts; the sun was entirely hidden and the sky had become a dull ashen gray which boded snow at no distant hour." The siren song of the prey lures the brothers down Long Island Sound, farther and farther away from the safety of home: "There must have been many hundreds in the flock, scattered about in clusters; there were so many that their continued, half-musical clangor had a most pleasing effect to the ear." The ducks ride the waves in "perfect unconcern," preening their "white-and-chestnut plumage," and uttering "the loud 'ha'-ha'-wee." The flock scares and rises into the air as the hunters "put all four barrels of no. 4 shot into them" and then four more. Amid swirling feathers they grab a half-dozen bodies. Only one of the wounded escapes.

Other old-squaws brace for the storm in the shelter of the shore, as the young hunters slip into icy shallows. Salt spray crystallizes on the gun barrels. Finally sensing danger, they turn "almost dead against the wind" and struggle to set the sheets as they tack toward home: "Under the rough touch of the wind the ice-covered shrouds sang like the chords of an Aeolian harp, a fitting accompaniment to the angry roar of the waves." The prose turns lyrical: "Sometimes there would be a few minutes lull and partial clearing off, and then with redoubled fury the fitful gust would strike us again, shrouding us from stem to stern in the scudding spoon drift." Out of the shroud looms a large coasting schooner headed straight at them. Startled, the hunters sing out "helm-a-lee, helm-a-lee" in warning to the captain. The schooner slides by, "going wing and wing, everything reefed down tight as could be."

The world spared the young men from destruction, but continued to warn them. A mournful cry arises, so "weird and airy was the sound that it stirred even our dulled senses, numbed and sluggish though the cold had made them, and we rose to our feet; as the storm lulled for an instant we saw but a short way off a great north-ern loon, riding on the tossing winter waves as easily and as lightly as if it had been a summer calm." The wail, a keening of sorts for the checker-back loon, unnerves the hunters as they struggle toward the safety of home: "He paid no heed to us, though we were near enough to see his eyes plainly, and again uttered the loud defiant call we had first heard." Nature defies.

"Sou' Sou' Southerly" is Roosevelt's most creative piece of youth-ful prose, displaying many of the techniques of fiction and the care-ful, objective, and scientific observation that would frame his later work. The original manuscript, now in the Houghton Library at Harvard University, reveals assured longhand strokes with few revi-sions, mostly for clarity. Confidence in the first draft is character-istic of the work he would do all his life as a writer. The hunting story shows him to be, as environmentalist Daniel Philippon notes, "a gifted and sensitive observer of his environment—a young man well on his way to becoming one of the late nineteenth century's most talented writers on nature."[6]

The young writer put the manuscript into a drawer and apparently never tried to publish it, as he would do later with nearly every word he committed to paper. But this brilliant experiment set the direction of the nature writing to come. Throughout his life Theodore Roos-evelt worked to put action and thought into journals, letters, scientific field reports, nature sketches, hunting tales, national histories, military memoirs, political speeches, academic essays, book and art reviews, editorials, and exhortations of all sorts. Almost always, he could turn to intense descriptions of the natural world to enhance those texts.

After becoming a respected reviewer and essayist himself, Roo-sevelt would theorize about nature writing in the *Outlook* essay, "A Hunter-Naturalist in Europe and Africa":

> The outdoor man who writes, the nature writer proper, should not only be a keen observer and a man of genuine literary capacity, abso-lutely trustworthy and able to tell with interest and charm what he has seen, but ought also to have the power to utilize, and to add to,

what science can teach; and he ought to be able to describe what goes on in our gardens, fields, and woods, but also to tell of the great epic tragedy of life which is unfolded in the stark wilderness.[7]

The outdoor man who writes blends science and literature in telling hunting and ranching tales, detailing histories of the opening of the West, remembering military exploits in Cuba and big-game hunting in Africa. We see stark wilderness and near tragedy in his perilous tale of exploring an unknown Brazilian river, when, over-weight, out of shape, and middle-aged, he got himself into difficulties that a less adventuresome man, less intent on living the strenuous life, would have avoided.

Book after astonishing book displays the protean nature of Theodore Roosevelt's mind and makes clear that whether he is writing about history or hunting or exploration, he is working in a genre pretty much of his own making.

In his second book, *Hunting Trips of a Ranchman* (1885), he often sees the natural world as a stark wilderness. Written in the years following the sudden and unexpected deaths of his wife and mother on Valentine's Day in 1884, the young man's descriptions of the landscape have built into them a powerful sense of foreboding and loss. He finds the landscape compelling; looking across it, in a moment of synesthesia, Roosevelt hears the rhythms of Edgar Allan Poe: "And when one is in the Bad Lands he feels as if they somehow *look* just exactly as Poe's tales and poems *sound*."[8]

The Dakota badlands are so called because of their dramatic contours: "This broken country extends back from the river for many miles, and has been called always, by Indians, French voyageurs, and American trappers alike, the Bad Lands, partly from its dreary and forbidding aspect and partly from the difficulty experienced in traveling through it." The shapes are fantastical and the colors bizarre: "When a coal vein gets on fire it makes what is called a burning mine, and the clay above it is turned to brick; so that where water wears away the side of a hill sharp streaks of black and red are seen across it, mingled with the grays, purples and browns." But that mood quickly lifts; Roosevelt can turn from starkness to the gentleness of that same landscape's nourishing grasses, and the offering of shelter from the furious storms that sometimes assail it.

He is often consoled by the domesticity of the badlands when they are not stark. Of the local meadowlark, he writes: "The plains air seems to give it a voice, and it will perch on top of a bush or tree and sing for hours in rich, bubbling tones." Roosevelt himself, in this mood and mode, writes prose that does much the same thing. He focuses his careful and knowing eye on the Missouri skylark: "The skylark sings on the wing, soaring overhead and mounting in spiral curves until it can hardly be seen, while its bright, tender strands never cease for a moment." In the book's most lyrical language, Roosevelt records the music of a flock of snow buntings:

> One bleak March day, when the snow covered the ground and the shaggy ponies crowded about the empty corral, a flock of snow-buntings came familiarly round the cow-shed, clamoring of the ridge-pole and roof. Every few moments one of them would mount into the air, hovering about with quivering wings and warbling a loud, merry song with some very sweet notes.[9]

These lovely descriptions lessen, but do not fully balance, the deep sense of grief and loss in *Hunting Trips of a Ranch Man*. A representative passage would be his chapter-long description of an antelope hunt. It is more about landscape and loneliness than about heroic manliness as he travels on horseback to the west of the badlands through the grand prairies in search of spiritual nourishment, the vast stretches of the American plains echoing the writer's mood:

> Nowhere, not even at sea, does a man feel more lonely than when riding over the far-reaching, seemingly never-ending plains; and after a man has lived a little while on or near them, their very vastness and loneliness and their melancholy monotony have a strong fascination for him.[10]

Nowhere else does a man feel so "far off from all mankind," Roosevelt confesses, "The plains stretch out in deathlike and measureless expanse." The landscape becomes for the lonely hunter almost a phantasm:

> Although he can see so far, yet all objects on the outermost verge of the horizon, even though within the ken of his vision, look unreal and strange; for there is no shade to take away from the bright glare, and at a little distance things seem to shimmer and dance in the hot rays of the sun.

At the distance of a mile, a white shape appears to be a prairie wagon, but as the rider draws near, "it changes into the ghastly staring skull of some mighty buffalo, long dead and gone to join the rest of his vanished race."

Passages such as these, which recur in the tales of hunting more and more dangerous and difficult game, demonstrate what results when an extremely gifted faunal naturalist is combined with a prose writer of skill and discipline. The genre is mixed: one admires and understands the natural world even as the hunting parts of the story demand a brutal and, to the modern reader, harsh description of killing of the antelope itself.

> I pulled up short, leaped from [my horse's] back, and blazed into the band as they went by not forty yards off . . . and as the smoke blew off I saw the buck roll over like a rabbit, with both shoulders broken. I then emptied the Winchester at the rest of the band, breaking one hind leg of a young buck. Hastily cutting the throat of, and opening, the dead buck I again mounted and started off after the wounded one. But, though only on three legs, it went astonishingly fast . . . and after following it over a mile I gave up the pursuit. . . . Returning to the carcass, I cut off the hams and strung them beside the saddle; an antelope is so spare that there is very little more meat on the body.[11]

Such writing displays the epic and Darwinian struggle for life on the plains, revealing as well the life of the hunter, which at last is, like it or not, about death.

The Rough Riders, Theodore Roosevelt's best known book, details

6. Theodore Roosevelt, home from Cuba, crafting *The Rough Riders* at a makeshift desk in Montauk. R560.3.EL61–017, olvwork384437, Houghton Library, Harvard University.

his one true military adventure, his "crowded hour," bringing together all his talents and inclinations as a writer and allowing him to write in every genre he had mastered in the first part of his life: military history, ornithology, nature writing, and hunting narrative.

The most remarkable passages in the war story sketch the natural world. As he moved into battle with Sergeant Hamilton Fish in the lead, followed by Captain Capron's troop and the Rough Riders under the command of Colonel Leonard Wood, the action stops, astonishingly, as Roosevelt on horseback takes in the scene: "The tropical forest was very beautiful, and it was a delight to see the strange trees, the splendid royal palms and a tree which looked like a flat-topped acacia, and which was covered with a mass of brilliant scarlet flowers."[12] Here we see the young ornithologist, listening intently for the sounds he loved:

> We heard many birdnotes, too, the cooing of doves and the call of a great brush cuckoo. Afterward we found that the Spanish guerillas imitated these birdcalls, but the sounds we heard that morning, as we advanced through the tropic forest, were from birds, not guerillas, until we came right up to the Spanish lines.

Then Roosevelt turns his pen to the hunting stories he had been telling since he was a teenager: "It was very beautiful and very peaceful, and it seemed more as if we were off on some hunting excursion than as if we were about to go into a sharp and bloody little fight." Once in the thrall of battle, Roosevelt describes incredible shots on both sides, bullets entering body after body, grim images of wounded and dead bodies opened by vultures and land crabs:

> We found all our dead and all the badly wounded. Around one of the latter the big, hideous land-crabs had gathered in a gruesome ring, waiting for life to be extinct. One of our own men . . . had been found by the vultures before we got to [him]; and [his body] was mangled, the eyes and wounds being torn.[13]

Epic tragedy and starkness combined with lyrical precision: Colonel Roosevelt can mix modes and moods brilliantly, in this genre of his own invention.

During his White House years Roosevelt was scrupulous about appearances and about keeping the office separate from his literary life. He wrote only one book during those years, *Outdoor Pastimes of an American Hunter* (1905), and he made it clear to his editor at Charles Scribner's Sons that it had been largely written before he was elected president.

But as his days in the White House came to a close, Roosevelt made plans to return to his life as a writer, making meticulous plans for a massive hunting safari and scientific collecting expedition to sub-Saharan Africa that would be chronicled in a book. The writing style of that book turned out to be a heightened version of his earlier hunter-naturalist tales, full of intricate and fulsome descriptions of stalking and shooting, interspersed with lush descriptions of the natural world. The method he develops to present his manuscript, however, becomes a genre of his own devising in style and in organization. His contract with Scribner's called for him to do something revolutionary: to write the book on the go, sending in quantities of manuscript as he got it done, having written up his adventures at the end of every day, until he had enough pages to make a chapter, which he titled and then sent off to Mombasa by runner to be shipped to Scribner's in New York. There, the chapters were set in type, published in *Scribner's Magazine*, and later gathered into a book under Roosevelt's already-decided-upon title of *African Game Trails: An Account of the African Wanderings of an American Hunter Naturalist*.

This new mode of writing, not knowing when or where or how the text was to end, was daring and so Rooseveltian. He knew that the public would read what he had written, if for no other reason than he was at that time one of the most famous men on earth. Moreover he had absolute faith in his literary abilities; he knew he could produce readable and skillful prose, steeped in the realities and lyricisms of the hunt, in a solid and commanding first draft. He was at this time of his life completely ready to embark upon a new career as a successful, professional man of letters.

The tone of the text is often grim, the starkness of the natural world either present or implicit, scientific detail always on call, and the pumping adrenaline of the hunt vividly apparent:

> We did not get an early start. Hour after hour we plodded on, under the burning sun, through the tall, tangled grass, which was often higher than our heads . . . . the hard, sun-baked earth and stiff, tinder-dry long grass made it a matter of extreme difficulty to tell if a trail was fresh . . . . Mounting a low ant-hill I saw rather dimly through the long grass a big gray bulk . . . it was a rhinoceros lying asleep on its side, looking like an enormous pig. It heard something, and raised itself on its forelegs, in a sitting posture, . . . I fired for the chest, and the heavy Holland bullet knocked it clean off its feet. Squealing loudly, it rose again, but it was clearly done for . . . . I [then] killed a calf, which was needed for the museum; the rhino I had already shot was a full-grown cow, doubtless the calf's mother . . . . They were totally different in look from the common rhino, seeming to stand higher and to be shorter in proportion to their height . . . the muzzle is broad and square, and the upper lip without a vestige of the . . . prehensile development . . . of a common rhino; the stomachs contained nothing but grass; it is a grazing, not a browsing animal.[14]

His prose displays all the aspects of writing that the outdoor man who writes should display: careful observation, careful structure, frank acknowledgement of starkness, dependability. This passage comes toward the end of the safari and its tone is a bit weary, but it is vivid and, as always with Roosevelt, frank and honest.

Following the glory of his big-game book, Roosevelt's autobiography seems anything but glorious or even coherent. He started writing it by dictation; early segments, especially the charming story of his boyhood infatuation with a dead seal and his desire to buy and dissect it and learn what the carcass had to tell, are full of promise. The task of writing about his political and personal irritations with Taft and then Wilson, after the bitter loss of his quixotic campaign for president in 1912 as the Progressive Bull Moose, overwhelmed him, and *The Autobiography*, quickly written in 1912 and 1913, largely

7. Roosevelt reading from his Pigskin Library in front of his tent in a Kenyan hunting camp, April 1910. Library of Congress Prints and Photographs. LC-DIG-ppmsca-36549.

failed as a literary effort. The ninth chapter, "Indoors and Outdoors," for example, was Roosevelt's favorite part of the book. One wonders why he did not start his story here, moving backward and forward from this splendid literary perch. He sings of his love for nature and literature, "the garden, fields, and woods," domestic nature as haunt and escape rather than stark wilderness: "Usually the keenest appreciation of what is seen in nature is to be found in those who have also profited by the hoarded and recorded wisdom of their fellow-men."[15] He takes his readers on a walk around Sagamore Hill to hear the familiar sounds of winter gulls, loons, and wildfowl. Then in the fields, he points to the shy mayflower, the delicate anemones, cherry blossoms, and the thronging dogwoods. From Long Island he moves in memory back to Yellowstone National Park with John Burroughs: "I was rather ashamed to find how much better his eyes were than mine in seeing the birds and grasping their differences." He remembers an evening meal at the White House with the "shy recluse" Joel Chandler Harris as they enjoyed eating bear meat. He turns his pen to the glory of the California sequoias and then to Yosemite as he narrates his camping trip with John Muir, who told him that the great poet Emerson, when he visited, had found himself too old and frail for such a hike.

Using the birds of Shakespeare and Shelley, Milton and Keats, Roosevelt segues into a memory of his walk in 1910 with Sir Edward Grey into the New Forest to see and hear British birds that he had known only from literature. Startlingly, he offers a paragraph that simply lists the forty-one birds they saw, with asterisks to mark the twenty-three they heard singing. He leans and all but whispers into his reader's ear that larks "spring from grass, circle upwards, steadily singing" a song that is "joyous, buoyant and unbroken." For him the movements and sounds of nature and the language of poets and prose writers flow together. Then Roosevelt circles back to Sagamore Hill, where he sits in his rocking chair:

> The thickly grassed hillside sloped down in front of me to a belt of
> forest from which rose the golden, leisurely chiming of the wood

thrushes, chanting their vespers; through the still air came the warble of the vireo and tanager; and after nightfall we heard the flight
song of the ovenbird from the same belt of timber. Overhead an
oriole sang in the weeping elm, now and then breaking his song to
scold like an overgrown wren.

The observation of the natural world brings considerable grace to
his life's story.

Roosevelt was restless and bored; after losing the election and the
unenthusiastic critical and public response to the autobiography,
he decided to make another long and daring trip to South America. It was to be a collecting expedition through the Amazon basin
of Brazil; he again contracted with Scribner's for a new book that
would deploy his on-the-go method, developed and perfected for
the African safari. Planning for this expedition, in part funded by
the Smithsonian Institution, took a surprising turn when the Brazilian government offered Roosevelt and his expeditionary companions a chance to join Candido Rondon, a Brazilian national hero
whose local fame was nearly equal to Colonel Roosevelt's. Rondon
had already planned to explore in a careful and scientific fashion
an unknown river, Rio da Duvida, in the vast, remote unexplored
reaches of the Amazon.

Roosevelt jumped at the chance. It was, he proclaimed, his "last
chance to be a boy." Edith, who had come with him to Brazil for
the first stages of the trip, agreed to let him go, but only if he could
be accompanied and watched over by his second son, Kermit. The
senior Roosevelt was delighted with the prospect of traveling with
Kermit, as in their African days, and was genuinely excited about
doing serious exploration of a significant, previously unexplored river.

The journey was exciting, although, as detailed by writers like
Candace Millard and Joseph Ornig, it proved to be far more dangerous and difficult than anyone could have guessed. Still, the resulting
book represents the most compelling success of Roosevelt's mixing
of genres. The natural world as seen on the River of Doubt is at once
stark and beautiful, tragic and peaceful—the expedition traveled

into the unknown, carried by strong currents often made worse by tropical deluges and dragged more or less into increasing danger.

In many ways this adventure hearkens back to that early, unpublished essay, "Sou' Sou' Southerly," in that the threat of the natural world leads almost to death. In that earlier story, however, the two Roosevelt brothers venture into their dilemma through naive innocence. In this late-in-life voyage, Roosevelt and his companions choose deliberately to put themselves into danger.

For the most part Roosevelt recounts an ominous world. Insects of all sorts assailed the men: termites ate their clothes and tents, stinging insects tormented them night and day, serpents of unknown varieties threatened them. Game, which they had thought to hunt for protein, was elusive or shockingly scarce, and hunger stalked the party. They were ill equipped for their travails and, as nutrition failed, they began to be troubled by yellow fever, malaria, vitamin deficiencies, dysentery, and sores. Roosevelt, as the expedition's oldest member, failed more rapidly than anyone else; he lost weight, suffered from fever, and weakened.

However ill, he stuck to his method. He donned netting and gloves so he could write every night. He observed the flora and fauna as a scientist, and wrote about the region's biodiversity in prose as good and compelling as any he ever got onto paper. One of the striking things about this book is its tone of urgency and fear:

> In a wilderness, where what is ahead is absolutely unknown, alike in terms of time, space and method—for we had no idea where we would come out, how we would get out, or when we would get out—it is of vital consequence not to lose one's outfit, especially the provisions; and yet it is of only less consequence to go as rapidly as possible lest all the provisions be exhausted and the final stages of the expedition be accomplished by men weakened from semi-starvation, and therefore ripe for disaster.[16]

But if this passage hints at unease, Roosevelt ends it in his accustomed register: "This evening the air was fresh and cool."

Roosevelt's writing is not always focused on the labor and peril

8. Theodore Roosevelt, in netting and gloves, writing *Through the Brazilian Wilderness*, in lantern slide of his Brazil expedition, 1913, taken by his son Kermit. Library of Congress Prints and Photographs. LC-DIG-ds-09857.

involved in the trip. When he turns his attention to his surroundings, his passages of nature writing are gratifying, not only to himself, but to readers as well:

> Yet while we were actually on the river, paddling and floating downstream along the reaches of swift, smooth water, it was very lovely. When we started in the morning the day was overcast and the air was heavy with vapor. Ahead of us the shrouded river stretched between dim walls of forest, half-seen in the mist. Then the sun burned up the fog, and loomed through it in a red splendor that changed first to gold and then to molten white. In the dazzling light, under the brilliant blue of the sky, every detail of the magnificent forest was vivid to the eye: the great trees, the network of bush ropes, the cav-

erns of greenery, where thick-leaved vines covered all things else. Wherever there was a hidden boulder the surface of the current was broken by waves. In one place, in midstream, a pyramidal rock thrust itself six feet above the surface of the river. On the banks we found fresh Indian sign.[17]

A few paragraphs on from this description of the river, Roosevelt continues with careful, scientifically accurate observations, while at the same time revealing the dangerous nature of their situation; the Brazilian forest does not contain teeming life of a kind the expedition could eat:

> There was not much bird life in the forest, but Cherrie kept getting species new to the collection. At this camp, he shot an interesting little ant-thrush. It was the size of a warbler, jet-black, with white under-surfaces of the wings and tail, white on the tail-feathers, and a large spot of white on the back, normally almost concealed, the feathers on the back being long and fluffy. When he shot the bird, a male, it was showing off before a dull-colored little bird, doubtless the female; and the chief feature of the display was this white spot on the back. The white feathers were raised and displayed so that the spot flashed like the 'chrysanthemum' on a prongbuck whose curiosity has been aroused. In the gloom of the forest the bird was hard to see, but the flashing of this patch of white feathers revealed it at once, attracting immediate attention. It was an excellent example of a coloration mark which served a purely advertising purpose; apparently it was part of a courtship display. The bird was about thirty feet up in the branches.

Such disinterest and close daily observation would be tested in the succeeding weeks, and, for a long time, abandoned. Soon, Roosevelt was so ill that his habit and disciplined task of writing at the end of each wearying day would become impossible. In the last analysis *Travels through the Brazilian Wilderness* represents him as the quintessential "outdoor man who writes." His writing touches all the prescribed notes: it is accurate, the hunting scenes are vibrant, the domestic landscapes are carefully presented, tragedy is never far from the writer's consciousness, the starkness of the wilderness is stark indeed. Few have ever written a better book about being lost in nature than Theodore Roosevelt.

Roosevelt's last epic battle was World War I. Even though President Woodrow Wilson refused to allow him to lead a regiment as he had done in Cuba, his four boys served in what Wilson asserted would be "a war to make the world safe for democracy." TR's frustrations were many and mounting. He knew fundamentally that he would have been a superior wartime president than Wilson, and yet all the while lived in fear that his boys might suffer serious injury or even death. His writings of the time were profuse: he wrote article after article, editorial after editorial, all of them filled with anger. His fury, and the tone in which he chose to express it, was intemperate. The many books he wrote in these last years were collections of polemic, ferociously written and ferociously titled, including *Fear God and Take Your Own Part* (1916) and *The Foes of Our Own Household* (1917). At times his enemies felt his language bordered on treason and sedition.

Yet, even as Roosevelt ranted, he wrote one last book having to do with nature, a charming omnium-gatherum, published in 1916, entitled *A Book Lover's Holiday in the Open*. Valedictory in tone and content, in it he says goodbye to the strenuous outdoor life. The final words of his introduction to these essays were, in true Rooseveltian fashion, upbeat: "The joy of living is his who has the heart to demand it." The phrase is a salve of sorts.

Then, in the wake of his son Quentin's death in July 1918, after his surviving boys have been wounded, as the war is at last being won, after his fury at and hatred of Woodrow Wilson have begun to subside somewhat, TR's writing calms a bit. His sorrow at Quentin's death seems to force him into some sort of reconciliation. His letters to men and women whose sons have died in the war are kind and gentle. His health, however, continued to decline. He spent weeks in the hospital in New York, desperate to recover from an attack of arthritis and from what appears to have been heart failure and congestion in his lungs, so that he could rouse himself to begin his campaign for president in the election of 1920. Frailer, weaker, sicker than even his children know, he and Edith talk quietly and read to each other, first in the hospital, then at Sagamore Hill.

In this gentler mood, Roosevelt's thoughts turn again to the outdoors, to the natural world, and he reads *Jungle Peace* (1918), a book by his friend William Beebe. So impressed is he by the writing and by the title that he decides, sick as he is, to write one last review for the *New York Times*. Beebe, the naturalist and writer who later invented the bathysphere and explored the ocean's underworld, had lived in and researched the flora and fauna of the wilderness of Guiana in the years before the war. He wrote this book from his field notes while serving as a pilot during World War I, writing in the evenings in his barracks as a release from his daily experiences flying his airplane, armed with bombs that he dropped on the German army. Sickened by such duties, Beebe found comfort in writing about his early days in Guiana—nature writing as escape or at least respite, a sensibility Roosevelt appreciated.

In his review Roosevelt touches once again on his definition of nature writing, and maintains that Beebe is an exemplary writer about the natural world:

> Nothing of this [book's] kind could have been done by the man who was only a good writer, only a trained scientific observer, or only an enterprising and adventurous traveler. Mr. Beebe is not merely one of these, but all three; and he is very much more in addition. He possesses a wide field of interest; he is in the truest sense of the word a man of broad and deep cultivation. . . . Nor are his interests only concerned with nature apart from man and from the works of man. He possesses an extraordinary sympathy with and understanding of mankind itself, in all its myriad types and varieties.[18]

Roosevelt, crippled by grief and worry, reads Beebe's words with compassion and, finally, a sense of forgiveness and deep understanding:

This volume was written when the writer's soul was sick of the carnage which has turned the soil of Northern France into a red desert of horror. To him the jungle seemed peaceful, and the underlying war among its furtive dwellers but a small thing compared to the awful contest raging [in France.] It is the same feeling that makes strong men, who have sickened of the mean and squalid injustice of so much of life . . . turn with longing to the waste places where no paths penetrate the frowning or smiling forests and no keels furrow the lonely rivers.

Roosevelt's understanding of the war is expressed in his striking phrase "the red desert of horror," which with Quentin's death he now fully comprehended. The passage's final words are just as poignant—"no keels furrow the lonely rivers." Its Tennysonian echoes call to mind one of Roosevelt's favorite poems, "Ulysses," as its aging hero ploughs the "sounding furrows" to "sail beyond the sunset," reinforcing his deep and abiding love for the wild where no paths penetrate. Theodore Roosevelt died on January 6, 1919.

Notes

1. *Independent*, December 28, 1905, 1535.

2. *Public Opinion*, January 6, 1906.

3. Theodore Roosevelt, *Outdoor Pastimes of an American Hunter* (New York: Charles Scribner's Sons, new and enlarged edition, 1908), 315.

4. Roosevelt, *Outdoor Pastimes of an American Hunter*, 330.

5. Theodore Roosevelt, "Sou' Sou' Southerly," *Gray's Sporting Journal* 13 (1988): 70–75. The essay was finally published more than seventy years after his death.

6. Daniel J. Philippon, *Conserving Words: How American Nature Writers Shaped the Environmental Movement* (Athens: University of Georgia Press, 2004), 41.

7. Theodore Roosevelt, "A Hunter-Naturalist in Europe and Africa," *Outlook*, September 16, 1911.

8. Theodore Roosevelt, *Hunting Trips of a Ranchman; Hunting Trips on the Prairie and in the Mountains*, Homeward Bound Edition (New York: Review of Reviews Co., 1910), 17.

9. Roosevelt, *Hunting Trips of a Ranchman*, 19.

10. Roosevelt, *Hunting Trips of a Ranchman*, 216.

11. Roosevelt, *Hunting Trips of a Ranchman*, 223.

12. Theodore Roosevelt, *The Rough Riders*, Homeward Bound Edition (New York: Review of Reviews Co., 1910), 48–49.

13. Roosevelt, *The Rough Riders*, 103.

14. Theodore Roosevelt, *African Game Trails: An Account of the African Wanderings of an American Hunter-Naturalist* (New York: Charles Scribner's Sons, 1910), 466–67.

15. Theodore Roosevelt, *Theodore Roosevelt: An Autobiography* (New York: Charles Scribner's Sons, 1913), 328–39.

16. Theodore Roosevelt, *Through the Brazilian Wilderness* (New York: Charles Scribner's Sons, 1914), 267.

17. Roosevelt, *Through the Brazilian Wilderness*, 285–86.

18. Theodore Roosevelt, *New York Times Book Review*, October 13, 1918.

3

"I So Declare It"

Theodore Roosevelt's Love Affair with Birds

DUANE G. JUNDT

Most Americans can identify Theodore Roosevelt as a former president of the United States, but relatively few are aware that Roosevelt was also an accomplished ornithologist and one of the most important figures in the history of American bird conservation. And TR was no latecomer to birding. He began a love affair with birds as a child and was faithful in his devotion to them to the end of his life. Historian Douglas Brinkley goes so far as to claim that, "with the exception of his family, birds probably touched him more deeply than anything else in his life."[1] Today, legions of American birdwatchers can thank Roosevelt for his role in rescuing their objects of affection, and identify a kindred spirit who gladly suffered their mutual addiction.

If one were to establish a great triumvirate of American birding, Theodore Roosevelt would have to be included in its ranks, along with John James Audubon and Roger Tory Peterson. Audubon (1785–1851), best known for his magisterial *The Birds of America*, produced not just an extensive catalog of American birds but also a masterpiece of art. Peterson (1908–96) greatly expanded the ranks of birders by producing the hobby's first true pocket-sized bird identification guide, *A Field Guide to the Birds*, in 1934. Roosevelt, while not as keen an observer or recorder of birds as either Audubon or Peterson, nonetheless could hold his own as an ornithologist based on his hunting, his extensive taxidermy experience, and his writings on American birds, ranging from simple bird lists to

9. One of ten bas reliefs in a statue sculpted by Vincenzo Miserendino, the monument to Roosevelt was erected in McHose Park, Boone, Iowa, in 1948. Used with permission by Ann E. Lundberg.

detailed descriptions of their behavior and coloration. These birding credentials, while impressive, are not enough to secure a place alongside the likes of Audubon and Peterson. Rather, TR's reputation rests on the considerable actions he took on behalf of birds and their conservation while president.

Roosevelt's discovery as a seven-year-old boy of a seal carcass at a New York open-air market is often cited by his biographers as a pivotal moment in the making of the aspiring scientist, but it was the observation, description, hunting, and mounting of birds that occupied much of Roosevelt's youth.[2] The seal may have lit a fuse, but birds sustained the fire. Ultimately the pursuit of big-game hunting would eclipse TR's birding and would earn for him much of his renown as an outdoorsman, but his fondness for birds was never extinguished, and appropriate credit for being their champion has finally started to accrue to him. As Don Freiday of New Jersey's Cape May Bird Observatory recounted in the August 2016 issue of *Bird Watching* magazine: "I recently spoke about worldwide bird conservation at a meeting of eastern North American wildlife professionals. I asked, 'Why are we doing as well as we are in North America?' Somebody immediately shouted out, 'Teddy Roosevelt!'"[3]

Notebooks filled with field observations of birds, diary entries detailing bird hunts, mounted specimens at home and in museums, and the publication of detailed bird lists all point to a young man dedicated to the study of birds and one seemingly destined for a career as a natural scientist.[4] The conclusion of four years of study at Harvard found Roosevelt on the cusp of a political career instead of joining the ranks of "Audubon, or [Alexander] Wilson, or [Spencer] Baird" as an ornithologist.[5] His alma mater's lack of interest in preparing Roosevelt to be a field scientist, his determined pursuit of Alice Hathaway Lee, and the loss of his Harvard classmate and birding partner, Henry "Hal" Minot, to a nervous breakdown combined to abort TR's first career choice.[6] Though his ambition to become a professional ornithologist may have been thwarted, his ability to influence the world of birds was actually enhanced by his choice of politics, as it gave Roosevelt access to power that he could wield on behalf of bird conservation.

Because of Roosevelt's obvious affinity for birds it is natural to assign him the label of *birdwatcher*, but in his case it might be more accurate to use the term *bird listener*, since it was mostly through birdcalls and songs that TR came to know his avian companions. One of the most remarked-upon episodes in Roosevelt's childhood is the revelation he experienced after he was finally fitted with glasses (or spectacles, as he called them), at the age of thirteen.[7] While his poor eyesight may have contributed to his reliance on hearing to identify birds as a child, he may also have been blessed with remarkably acute recognition of birdcalls and songs, and anyone reading TR's writings on birds will discover that his depiction of them is decidedly musical:

10. The meadowlark may have been Roosevelt's favorite bird. Many other Americans shared his enjoyment of it, as exemplified in this Arm & Hammer bird conservation card dated 1915. Duane Jundt Collection.

Among the earliest sounds of spring is the cheerful, simple, homely song of the song-sparrow; and in March we also hear the piercing cadence of the meadowlark—to us one of the most attractive of all bird calls. Of late years now and then we hear the rollicking, bubbling melody of the bobolink in the pastures back of the barn; and when the full chorus of these and of many other of the singers of spring is dying down, there are some true hot-weather songsters, such as the brightly hued indigo buntings and thistlefinches. In our ears the red-winged blackbirds have a very attractive note.[8]

Roosevelt's use of hearing to identify and enjoy birds meant that their songs left a deep and lasting impression on him, and over the course of his life he formed associations between birds, their songs, and the places and times he encountered them, from his home on Long Island and his ranches in Dakota to the mountain ranges of the American West. As Roosevelt remarked, "it is hard to tell just how much of the attraction in any bird-note lies in the music itself and how much in the associations."[9]

Although it may prove impossible to identify Roosevelt's single

"USEFUL BIRDS OF AMERICA"
SET OF 30 DESIGNS.

Full set (thirty in all) will be sent on receipt of six two-cent stamps, with your Name and Post Office address. State and County must be plainly written.

If you want the best BAKING SODA be sure and buy the ARM and HAMMER BRAND BAKING SODA (BI-CARBONATE OF SODA) in packages. Bulk Soda may be of anybody's manufacture, generally of a poor quality.

CHURCH & DWIGHT COMPANY,
27 Cedar St., New York.

19. MEADOWLARK. (Sturnella magna) Open grass lands and sloughs running back from the sea are favorite haunts for this yellow breasted bird whose jet "necktie" is a distinguishing feature. He is trustful, fond of human company and very curious. His song is not the greatest of bird melodies but it is cheerful and confident. As an insect and weed seed destroyer he ranks high, his average bill of fare being 73 per cent insects, 5 per cent grain, 12 per cent weed seed.

FOR THE GOOD OF ALL,
DO NOT DESTROY THE BIRDS.

II. The reverse of the Arm & Hammer bird conservation card celebrates the meadowlark as one of the "Useful Birds of America." Duane Jundt Collection.

favorite bird, one type that seems to have made a great impression on him, and that appears frequently in his writings, is the grassland songbird, the meadowlark.[10] TR found the eastern meadowlark in the environs of Sagamore Hill and its close relation the western meadowlark in the badlands. Of the former, Roosevelt wrote that its "strong, plaintive note . . . is one of the most noticeable and most attractive sounds"[11] and the latter he described as "most wonderful of all; the meadow-lark has found a rich, strong voice, and is one of the sweetest and most incessant singers we have."[12]

One of the most lyrical passages that Roosevelt penned about the western meadowlark can be found in the pages of *The Wilderness Hunter* (1893), the final volume of Roosevelt's trilogy on his experiences in Dakota Territory. Revelatory and romantic, this selection conveys the hold that this bird's song had on TR and how it shaped his memory of the badlands:

> The meadow lark is a singer of a higher order, deserving to rank with the best. Its song has length, variety, power and rich melody; and there is in it sometimes a cadence of wild sadness, inexpressibly touching; . . . for to me it comes forever laden with a hundred memories and associations; with the sight of dim hills reddening in the dawn, with the breath of cool morning winds blowing across lonely plains, with the scent of flowers on the sunlit prairie, with the motion of fiery horses, with all the strong thrill of eager and buoyant life.[13]

The selection is also noteworthy for its charting of Roosevelt's emotional journey in the badlands. The beginning of the passage notes that the meadowlark's song could prompt feelings of sadness in Roosevelt, but the passage concludes in an upbeat and optimistic tone. In effect the quotation mirrors Roosevelt's time in the badlands, which saw him both grieve and recover from the devastating loss of his wife and his mother. For TR, the meadowlark provided the soundtrack along the path from pain and suffering to pleasure and delight in his life and surroundings.

In *Ranch Life and the Hunting-Trail* (1888) Roosevelt penned another autobiographical bird passage that revealed feelings he would not allow himself to express in any other form. Beautifully written, with an eye for detail, TR's description of the call of the mourning dove as heard from the veranda of the Elkhorn ranch house epitomizes his belief that "with all bird-music much must be allowed for the surroundings, and much for the mood, and the keenness of sense, of the listener."[14]

> In the hot, lifeless air all objects that are not nearby seem to sway and waver. There are few sounds to break the stillness. From the upper branches of the cottonwood trees overhead, whose shimmering, tremulous leaves are hardly ever quiet, but if the wind stirs at all, rustle and quiver and sigh all day long, comes every now and then the soft, melancholy cooing of the mourning dove, whose voice always seems far away and expresses more than any other sound in nature the sadness of gentle, hopeless, never-ending grief.[15]

Written when the death of his first wife, Alice Lee, remained achingly fresh, Roosevelt not only provides the reader with an apt description of the mourning dove's call, but also conveys the emotions that its call summoned forth, giving the reader a rare glimpse of his recently shattered, still-fragile psyche.[16]

While birds like the meadowlark and mourning dove may have reminded Roosevelt of his personal loss, the plight of many bird species at the turn of the twentieth century prodded him to use his political power and influence to prevent their disappearance from the American landscape. As a historian of the American West, Roosevelt was aware of the near extermination of the beaver, and he had, to a limited degree, participated in the destruction of the great American buffalo herds in the late nineteenth century. TR's correspondence and writing about birds not only convey a sense of loss, but also literally make frequent use of the term to express what the future would hold if conservation measures were not taken to stop the slaughter of birds. In February 1899, the recently elected governor of New York wrote to the noted ornithologist Frank Chapman:

When the bluebirds were so nearly destroyed by the severe winter a few seasons ago, the *loss* was like the *loss* of an old friend, or at least like the burning down of a familiar and dearly loved house. The destruction of the wild pigeon [passenger pigeon] and the Carolina paraquet [*sic*] has meant a *loss* as severe as if the Catskills or the Palisades were taken away. When I hear of the destruction of a species I feel just as if all the works of some great writer had perished; as if we had *lost* all instead of only part of Polybius or Livy.[17]

For Theodore Roosevelt the extinction of a bird species was not just a loss to science or to a particular ecosystem, but a blow to the larger American civilization; for when it came to birds he could not divorce his feelings for them from his ardent nationalism. As a child and a young man Roosevelt had traveled to Europe and was well versed in the treasures to be found in the Old World, but he believed that America had its own unique repository of masterpieces in the form of its myriad parks, forests, and canyons, and in the birds and other animals that dwelled within. Roosevelt frequently compared the landscape and wildlife jewels of the United States to the cathedrals of Europe, arguing that the former deserved preservation as much as the latter:

> A grove of giant redwoods or sequoias should be kept just as we keep a great and beautiful cathedral. The extermination of the passenger-pigeon meant that mankind was just so much poorer; exactly as in the case of the destruction of the cathedral at Rheims. And to lose the chance to see frigate-birds soaring in circles above the storm, or a file of pelicans winging their way homeward across the crimson afterglow of the sunset; . . . why, the loss is like the loss of a gallery of the masterpieces of the artists of old time.[18]

A unique combination of circumstances coalesced during Roosevelt's presidency that provided him with the opportunity to act in an unprecedented way on behalf of America's avian treasures. A fashion trend in the millinery trade, the use of bird feathers to adorn elaborate hats for women, posed a formidable threat to birds of all kinds, but especially to the populations of egrets and herons along the Gulf Coast whose feathers were especially prized in the trade. Lacking hunting regulations and protected preserves, bird populations were being decimated by the unchecked harvest of their feathers. Once again a fashion fad in the hat trade portended the destruction of a swath of American wildlife (beavers had fallen victim to the craze for beaver felt hats in previous centuries). Roosevelt minced no words in his condemnation of the trade: "The butchery of terns and herons for 'fun,' or for woman's headgear, has been atrocious—I can use no other word. [Birds] look a great deal better in the swamps and on the beaches and among the trees than they do on hats."[19]

Imperiled by their own beauty, America's bird populations were set on a flight path of recovery by a president who not only happened to be a lifelong lover of birds and a published ornithologist, but whose conception of the role and capacities of his office allowed him to translate his affection into action. Taking his cue from Abraham Lincoln, his presidential role model, Roosevelt believed in a strong executive who exercised power with the widest leeway possible given the constraints of Congress and the Constitution. TR freely admitted that he enjoyed the presidency and pulling the levers of power: when given the chance to affect an issue that captured his imagination—building an isthmian canal, deploying the American navy on a global tour, setting aside forest reserves, or establishing a continent-wide system of bird reservations—he intended to act on behalf of what he considered to be the greater public good. In March 1903 Roosevelt issued an executive order establishing Pelican Island, Florida, as the first federal bird reservation—an executive order that reportedly depended on the classic Rooseveltian use of a loophole. Querying legal counsel about whether any law forbade him from designating the sanctuary and hearing that there was none, TR uttered the now-famous line: "Very well, then I so declare it." In one form or another, he would employ that same declaration an additional fifty times during the course of his presidency, in effect establishing what would become the national wildlife refuge system.[20]

Authors who have made a study of Roosevelt and the outdoors have variously assigned him the monikers of *hunter-conservationist* and *naturalist*, but perhaps the best summation of TR's relationship to the natural world can be found in the title he assigned to himself.[21] The subtitle of *African Game Trails: An Account of the African Wanderings of an American Hunter-Naturalist* is revelatory. Roosevelt employed the hyphen to join *hunter* and *naturalist*; he did not see himself as having two distinct roles, but as embodying a blend of the two. This manifests itself in Roosevelt's vast hunting corpus, where he frequently departs from the main subject at hand—the hunting of big game—to describe the landscape, the plants, and the birds and their songs. Works such as *Ranch Life and the Hunting Trail*, *The Wilderness Hunter*, and *Outdoor Pastimes of an American Hunter* are all leavened by numerous passages devoted to bird study. Roosevelt encouraged his fellow hunters to hone the skills needed to bag game and to open their eyes and employ their pens to sharpen their observational skills: "I wish that members of the Boone and Crockett Club, and big game hunters generally, would make a point of putting down all their experiences with game, and with any other markworthy beasts or birds, in the regions where they hunt, which would be of interest to students of natural history."[22]

In April 1909 Roosevelt embarked upon his great African safari, and although the expedition centered on hunting and the collection of thousands of specimens for the Smithsonian Institution, TR, as always, took careful note of the bird life that accompanied his march up the continent. In *African Game Trails*, his account of the safari written as it unfolded over the course of two calendar years, Roosevelt describes many of the birds he encountered (to a large extent by comparing them to familiar American birds), but one passage in particular stands out. In what could best be described as a peculiar mix of homesickness and patriotic ornithology, Roosevelt makes a case for the superiority of American birdsong from the depths of Africa:

Many of them [African bird songs] are beautiful, though to my ears none quite as beautiful as the best of our own bird songs. At any rate there is nothing that quite corresponds to the chorus that during May and June moves northward from the Gulf States and southern California to Maine, Minnesota, and Oregon, to Ontario and Saskatchewan; when mocking-birds and cardinals sing in the magnolia groves of the South, and hermit thrushes, winter wrens, and sweetheart sparrows in the spruce and hemlock forests of the North; when bobolinks in the East and meadow larks East and West sing in the fields; and water ousels by the cold streams of the Rockies, and canyon wrens in their sheer gorges; when from the Atlantic seaboard to the Pacific wood thrushes, veeries, rufous-backed thrushes, robins, bluebirds, orioles, thrashers, cat-birds, house finches, song sparrows—some in the East, some in the West, some both East and West—and many, many other singers thrill the gardens at sunrise; until the long days begin to shorten, and tawny lilies burn by the roadside, and the indigo buntings trill from the tops of little trees throughout the hot afternoons.[23]

Although he found much to observe and describe in the midst of Africa's bird life, Roosevelt nonetheless waxed lyrical about the birds whose songs he had come intimately to know and love. In this case distance did indeed make the heart grow fonder.[24]

Before returning to the United States, Roosevelt made a tour of Europe's capital cities, with major addresses in Paris, London, and Christiania (Oslo), belatedly to accept his 1906 Nobel Peace Prize. On the day before he was scheduled to sail for home, TR set out on a bird walk in southern England with Sir Edward Grey, because he "had always much desired to hear the [English] birds" that he had read so much about in the works of Shakespeare, Milton, and Wordsworth.[25] This episode, which Roosevelt details in his autobiography, confirms his preference for the company of birds and for companions like Grey ("a keen lover of outdoor life in all its phases") over the many crowned heads of Europe who had competed for his time and attention.[26] Roosevelt writes of this June 1910 outing that "I passed no pleasanter twenty-four hours during my entire European trip."[27]

Reading Roosevelt's writing on birds also reveals the great joy they brought him. The frequent departures from the hunting narrative that punctuate so much of his work are not the product of having to provide filler, but should rightfully be seen as an expression of his love of birds and his desire to transmit those feelings to the reader. Roosevelt closes "A Colorado Bear Hunt" in *Outdoor Pastimes of an American Hunter* by reporting that his hotel in Denver was the home to numerous "pretty, musical house finches" at the expense of the upstart invasive species, the house sparrow. TR relishes the victory of the native house finch over the "thoroughly unattractive and disreputable" sparrow, and concludes the chapter by parceling out a most remarkable piece of civic praise. "The cities of the Southwestern States are to be congratulated," writes the president of the United States, not for their irrigation and reclamation projects or their gleaming new opera houses, but for "having this spirited, attractive little songster as a familiar dweller around their houses and in their gardens."[28]

Given his own ardor for birds, it is not surprising that Roosevelt reveled in the fellowship of those who shared his feelings while he struggled to understand the lack of enthusiasm for bird life evinced by others. This dichotomy found its fullest expression in Roosevelt's friendship with the naturalists John Burroughs and John Muir, and it played out during TR's great western tour of 1903, when both men accompanied the president for a time during his travels. Roosevelt admired Burroughs's writings and readily acknowledged (despite his own formidable birding skills) that he looked to him for advice on bird identification.[29] The birding duo explored Yellowstone National Park together in April in the early stages of the president's tour, and the results compelled TR to admit that he "was rather ashamed to find how much better his eyes were than mine in seeing the birds and grasping their differences."[30] Muir, whom Roosevelt knew by his reputation and his writings, served as TR's tour guide through Yosemite National Park and lobbied Roosevelt for more federal protection of the park's surrounding lands. While camping in Yosemite with his famous guide, Roosevelt "was interested and a little surprised to find that, unlike John Burroughs, John Muir cared little for birds or bird songs, and knew little about them. The hermit thrushes meant nothing to him, the trees and the flowers and the cliffs everything."[31] Nearly twelve years later, in early 1915, Roosevelt still confessed to being "surprised" at Muir's lack of interest in birds and their songs.[32] Roosevelt found it hard to grasp that Muir would not succumb to the charm of birds, especially ones with songs as beautiful as those of the hermit thrushes that serenaded them in their first night in Yosemite.

In *Colonel Roosevelt*, the third and final volume of his biography of TR, Edmund Morris writes: "[William Howard] Taft remarked that on occasion Theodore Roosevelt was possessed of 'the spirit of the old berserkers.' If so, the Colonel's savage beast was as often soothed by the bird music he heard at Oyster Bay, spring after warming spring."[33] The image of a bloodthirsty Roosevelt remains all too common, especially in the popular culture, and while extensive reading of Roosevelt's hunting literature might appear to confirm this belief, his writings on birds reveal a gentler, softer side of a man not afraid to liberally employ the word *sweet* to describe his favorite birdsongs.[34] For example, in *Hunting Trips of a Ranchman*, Roosevelt uses forms of that word three times in a single paragraph: "In the spring, when the thickets are green, the hermit thrushes sing sweetly in them. . . . One of our sweetest, loudest songsters is the meadow-lark. Snow-buntings came familiarly round the cowshed . . . warbling a loud, merry song with some very sweet notes."[35] Who but a tenderhearted man would refer to the waves of colorful spring migrants as "my friends, the warblers"?[36] Recent research supports the idea that TR may very well have been "soothed" by birdsong. Writing in the *Wall Street Journal*, Robert Lee Hotz reports that "psychologists are discovering that natural sounds—from the wind rustling the trees to the warble of songbirds—have benefits for humans, and can lower stress, elevate mood, boost cognitive abilities and perhaps enhance healing."[37]

Contemporary birdwatchers would recognize many of the skills and habits of their hobby in Theodore Roosevelt's bird literature. Seemingly at odds with the notion of TR as the "steam engine in trousers" or as someone who was "pure act," he could not have closely listened to, observed, and described birds were it not for a significant reservoir of patience that allowed him to remain "standing under trees, motionless, for long periods of time."[38] In *Hunting Trips of a Ranchman*, Roosevelt writes: "I have sat on my horse and listened to one [Sprague's pipit] singing for a quarter of an hour at a time without stopping."[39] On a trip to Tennessee TR spent two blissful hours listening to the singing of a northern mockingbird from his bedroom window.[40]

Roosevelt's patience allowed him to act as a keen observer of birds, and he added to that the power to ably and eloquently translate those observations into words. Praising the work of an ornithologist named E. W. Nelson, TR could just as well have been describing himself when he wrote that "to extraordinary powers of observation, and intense love of the wilderness and wild creatures, he adds the ability to write with singular power and charm."[41] In the following passage, Roosevelt touches on three important characteristics used by birders in identification: behavior (what the bird is doing), sound (description of its song and call), and appearance (color and shape):

> A little black woodpecker with a yellow crest ran nimbly up and down the tree-trunks for some time and then flitted away with a party of chickadees and nut-hatches. Occasionally a Clark's crow soared about overhead or clung in any position to the swaying end of a pine branch, chattering and screaming. Flocks of crossbills, with wavy flight and plaintive calls, flew to a small mineral lick nearby, where they scraped the clay with their queer little beaks.[42]

Although Roosevelt birded primarily by ear, he resorted to using the indispensable tool of birding, what he called glasses or field glasses (today's binoculars), "to examine any bird as to the identity of which I am doubtful."[43] Before the introduction of the field guide, TR and birders of his era had to resort to bulky bird books (ornithologies) that remained on a shelf and that compelled them to make their identifications at a remove from the birds under study.[44] Contemporary birders have access to binoculars that make watching birds akin to viewing them in high definition, and there are dozens of paperback bird guides and smartphone apps that can be used in the field. Technology has enhanced but not fundamentally altered the practices of birding. Were Roosevelt alive today, he could seamlessly join in a morning bird hike, calling out species after species to be added to the group's list, no doubt recalling the list he compiled as president from his morning strolls around the White House grounds.[45]

During the course of his life Theodore Roosevelt birded across the country and around the globe—in Africa, Europe, and South America—but like many birdwatchers he was particularly fond of the birds found in his own yard. Backyard birdwatching allows those who cannot venture far afield (like Roosevelt himself in the last year of his life) to enjoy birds from a porch or patio or kitchen window, and over time the birder gains a familiarity with, and extensive knowledge of, the birds found around his home. As a birder Roosevelt was fortunate because his home at Sagamore Hill drew birds attracted to grasslands, forests, and the seashore. TR's extensive writings on birds frequently feature the birds of his home, but his most remarkable paean to them can be found in the pages of his autobiography: "At Sagamore Hill we love a great many things—birds and trees and books, and all things beautiful, and horses and rifles and children and hard work and the joy of life."[46] Roosevelt not only places birds at the vanguard of the things he loves about Sagamore Hill, but also devotes ten consecutive pages of his memoir to them.[47] There are few better examples of the hold that birds had on TR than this: that he was willing to pare the discussion of his own accomplishments and legacy to share the spotlight with his many feathered friends.

There were many places that could have asserted a claim to be the site of Theodore Roosevelt's grave. As a combat veteran and commander in chief, he could have been laid to rest in Arlington

NAT. SIZE.

COPYRIGHT. 1898. BY THE SINGER MFG. CO. N.Y.   BOBOLINK.

12. Roosevelt knew birds primarily by their songs. The bobolink, seen here
in this 1898 card from the Singer Manufacturing Company, could be found
around Roosevelt's Long Island home. Duane Jundt Collection.

National Cemetery. Certainly New York City, his place of birth and the home to so much of his history—from mayoral candidate to police commissioner—could have made a strong case. And no one would have blamed Roosevelt for choosing to return to his beloved badlands. But he chose to be buried at Youngs Cemetery overlooking the hamlet of Oyster Bay, in part because "he had always enjoyed the birdsong in that fir-forested corner."[48] The remains of the nation's only birdwatcher-in-chief are treated to the music of the dawn chorus thanks to the Theodore Roosevelt Sanctuary and Audubon Center, which hugs the hillsides of the cemetery. One imagines that the denizens of the nation's first Audubon songbird sanctuary put forth their best for their distinguished neighbor, ensuring that his love for them will not go unrequited.

Notes

1. Douglas Brinkley, *The Wilderness Warrior: Theodore Roosevelt and the Crusade for America* (New York: HarperCollins, 2009), 8.

2. Edmund Morris, *The Rise of Theodore Roosevelt* (New York: Coward, McCann & Geoghegan, 1979), 46; H. W. Brands, *TR: The Last Romantic* (New York: BasicBooks, 1997), 29; Darrin Lunde, *The Naturalist: Theodore Roosevelt, a Lifetime of Exploration, and the Triumph of American Natural History* (New York: Crown Publishers, 2016), 9–10.

3. Don Freiday, "Game Changer," *Bird Watching* 30, no. 4 (August 2016): 37.

4. On Roosevelt's bird lists, see Gregory A. Wynn, "Roosevelt's Birds," *Theodore Roosevelt Association Journal* 31, no. 3 (Summer 2010): 16–20.

5. Theodore Roosevelt, *Theodore Roosevelt: An Autobiography* (1913; repr., New York: Charles Scribner's Sons, 1925), 23.

6. On Roosevelt's heartfelt response to Minot's condition, see Edward P. Kohn, ed., *A Most Glorious Ride: The Diaries of Theodore Roosevelt, 1877–1886* (Albany: State University of New York Press, 2015), 48–50.

7. Morris, *Rise of Theodore Roosevelt*, 62.

8. Roosevelt, *Autobiography*, 328.

9. Roosevelt, *Autobiography*, 328.

10. Roosevelt also treasured the singing of the northern cardinal, the northern mockingbird, and the American dipper.

11. Theodore Roosevelt, *Outdoor Pastimes of an American Hunter* (1905; repr., New York: Charles Scribner's Sons, 1923), 382.

12. Theodore Roosevelt, *Ranch Life and the Hunting-Trail* (1888; repr., Lincoln: University of Nebraska Press, 1983), 38.

13. Theodore Roosevelt, *The Wilderness Hunter* (1893; repr., New York: G. P. Putnam's Sons, 1909), 65.

14. Roosevelt, *The Wilderness Hunter*, 64.

15. Roosevelt, *Ranch Life and the Hunting-Trail*, 39–40.

16. Compare the passage examined above, published in 1888, with the following from *The Wilderness Hunter*, published in 1893: "Through the still, clear, hot air, the faces of the bluffs shone dazzling white; no shadow fell from the cloudless sky on the grassy slopes, or the groves of timber; only the faraway cooing of a mourning dove broke the silence." Five years later the call of the mourning dove (in the same setting) elicits no emotional reaction from Roosevelt. Roosevelt, *Wilderness Hunter*, 53.

17. Theodore Roosevelt to Frank Michler Chapman, February 16, 1899, in *Theodore Roosevelt: Letters and Speeches*, ed. Louis Auchincloss (New York: The Library of America, 2004), 167 (emphasis added).

18. Theodore Roosevelt, "The Bird Refuges of Louisiana," *Scribner's Magazine* 59, no. 3 (March 1916): 280.

19. Theodore Roosevelt, "A Hunter-Naturalist in Europe and Africa," in *Forgotten Tales and Vanished Trails*, ed. Jim Casada (New York: Skyhorse Publishing, 2014), 191.

20. In a nod to the importance of birds in relaying the story of Roosevelt the conservationist, Douglas Brinkley opens *The Wilderness Warrior* with an account of the creation of the Pelican Island preserve; the inside front and back covers of the hardcover edition of the book feature photographs of Roosevelt on the beach of one of his many bird set-asides. Brinkley, *Wilderness Warrior*, 1–19; Harold H. Bruff, *Untrodden Ground: How Presidents Interpret the Constitution* (Chicago: University of Chicago Press, 2015), 200.

21. R. L. Wilson, *Theodore Roosevelt: Hunter-Conservationist* (Missoula MT: Boone & Crockett Club, 2009); Lunde, *The Naturalist*.

22. Roosevelt, "Hunting in the Cattle Country," in Casada, ed., *Forgotten Tales and Vanished Trails*, 44.

23. Theodore Roosevelt, *African Game Trails: An Account of the African Wanderings of an American Hunter-Naturalist* (New York: Syndicate Publishing Company, 1910), 279–80.

24. Roosevelt expressed similar sentiments as he came to the end of his exploration of Brazil's River of Doubt in the spring of 1914. In *Through the Brazilian Wilderness* he wrote of his longing to return home to Sagamore Hill to listen to the "robin and blue-bird, meadow-lark and song sparrow, [that] were singing in the mornings at home; the rapture of the hermit thrush in Vermont, the serene golden melody of the wood-thrush on Long Island, would be heard before we were there to listen." Theodore Roosevelt, *Through the Brazilian Wilderness*, vol. 28 of *The Works of Theodore Roosevelt* (New York: Charles Scribner's Sons, 1920), 329.

25. Roosevelt, *Autobiography*, 322.

26. Roosevelt, *Autobiography*, 322.

27. Roosevelt, *Autobiography*, 326.

28. Roosevelt, *Outdoor Pastimes of an American Hunter*, 110–11.

29. Roosevelt, "John Muir: An Appreciation," in Casada, ed., *Forgotten Tales and Vanished Trails*, 172.

30. Roosevelt, *Autobiography*, 321.

31. Roosevelt, *Autobiography*, 322.

32. Roosevelt, "John Muir: An Appreciation," in Casada, ed., *Forgotten Tales and Vanished Trails*, 172.

33. Edmund Morris, *Colonel Roosevelt* (New York: Random House, 2010), 139.

34. For a recent depiction of a violence-prone Roosevelt, see the graphic novel series *Rough Riders* (2016) and *Rough Riders: Riders on the Storm* (2017) from AfterShock Comics. In a review of *The Illustrated Art of Manliness*, Dave Shiflett says that "the book evokes a golden age where Teddy Roosevelt was the ideal and any man worth his moustache knew how to shoot guns, [and] pummel thugs." Roosevelt is invoked two more times in the course of the review. Dave Shiflett, "Testosterone Not Included," *Wall Street Journal*, May 27–28, 2017, C12.

35. Theodore Roosevelt, *Hunting Trips of a Ranchman* (New York: G. P. Putnam's Sons, 1885), 13–14.

36. Theodore Roosevelt to Archie Roosevelt, May 17, 1908, in *Theodore Roosevelt's Letters to His Children*, ed. Joseph Bucklin Bishop (New York: Charles Scribner's Sons, 1923), 228.

37. Robert Lee Hotz, "Natural Healing: Sounds Aid Humans," *Wall Street Journal*, May 5, 2017, A3.

38. Edmund Morris, *Theodore Rex* (New York: Random House, 2001), 108.

39. Roosevelt, *Hunting Trips of a Ranchman*, 13.

40. Roosevelt, *Wilderness Hunter*, 66–68.

41. Roosevelt, "The Conservation of Wild Life," in Casada, ed., *Forgotten Tales and Vanished Trails*, 179.

42. Theodore Roosevelt, *Hunting the Grisly and Other Sketches* (1889; repr., New York: Barnes & Noble Publishing, 2003), 55.

43. Roosevelt, "Small Country Neighbors," in Casada, ed., *Forgotten Tales and Vanished Trails*, 78.

44. A wonderful example of one of these books, a gift to a young Roosevelt from his parents, is on display at the Theodore Roosevelt Museum at Old Orchard at Sagamore Hill National Historic Site.

45. See Roosevelt's White House bird list at https://www.theodorerooseveltcenter .org/Research/Digital-Library/Record?libID=o287125.

46. Roosevelt, *Autobiography*, 329.

47. Roosevelt, *Autobiography*, 319–28.

48. Morris, *Colonel Roosevelt*, 557.

4

Urban Wild

Theodore Roosevelt's Explorations of Rock Creek Park

MELANIE CHOUKAS-BRADLEY

The Theodore Roosevelt Trail in Washington DC's Rock Creek Park winds through a picturesque forest of oaks, beeches, and mountain laurel, leading uphill to the top of a dramatic, jagged outcrop known as Pulpit Rock. During his presidency, climbing Pulpit Rock was one of Theodore Roosevelt's favorite outdoor activities. However, his preferred route to the top did not incorporate the trail that now bears his name. Instead, according to many harrowing accounts, and at least one photograph housed at the Library of Congress, TR loved scaling the face of Pulpit Rock and other rock outcrops in the Washington area, often with less robust friends and colleagues struggling to keep up with him.[1] "Scrambling" up the face of Pulpit Rock was a welcome respite from administrative chores and political challenges during his nearly eight-year presidency, from 1901 to 1909.

The Rock Creek stream valley that comprises the heart of the national park running through the nation's capital is no North Dakota badlands, African plain, or River of Doubt. Yet Roosevelt's adventures in the park are nevertheless fascinating, partly because they remind us of how insistent TR was about getting strenuous exercise, even in the confines of the presidency, and partly because his forays there reveal that Washington DC provides more "wilderness" than one might think. Roosevelt wrote about his Rock Creek Park outings with exuberance and humor. His greatest adventures occurred far from the national capital, but he managed to challenge, sometimes appall, his friends and colleagues in Rock Creek Park,

13. President Roosevelt is "scrambling" up a rock wall often misidentified as an image of Pulpit Rock. The actual location is about a third of a mile farther upstream next to Boulder Bridge. Melanie Choukas-Bradley, who discovered the precise location in January 2019—a hundred years after Roosevelt's death, can testify that this climb is far more challenging than it appears in the photograph! Library of Congress Prints and Photographs Division. https://www.theodorerooseveltcenter.org/Research/Digital-Library/Record?libID=o282138. Theodore Roosevelt Digital Library. Dickinson State University.

and at times even found it possible to do himself some bodily injury. This surprisingly challenging landscape afforded an energetic president a ready outlet for rock scrambling, horseback riding, swimming, wading, birding, and other naturalist pursuits near 1600 Pennsylvania Avenue. Often accompanied by his "Tennis Cabinet," whose local membership was extended to include various visiting friends and colleagues, TR sought every opportunity for woodland adventures. In his autobiography Roosevelt wrote: "Often, especially in the winters and early springs, we would arrange for a point to point walk, not turning aside for anything—for instance, swimming Rock Creek or even the Potomac if it came in our way."[2]

Rock Creek Park's habitats are a mix of deciduous floodplain forest composed of sycamore, river birch, musclewood, and other bottomland trees and upland woods heavily populated with several oak species and American beech. The trees and shrubs of the upper and lower canopy are teeming with migrating birds in the spring and fall, and home to many year-round residents as well as nesting songbirds who winter in Central and South America. Much of the park's geology, including the Pulpit Rock outcrop, is composed of half-billion-year-old metamorphic rock known as the Laurel Formation. Rock Creek itself is a thirty-three-mile-long stream, the main stem of which originates in Laytonsville, Maryland. The creek flows for twenty-two miles in Maryland before arriving in the nation's capital and entering the national park; its course through the Old Line State is protected by Montgomery County stream valley parkland.

Created by an act of Congress on September 27, 1890, a little more than a decade before Roosevelt's first term as president, Rock Creek Park is the oldest urban national park in the country; it even predates the designation of Yosemite National Park by a few days. Twice the size of Central Park in New York City, Rock Creek Park remains a wild, wooded stream valley to this day, running through the center of the city from the Maryland-DC border to the Potomac River. That is just as Congress intended when it encumbered the funds necessary to purchase the land from willing sellers so that the resulting site would be "perpetually dedicated and set apart as a public park or pleasure ground for the benefit and enjoyment of the people of the United States."[3] No citizen enjoyed this rugged terrain more than TR, whose favorite destinations in the park were within a few miles of the White House, providing a perennial temptation:

> While in the White House I always tried to get a couple of hours' exercise in the afternoons—sometimes tennis, more often riding, or else a rough cross-country walk, perhaps down Rock Creek, which was then as wild as a stream in the White Mountains, or on the Virginia side along the Potomac. My companions at tennis or on these rides and walks we gradually grew to style the Tennis Cabinet; and then we extended the term to take in many of my old-time Western friends.[4]

Although Theodore Roosevelt is appropriately recognized as our foremost conservationist president, as a naturalist he was in good company with some of his predecessors, most notably George Washington—who is survived at his Mount Vernon home by at least two trees that he planted—and Thomas Jefferson, who planned, designed, and executed the first street tree planting on record in the District of Columbia. Both men were serious tree and nature lovers whose Mount Vernon and Monticello estates are testament to their passions for farming and gardening. Washington had spent his youthful years as a land surveyor in the wilds of western Virginia. Both early presidents were innovative horticulturists who took pride in the native plants of the country they were forming and also sought to extend what they could grow by acquiring seeds and plant materials from distant lands. John Quincy Adams—who increased the size and diversity of the White House gardens and trees and tried to jump-start a silk industry with white mulberries and the silkworms that were tended by his wife, Louisa—was known as the "Tree Planting Mr. Adams."[5]

When Roosevelt first arrived in Washington in 1889 as a U.S. civil service commissioner, he had landed in a region rich in biological diversity. The capital city lies on the fall zone between the hilly Piedmont region and the Atlantic coastal plain, where plant communities and species native to both intersect. Many southern and northern species overlap as well. Citizens immigrating from all over the world brought their favorite trees to Washington's welcoming climate; around the time of Roosevelt's administration, Washington became known as the "City of Trees" for its tree-lined avenues and international tree population.[6]

In addition to Rock Creek Park, Roosevelt explored another nearby stream valley, Northwest Branch, and also the Potomac Gorge, running from the Great Falls of the Potomac to Mason's Island—since renamed Theodore Roosevelt Island. The Potomac Gorge is considered one of the most botanically diverse areas in the country, with some of its native plants having arrived there from the upper watershed, washed far downriver to make their homes in several rare and unique habitat niches.

Rock Creek Park was Roosevelt's most easily accessed wild playground near the White House. Fortunately for posterity, he took time to recount many of his adventures there, not only in his autobiography but also in letters to friends, colleagues, and family members. In entertaining and poetic prose, his letters reveal the athletically extreme nature of many of his outings as well as his appreciation for local nature and natural beauty.

One of President Roosevelt's regular hiking companions was the French ambassador Jean Jules Jusserand, who was widely reputed to have been one of the few men who could keep up with him. In his autobiographical work, *What Me Befell,* Jusserand wrote of his Rock Creek Park adventures with TR: "What the President called a walk was a run: no stop, no breathing time, no slacking of speed, but a continuous race, careless of mud, thorns and the rest."[7] He clearly struggled to stay abreast with the intrepid twenty-sixth president, as did most of the many other companions whom Roosevelt lured into Rock Creek Park for a day's outing. On January 21, 1906, Roosevelt wrote in a letter to his sixteen-year-old son Kermit, then a student at Groton School: "Yesterday we took a scramble down Rock Creek, Uncle Douglas, Grant La Farge, Bob Bacon, and the French Ambassador [Jusserand] going with me. We had a first-rate time, although the French Ambassador found it a little too much for him; but he is a trump and did his best. Today is a mild, beautiful day, and Mother and I are going for a good long ride together."[8]

A stone bench in Rock Creek Park memorializes the game French ambassador. Located just off Beach Drive, which runs through the center of the park from north to south, the bench is a bit off the beaten path and not very accessible for visitors today. A colorful and oft-told tale about TR and Jusserand fording a body of water together is perhaps better known than the stone memorial to posterity. While some historians have placed the crossing at Rock Creek, in *What Me Befell*, Jusserand himself located it near Chain Bridge, which crosses the Potomac River northwest of the White House. Roosevelt wrote in his autobiography in a section largely devoted to Rock Creek exploits: "On several occasions we . . . swam Rock Creek in the early spring when the ice was floating thick upon it. If we swam the Potomac, we usually took off our clothes."[9] That passage seems to imply that the incident took place in the Potomac, which aligns with Jusserand's own telling. However, I cannot help sharing biographer William Roscoe Thayer's entertaining rendering of the tale that places it, most likely erroneously, in Rock Creek. "In Washington," Thayer wrote, "the President continued this practice of [point-to-point] hiking, but in a somewhat modified form. His favorite resort was Rock Creek, then a wild stream, with a good deal of water in it, and here and there steep, rocky banks. To be invited by the President to go on one of those hikes was regarded as a mark of special favor. He indulged in them to test a man's bodily vigor and endurance, and there were many amusing incidents and perhaps more amusing stories about them . . . What must have been the surprise in the French Foreign Office when it received the following dispatch:

> 'Yesterday,' wrote Ambassador Jusserand, 'President Roosevelt invited me to take a promenade with him this afternoon at three. I arrived at the White House punctually, in afternoon dress and silk hat, as if we were to stroll through the Tuileries Garden or in the Champs

Elysees. To my surprise, the President soon joined me in a tramping suit, with knickerbockers and thick boots, and soft felt hat, much worn. Two or three other gentlemen came, and we started off at what seemed to me a breakneck pace, which soon brought us out of the city. On reaching the country, the President went pell-mell over the fields, following neither road nor path, always on, on, straight ahead! I was much winded, but I would not give in, nor ask him to slow up, because I had the honor of La belle France in my heart. At last we came to the bank of a stream, rather wide and too deep to be forded. I sighed relief, because I thought that now we had reached our goal and would rest a moment and catch our breath, before turning homeward. But judge of my horror when I saw the President unbutton his clothes and heard him say, 'We had better strip, so as not to wet our things in the Creek.' Then I, too, for the honor of France, removed my apparel, everything except my lavender kid gloves. The President cast an inquiring look at these as if they, too, must come off, but I quickly forestalled any remark by saying, 'With your permission, Mr. President, I will keep these on, otherwise it would be embarrassing if we should meet ladies.' And so we jumped in the water and swam across.'"[10] Gifford Pinchot later referred to the French Ambassador as "the man who wore gloves when swimming."[11]

In a letter to his son Kermit, dated February 16, 1908, TR described a Rock Creek swim that is just as colorful for the clothes that were left *on* during the plunge. The second paragraph of the letter reads:

Yesterday afternoon Fitz Lee and John McIlhenney and I took Colonel Cecil Lyon, of Texas, for a walk down Rock Creek. The ice had just broken and the creek was a swollen flood, running like a millrace. We did the usual climbing stunts at the various rocks, and then swam the creek; and it was a good swim, in our winter clothes and with hobnail boots and the icy current running really fast. Colonel Lyon balked at the swim; or, rather, he would have swum all right, but I was afraid to let him when I found he was doubtful as to his ability to get over; for I did not want a guest to drown on one of my walks.[12]

14. Portrait of J. J. Jusserand, French ambassador to the United States, circa 1903. *The World's Work,* 1903. Wikimedia Commons.

TR's Rock Creek woodland rides could be every bit as harrowing as his rock scrambling, hiking, and swimming. According to Scott Einberger, author of *A History of Rock Creek Park*:

Mr. and Mrs. Roosevelt often went horseback riding in Rock Creek Park. The duo was usually accompanied by Cavalry officer Cornelius McDermott, who rode a few trots behind to give the president and first lady some privacy. On at least one occasion Mr. and Mrs. Roosevelt enjoyed a quiet Thanksgiving ride through the sylvan woods, but on at least two other occasions the president was thrown off his horse—both times at practically the same location at a ford near Boulder Bridge. The first of these incidents led to a bloody-faced Theodore Roosevelt, and the second involved an "untried horse" getting spooked in the water. The horse jumped up on its hind legs but slipped at the same time. Before the horse fell backwards onto its back, the alert Roosevelt was able to jump off, probably saving himself from very serious injury. Nevertheless, while landing in the water helped break his fall, Rock Creek was only running two-feet deep at the location and was also full of boulders; the president bruised in several places.[13]

Boulder Bridge is a picturesque stone bridge that was built in 1902 and still carries Beach Drive traffic over Rock Creek. On weekends and holidays Beach Drive is closed to motorized vehicles, allowing walkers, runners, and cyclists to command the roadway. An additional tale connects the twenty-sixth president with a newly built Boulder Bridge. Apparently TR lost a ring during one of his Rock Creek adventures and subsequently posted this ad in the July 14, 1902 edition of *The Washington Star*: "Lost by the President, an all-gold seal ring on left bank of Rock Creek, 100 yards above Boulder Bridge. $25 for its recovery." It was never located.[14]

Its loss did not dampen the president's ardor for the park's subtle charms. His sensitive reading of its natural beauty, which changed with the seasons, emerges in a letter he wrote to Kermit dated February 19, 1903:

The blizzard came along and we had enough snow to completely cover the roads, and then so much cold weather that it has not melted. In consequence, yesterday and the day before I had two first-class horseback rides, being able to start from the White House, as I could go at a good swinging trot along the snow-covered streets instead of having a long, tiresome, gingerly walk or skate over the asphalt. Rock Creek Park was beautiful. It is really a wonderfully wild piece of scenery. The steep hillsides were covered with snow which lay in strips on the limbs of trees, and the stream churned noisily between the ice-rimmed banks and among the ice-coated boulders.[15]

TR commented on Rock Creek Park's springtime splendors in another letter to Kermit dated May 15, 1907: "Mother and I with Ethel and Senator Lodge had a beautiful ride yesterday. The azalea (I always rather like its old New York Dutch name of pinkster) is in bloom and the woods are beautiful, while the bridle trails thru them along Rock Creek really add very greatly to the pleasure of riding. Fifteen years ago there were no wire fences around Washington; the scenery was not built up; and Lodge and I used to go everywhere, jumping an occasional fence; but this no longer can be done and the bridle trails in Rock Creek Park are really the best substitute."[16]

I imagine the president would be happy to know that the wild native pinkster azalea (more often spelled *pinxter* today) still thrives along the bridle trails of Rock Creek Park, to the enjoyment of modern-day riders and walkers. He might also revel in the fact that the wood thrush, one of the Rock Creek Park bird species that he mentioned in his autobiography, has since become the official bird of the District of Columbia. Each spring nature lovers await its arrival from its wintering grounds in Central America, eager to hear its melodious song echo through the stream valley.

Although the accounts of Roosevelt's birding in Rock Creek Park do not seem to be as extensive as those that mention his more athletic exploits, this passage from Darrin Lunde's *The Naturalist* shows how much the president continued to enjoy birding while residing in the White House:

Even from the presidential residence, Theodore Roosevelt found ways to engage with his beloved nature. The White House, with its patchwork of trees, shrubs, and open lawns, was a perfect songbird habitat . . . Roosevelt sometimes paid more attention to the birds perched outside the White House windows than to the statesmen seated inside. One morning he burst into a Cabinet meeting with startling news. "Gentlemen, do you know what has happened this morning?" he squawked. Every man in the room feared national crisis, but, to their surprise, the president chirped, "I just saw a chestnut-sided warbler—and this only in February!"[17]

Rock Creek Park provided a pleasing destination for Roosevelt family outings. In his autobiography, TR wrote: "The country is the place for children, and if not the country, a city small enough that one can get out in the country. When our own children were little, we were for several winters in Washington, and each Sunday afternoon the whole family spent in Rock Creek Park, which was then very real country indeed. I would drag one of the children's wagons; and when the very smallest pairs of feet grew tired of trudging bravely after us, or of racing on rapturous side trips after flowers and other treasures, the owners would clamber into the wagon."[18]

Roosevelt is known for preserving approximately 230 million acres of public land during his presidency. As a frequent visitor to Rock Creek Park, he was not shy about demanding its protection and maintenance. His interest in saving an individual tree in the park from erosion reveals that the smallest act of conservation mattered to him as much as the grand gesture creating a national forest, park, or monument. In June 1903 the president wrote to Colonel John Biddle, district commissioner of Washington D C, who oversaw the park's management:

My dear Colonel Biddle: A month ago Mrs. Roosevelt spoke to you about preserving that beautiful purple beech in the Pierce's [now spelled *Peirce*] Mill meadow in Rock Creek. Not one thing has been done towards its preservation. The bank has eaten away under it so that a severe flood might at any time destroy it, and we should

15. The Theodore Roosevelt Trail in Rock Creek Park climbs from the creek to Pulpit Rock, winding through a native forest of oak, beech and mountain laurel. Photo by Melanie Choukas-Bradley.

lose one of the most beautiful trees in the Park. I think that steps should be taken without a day's delay to build some flood wall or something of the kind which would ensure the tree's preservation. Please let me know what can be done and when it can be done.[19]

Later that year Colonel Biddle received another letter from the president that may have caused Biddle a bit of consternation. The letter, dated November 28, 1903, reveals how much the preservation of the pristine nature of Rock Creek Park meant to Roosevelt:

My dear Colonel Biddle,

You have charge of Rock Creek Park have you not? If so, I wish to lay before you certain facts. The other day to my surprise—and I might almost say to my horror—I found that preparations were being made for flagging one or more of the footpaths through the park; that is, for changing them from woodland footpaths into stone sidewalks. Now, I think that is a real and serious mistake, and I wish most emphatically to protest against it. When people go into the park to walk, they go to get off the pavements, and it is worse than absurd, carefully and at much expense to see that they are unable to get off. I had noticed for some time these masses of big stone flags at certain places in the creek bottom, but, frankly, it never occurred to me that there would be any intention of using them for so foolish a purpose. But the other evening in walking down I was astounded to find that some of the flags had already been laid where the path on the west side of the stream crosses the meadow a little above the northern boundary of the Zoological Park. Such a flag path is hideous to look at and will greatly detract from the beauty of the park, and it is uncomfortable to walk on. It has not a single merit. If anyone wants to walk on a pavement, let him keep in the city and not go off into the woods. Personally, I would far rather see a good dirt road in a park than the macadamized roads, but I do not make a point of this. When, however, the question is of doing all that can be done to ruin the park for the only people who care to walk in it, by laying down these flag paths, I feel that the situation at least calls for an explanation.[20]

President Roosevelt's love of Rock Creek Park created an indelible memory for an august foreign visitor who accompanied him on a winter ride in the park. On February 28, 1903, this telegram was delivered to 1600 Pennsylvania Avenue from Prince Heinrich of Prussia: "Can not help reminding you of our charming little excursion on horse back in Rock Kreek [sic] Valley, just a year ago today. Greetings. Henry of Prussia"[21] As the prince's telegram suggests, Roosevelt's full-body immersion in the local park's wildness is inextricably linked to his intimate knowledge of its seasonal beauties, wildlife habitats, dramatic rock outcrops, and rushing waters. As important, Roosevelt's vigorous championing of this urban landscape is indistinguishable from his spirited advocacy for all public lands. Roosevelt was already a consummate naturalist and conservationist when he first explored Rock Creek Park; by introducing so many others—family, friends, military officers, public officials, and diplomats—to its athletic rigors and natural charms he helped convert them to the conservationist cause.

Notes

1. *Climbing in Rock Creek Park*, 1901–08, Library of Congress Prints and Photographs Division, http://www.theodorerooseveltcenter.org/Research/Digital-Library/Record ?libID=0282138, Theodore Roosevelt Digital Library, Dickinson State University. The photograph description reads: "President Roosevelt and some unsuspecting and unprepared friends go for 'a little walk in Rock Creek Park.' Roosevelt enjoyed rock climbing and referred to it as 'scrambling.'"

2. Theodore Roosevelt, *The Autobiography of Theodore Roosevelt* (New York: Charles Scribner's Sons, 1913), 30.

3. The Rock Creek Park Authorization, Fifty-First Congress, Session One, Ch. 1001, 1890, https://www.nps.gov/rocr/learn/historyculture/adhiaa.htm

4. Theodore Roosevelt, *The Autobiography of Theodore Roosevelt* (New York: Charles Scribner's Sons, 1913), 30.

5. Melanie Choukas-Bradley, *City of Trees: The Complete Field Guide to the Trees of Washington, D.C.*, 3rd ed. (Charlottesville: University of Virginia Press, in association with the Center for American Places, 2008).

6. Choukas-Bradley, *City of Trees*.

7. J. J. Jusserand, *What Me Befell—The Reminiscences of J.J. Jusserand* (Boston: Houghton Mifflin Company, 1933), 332.

8. Jusserand, *What Me Befell*, 335–36; Theodore Roosevelt to Kermit Roosevelt, January 21, 1906, Harvard College Library, http://www.theodorerooseveltcenter.org/Research /Digital-Library/Record?libID=0280690, Theodore Roosevelt Digital Library, Dickinson State University.

9. Roosevelt, *Autobiography*, 30.

10. William Roscoe Thayer, *Theodore Roosevelt: An Intimate Biography* (Boston: Houghton Mifflin, 1919), 262–63.

11. Gifford Pinchot to Theodore Roosevelt, undated, Library of Congress Manuscript Division, http://www.theodorerooseveltcenter.org/Research/Digital-Library/Record ?libID=0188524, Theodore Roosevelt Digital Library, Dickinson State University.

12. Theodore Roosevelt to Kermit Roosevelt, February 16, 1908, Harvard College Library, http://www.theodorerooseveltcenter.org/Research/Digital-Library/Record?libID =0281023, Theodore Roosevelt Digital Library, Dickinson State University.

13. Scott Einberger, "The Rock Creek Conservancy," January 30, 2018, https://www .rockcreekconservancy.org/get-involved/rock-creek-blog/527-theodore-roosevelt-in-rock -creek-park; see also Scott Einberger, *A History of Rock Creek Park: Wilderness & Washington, D.C.* (Washington DC: The History Press, 2014).

14. *The Washington Star*, July 14, 1902.

15. Theodore Roosevelt to Kermit Roosevelt, February 19, 1903, https://www .theodorerooseveltcenter.org/Research/Digital-Library/Record?libID=0280363. Theodore Roosevelt Digital Library. Dickinson State University.

16. Theodore Roosevelt to Kermit Roosevelt, May 15, 1907, Harvard College Library, http://www.theodorerooseveltcenter.org/Research/Digital-Library/Record?libID=0280363, Theodore Roosevelt Digital Library, Dickinson State University.

17. Darrin Lunde, *The Naturalist: Theodore Roosevelt, A Lifetime of Exploration, and the Triumph of American Natural History* (New York: Crown Publishers, 2016), 170–71.

18. Roosevelt, *Autobiography*, 187.

19. Theodore Roosevelt to Colonel John Biddle, June 19, 1903, Library of Congress Manuscript Division, http://www.theodorerooseveltcenter.org/Research/Digital-Library/Record?libID=0185132, Theodore Roosevelt Digital Library, Dickinson State University.

20. Theodore Roosevelt to Colonel John Biddle, November 28, 1903, Library of Congress Manuscript Division, http://www.theodorerooseveltcenter.org/Research/Digital-Library/Record?libID=0186554, Theodore Roosevelt Digital Library, Dickinson State University.

21. Prince Heinrich, Telegram to Theodore Roosevelt, February 28, 1903, Library of Congress Manuscript Division, https://www.theodorerooseveltcenter.org/Research/Digital-Library/Record/ImageViewer?libID=040538, Theodore Roosevelt Digital Library, Dickinson State University.

PART 2

Outside Influences

5

For "Generations Yet Unborn"

George Bird Grinnell, Theodore Roosevelt,
and the Early Conservation Movement

JOHN F. REIGER

It is probably safe to say that most adult Americans have heard of President Theodore Roosevelt. They may even think they know something about him—that he was a brave and dynamic leader who hunted big game, charged up San Juan (actually Kettle) Hill in the Spanish-American War, busted trusts, and energized the conservation movement to protect and manage the country's natural resources. After all, was it not for this last reason that Roosevelt's head is carved into Mount Rushmore?

It is also probably fair to say that most adult Americans, even those within the contemporary environmental movement, have never heard of the pathbreaking conservationist, and Roosevelt mentor, George Bird Grinnell. The reasons for this lack of fame are not hard to discern. He never held public office, usually preferring to have others take credit for initiatives he had launched and carried through, and even though he owned and edited the most popular outdoor newspaper of his time, *Forest and Stream*, his name rarely appeared in the weekly.

Despite his efforts to keep in the background, many in the New York upper-class circles in which he traveled knew who Grinnell was and admired his writings on natural history, hunting, and conservation. One of these individuals was a young Theodore Roosevelt. It was not, however, a positive reaction to Grinnell's writing in *Forest and Stream* that would bring the two men together, but a critical review the editor published of Roosevelt's 1885 book on hunting in the West.[1] Ironically it was the visit by an indignant Roosevelt to Grinnell's newspaper office in Manhattan that would lead to their close friendship and a conservation partnership that would have a profound impact on American history. Before we can understand how that partnership came to be, we need to examine George Bird Grinnell's life before his withering review appeared in *Forest and Stream.*

Born in Brooklyn, New York, on September 20, 1849, George Bird Grinnell was the oldest of five children of George Blake and Alvord Lansing Grinnell. During the nearly nine decades of his life, he was an explorer, big-game hunter, rancher, scientist, ethnographer, publicist, editor, author, and conservationist. The range of his associations was tremendous. He was on familiar terms with Native Americans in the West, as well as the leading representatives of the Eastern upper class: Theodore Roosevelt, Madison Grant, and many others. It is, however, with the first group that Grinnell is often linked today. Living with several tribes for weeks at a time and recording their stories and oral histories, he compiled works that are considered classics in American Indian ethnography.[2]

It was not in ethnography but in conservation that Grinnell made his greatest impact on American history. He was an aesthetic and utilitarian conservationist who understood that, to be successful, all efforts to preserve the natural world required continuous, apolitical, scientifically based management. Among his amazing array of accomplishments was the founding of the Audubon movement for the protection of birds, with the formation of the first Audubon Society in 1886; his key role in launching the national forest system; and his leadership of the campaign to create Glacier National Park, finally established in 1910. In a lengthy obituary, published a day after Grinnell died on April 11, 1938, the *New York Times* referred to him as the "father of American conservation."[3]

In 1866, the same year Grinnell entered Yale, the college awarded Othniel C. Marsh the first chair of paleontology in the United States. Several years later, as he was about to graduate, Grinnell learned that Marsh was going to lead an expedition that summer to

16. George Bird Grinnell and his wife, Elizabeth, standing on the glacier named for him in Glacier National Park. Among his many conservation accomplishments, Grinnell is probably best known today for his successful campaign to set aside this magnificent area as a national park, which he achieved in 1910. Glacier National Park.

the unmapped West in search of fossils. Marsh's acceptance of him as one of a dozen volunteer assistants from the college would prove pivotal in determining the course of Grinnell's life. Following the tracks of the recently completed transcontinental railroad, the 1870 Marsh expedition proved to be everything Grinnell had hoped it would be, and more. He would see free-ranging Plains Indians, get to know legendary scouts William F. "Buffalo Bill" Cody and Major Frank North, and travel among huge bison herds before the commercial hide hunters found them. In eastern Nebraska, for example, a herd stopped his train, taking three hours to cross the tracks! Grinnell's love affair with the West had begun; almost every summer thereafter he would return to explore, hunt, and collect fossils, birds, and other specimens, or study Indian cultures.

Not only was the Marsh expedition Grinnell's introduction to the West, it was also the beginning of a friendship between the two men, for Grinnell became one of the scientist's favorite graduate students. It was for Yale's Peabody Museum that Marsh sent him to collect specimens on the 1874 Custer expedition to the Black Hills and the 1875 Ludlow reconnaissance of the Yellowstone wilderness. The large collections Grinnell and others added to the museum took years to catalog and classify; it was not until 1880 that Grinnell was able to submit his dissertation, "The Osteology of *Geococcyx californianus*" (the roadrunner), and be awarded the PhD. In achieving this, Grinnell proved that he now possessed an awareness of some of the great transformations the earth had undergone, which made him realize that it was not invulnerable to human impact, as many of his contemporaries seemed to believe. When the concept of a vulnerable natural world was taken out of the past and applied to his own time, it naturally led him to be concerned about the rapid destruction of wildlife he was witnessing firsthand in the 1870s and 80s.

It was in fact Grinnell's anger over the slaughter of large mammals by commercial hide hunters in Yellowstone Park that led to his first published protest as a conservationist. In 1872 Congress had set aside the region as the nation's first national park, but with the idea that the area was a "museum" of "curiosities" or "wonders"—not a

17. George Bird Grinnell in 1870, the year he first traveled into the "Great West," a land still characterized by huge bison herds and free-ranging Plains Indians. *Images of Yale Individuals*, ca. 1750–2001 (inclusive). Manuscripts & Archives, Yale University.

national park in anything like the present conception of that term. Because the park's boundaries were drawn with little real knowledge of the terrain, expeditions were sent into the region to see exactly what Congress had in fact preserved. The Ludlow reconnaissance of 1875 was one of these. As the expedition's column traveled through the Yellowstone country, it continually encountered skin hunters. The completion of the transcontinental railroad to the south had made this great game region readily accessible to the eastern tanneries that called for the hides of all the larger mammals. The slaughter was almost beyond imagining, and Grinnell was outraged. His official standing as the Ludlow expedition's naturalist gave him a vehicle for expressing his anger.

Preceding his zoological report, published by the federal government as part of the papers of the reconnaissance, he included a "Letter of Transmittal," dated June 1, 1876, that he addressed to Captain Ludlow:

> It may not be out of place here to call . . . attention to the terrible destruction of large game, for the hides alone, which is constantly going on in those portions of Montana and Wyoming through which we passed. Buffalo, elk, mule deer, and antelope are being slaughtered by the thousands each year, without regard to age or sex, and at all seasons . . . Females of all these species are as eagerly pursued in the spring, when just about to bring forth their young, as at any other time . . . It is certain that unless in some way the destruction of these animals can be checked, the large game still so abundant in some localities will ere long be exterminated.[4]

Grinnell had no objection to hunting big game for food and a trophy—he was an avid hunter himself—but he despised those who killed game by the wagonload, without regard to sex or season, taking only the hides and leaving the meat to rot. He realized that those who hunted for sport were no threat to wildlife. Instead it was the commercialization of game that encouraged its unlimited, systematic destruction, threatening so many species with extinction.

In 1876, the same year Grinnell submitted his letter, he became the natural history editor of *Forest and Stream*, a weekly newspaper for sport fishermen and hunters. Several years later, as he was completing the research and writing for the PhD, Grinnell decided to leave the Peabody Museum, where the long hours had taken a toll on his health. He heeded the urgings of the paper's stockholders to go to New York and become the owner, publisher, and editor in chief of *Forest and Stream*.[5] When he assumed his new post on January 1, 1880, it was a monumental event in the history of American conservation. Controlling the weekly until 1911, Grinnell would pour forth a continual stream of front-page editorials that, when combined with his private efforts, made his influence on conservation incalculably great.

From the beginning of his tenure at *Forest and Stream*, Grinnell worked tirelessly to urge sportsmen to take responsibility for the game fishes, birds, and mammals they pursued. For this to happen they had to first understand that they were different from, and superior to, other fishermen and hunters who killed wildlife for commercial profit or simply to eat, without any higher understanding of the aesthetics, even the spirituality, of sport. In issue after issue Grinnell exhorted his readers to adopt the "code of the sportsman."[6] This was a kind of contract between hunters and anglers and their quarry that game should not be killed in the breeding season or sold for profit; that it should only be taken in reasonable numbers, without waste; and that it should be pursued solely by sporting methods. Of those who defied this code, the most despised were the market hunters that Grinnell encountered in Yellowstone Park in 1875. For him they became a symbol of the unrestrained greed sweeping the country after the Civil War, as well as of the abject failure of the federal government to protect and manage the natural resources of the American people. Yellowstone would be the test for whether or not that government could change; the park would be at the center of the early conservation movement.

In the December 14, 1882 issue of *Forest and Stream*, Grinnell launched what would prove to be a continuous editorial campaign, over the dozen years it took to achieve success, to make Yellowstone

Park an inviolate wildlife and wilderness preserve. Like all of his editorials, this one appeared unsigned, because he knew that the viewpoint of a prestigious newspaper carried more weight than the opinion of any one person. In "Their Last Refuge," Grinnell wrote:

> We have seen it [the West] when it was, except in isolated spots, an uninhabited wilderness; have seen the Indian and the game retreat before the white . . . tide of immigration. . . . There is one spot left, a single rock about which this tide will break, and past which it will sweep, leaving it undefiled by the unsightly traces of civilization. Here in this Yellowstone Park the large game of the West may be preserved from extermination; here . . . it may be seen by generations yet unborn. It is for the Nation to say whether these splendid species shall be so preserved, in this, their last refuge.[7]

Grinnell's poignant plea that we must work to ensure that wildlife in this reserve "may be seen by generations yet unborn" undoubtedly touched many of his readers. One of the most avid of these was a young Theodore Roosevelt, who would soon become a close friend of Grinnell's, joining him in his fight to save wildlife and its habitat in Yellowstone. In the years ahead it would be for those future generations that both men would fight their conservation battles.

The high regard in which Roosevelt and his family would come to hold Grinnell is shown by the request of Roosevelt's widow that Grinnell write the introduction to the first volume of *The Works of Theodore Roosevelt*, published by Scribner's in 1926.[8] Edith wanted the world to know the interesting story of how Grinnell's largely negative review in *Forest and Stream* of her late husband's *Hunting Trips of a Ranchman* (1885) would, ironically, lead to their close personal friendship. While the editor thought that "Roosevelt's accounts of life on a ranch are delightful for their freshness," he was "sorry to see that a number of hunting myths are given as fact, but it was, after all, scarcely to be expected that with the author's limited experience, he could sift the wheat from the chaff and distinguish the true from the false." Grinnell later justified the patronizing tone of his critique by reminding the reader that, at the time it was written, "there were not many active writers who had seen so much of the West as I, and who in travelling through it, had also given the same careful attention to the ways of the wild creatures."[9] While his criticism of *Hunting Trips* may have been justified, Roosevelt was piqued by the review and came to Grinnell's office soon after it appeared to ask for an explanation. "We talked freely about the book," Grinnell remembered, "and took up at length some of its statements." The editor must have made a strong case, for Roosevelt "at once saw my point of view":

> after we discussed the book and the habits of the animals he [Roosevelt] had described, we passed on to the broader subject of hunting in the West, which was still to some extent unexplored and unhunted, and to the habits of the animals as modified by their surroundings. I told him . . . about game destruction in Montana for the hides, which, so far as small[er] game was concerned, had begun in the West only a few years before that, though the slaughter of the buffalo for their skins had been going on much longer, and by this time . . . the last of the big herds had disappeared.

Because of their deep mutual interests, "Roosevelt called often at my office to discuss the broad country . . . we both loved, and we came to know each other extremely well."[10] The two men had, indeed, much in common. They had begun their active involvement with the natural world by hunting and collecting specimens, particularly birds. They had been introduced to the "Wild West" through the adventure tales of novelist Mayne Reid. They had gone to the most prestigious colleges, Yale and Harvard. They had experienced ranch life in the West, and they had been born into the New York upper class. These "patricians"[11] possessed an American version of noblesse oblige that required them to take a leadership role in correcting what was wrong with American society, especially its government.

After Grinnell became intimately associated with Roosevelt, he emphasized the need for an effective sportsmen's society, to do for the larger mammals what the Audubon Society—founded by Grinnell in 1886—was doing for birds. Roosevelt agreed;[12] in December

1887 he invited Grinnell and nine other sportsmen friends, all prominent, wellborn New Yorkers, to a dinner party in Manhattan. At it he proposed the formation of a national conservation organization, the Boone and Crockett Club, named after two of America's most famous hunter-heroes. Soon after that initial meeting, another was held at which Roosevelt, Grinnell, and Archibald Rogers, another club member, "formulated the purposes and objects of the organization."[13] Four of these articles had to do with promoting big-game hunting, exploration, and natural history study, but Grinnell clearly was the inspired source of article three: "To work for the preservation of the large game of this country, and, so far as possible, to further legislation for that purpose, and to assist in enforcing the existing laws."[14] Regular membership was limited to one hundred men, all of whom had to have taken at least one individual of three different species of big game by "fair chase," which meant that all unsportsmanlike methods, like hunting swimming animals from a boat or ones immobilized by deep snow, were strictly forbidden. The emphasis the club's constitution placed on fair chase meant that the reform potential of the sportsman's code was at last going to be realized. It was undoubtedly Grinnell who first pointed out that some provision in the membership requirements should be made for nonhunters, like his friends the geologist Arnold Hague and the Supreme Court lawyer William Hallett Phillips, who were interested in wildlife preservation and Yellowstone Park, and who could aid the club in its efforts. After some consideration it was decided that nonhunters could be elected to associate or honorary membership.[15] This rule and article three of the constitution were indications that the society would be more than a dining club of select outdoorsmen.

From the beginning of its existence the Boone and Crockett Club turned its attention to Yellowstone Park. Describing his early relationship with Roosevelt, Grinnell later recalled that, "as soon as he understood about the conditions in Yellowstone Park, he gave time and thought to considering its protection."[16] By April 1890 Grinnell could write Hart Lyman of the *New York Tribune* that

Roosevelt could now be counted among the reserve's most enthusiastic defenders. Like Phillips, Hague, and the other guardians, Grinnell believed that Roosevelt had no other "motive in this matter except the proper preservation of the Park."[17]

A problem soon arose, however, when Grinnell realized that his idea of park preservation went farther than what Roosevelt was at first willing to accept. Grinnell wanted not only the elimination of hide hunting, especially of the last free-ranging bison in the United States, but also an end to forest destruction, as well as of concessions around attractions like the park's geysers and waterfalls. Grinnell was also opposed to proposals for the construction of a private railroad inside the park to make it more accessible to tourists. Roosevelt toured the park in late 1890 to gain a better idea of its needs. He returned convinced that a railroad would be beneficial, because it would reduce Western opposition to the reservation while doing the park little material harm. Grinnell was particularly upset about this development, both because of his friendship with Roosevelt and because it would remove one of the park's most influential allies.[18] Despite these considerations Grinnell's commitment to his principles was then, as always, more important than friendship. He asked Hague and Rogers to attempt to "win Roosevelt back to his allegiance on this matter." If they could not, "of course, we must throw him overboard."[19] Luckily such a drastic move proved unnecessary, as one or both of these men managed to bring Roosevelt back to his original position. On December 24, 1890, Grinnell wrote Rogers: "I am glad to hear that Roosevelt is going to stand back on the question of railways in the Park and not to work against us."[20]

That hurdle cleared, in 1891 the leaders of Boone and Crockett galvanized themselves for a renewed effort on behalf of Yellowstone. The club's annual dinner was going to be held at the Metropolitan Club in Washington DC, and Roosevelt wanted to use the occasion to emphasize to government officials, like the Speaker of the House, secretary of the interior, and secretary of the Smithsonian, the need for action. Grinnell was so busy at the time with *Forest and Stream* that he thought he would be unable to attend, only changing his mind after receiving an urgent plea from Roosevelt.[21] At a business meeting beforehand, Grinnell and Roosevelt drew up a series of resolutions that were read at the dinner:

> *Resolved,* That the Boone and Crockett Club, speaking for itself and hundreds of [sportsmen's] clubs and associations throughout the country, urges the immediate passage by the House of Representatives of the Senate bill for the protection and maintenance of the Yellowstone National Park. *Resolved,* That this club declares itself emphatically opposed to the granting of a right of way to the Montana Mineral Railroad or to any other railroad through the Yellowstone National Park.[22]

After Roosevelt and Phillips made short speeches, the discussion turned to the subject of large game. As if on cue, Smithsonian secretary Samuel Pierpont Langley, "in response to a request from Roosevelt, said that he believed from what he had heard, that the large game of the Continent would be practically exterminated except in such preserves as Yellowstone Park, within the life of the present generation of men." To document that supposition, "Roosevelt . . . asked me," Grinnell wrote Rogers, "to say something of the way in which game had disappeared in my own time, and I told them a few 'lies' about buffalo, elk, and other large game in the old days."[23] Clearly, Grinnell's long and varied experience in the presettlement West had entitled him to Roosevelt's esteem.

By 1892 Yellowstone Park faced a new threat, what Grinnell called "segregation."[24] What he meant by this was that land speculators in Cooke City, Montana, wanted to delete (or segregate) some 622 square miles in the northeastern portion of the park and return it to the public domain so that they could develop it. They were pushing for a railroad in the park, but their efforts had been effectively blocked on the grounds that it would be an infringement on the park's integrity. The speculators reasoned that the perfect resolution to their dilemma was to have the area in question removed from the park. Grinnell published a scathing editorial attack on the Cooke City lobbyists, which Roosevelt, then a member of the U.S.

18. The 1874 George Armstrong Custer expedition to the Black Hills: Custer is lying down in the middle, and George Bird Grinnell is one of the three men standing together to the left of the tent, wearing a wide-brimmed hat. It was his early western expeditions that so endeared him to Theodore Roosevelt and that gave Grinnell the credibility to speak authoritatively, and urgently, about the decline of western big game. John Reiger Collection.

Civil Service Commission, enthusiastically endorsed in his letter of December 5, 1892 in *Forest and Stream*:

> I have just read the article, "A Standing Menace," printed in the *Forest and Stream*, in reference to the attempts made to destroy the National Park in the interests of Cooke City. I heartily agree with this article. It is of the utmost importance that the Park shall be kept in its present form as a great forestry preserve and a National pleasure ground, the like of which is not to be found on any other continent than ours; and all public-spirited Americans should join with *Forest and Stream* in the effort to prevent the greed of a little group of speculators, careless of everything save their own selfish interests, from doing the damage they threaten to the whole people of the United States, by wrecking the Yellowstone National Park. So far from having this Park cut down, it should be extended, and legislation adopted which would enable the military authorities

who now have charge of it to administer it solely in the interests of the whole public, and to punish in the most vigorous way people who trespass upon it. The Yellowstone Park is a great park for the people, and the representatives of the people should see that it is molested in no way.[25]

Although Grinnell, Roosevelt, and the Boone and Crockett Club were making steady progress in alerting the public to the dangers facing America's first national park, they would not achieve Grinnell's ultimate goal of establishing what he called a "government" for the park until they received the unwilling aid of the notorious poacher, Edgar Howell.[26] In the Pelican Creek area of Yellowstone in March 1894, he was caught shooting some of the last free-ranging bison for their heads and robes, which would bring large sums from taxidermists who wanted to stock up before the species became extinct. What made this more than an isolated incident in the remote western wilderness was the presence of a *Forest and Stream* reporter, Emerson Hough, whom Grinnell had sent into the park. When Hough telegraphed his editor with the news, Grinnell knew this was the opportunity for which he had been waiting. On March 24, 1894, in "A Premium on Crime," he published a strong protest in *Forest and Stream*: "The occurrence calls public attention again and most forcibly to the criminal negligence of which Congress has been guilty for all these years in failing to provide any form of government for the Park, or to establish any process of law by which crimes against the public committed within its borders can be punished."[27] Grinnell hammered away in the same vein in succeeding issues. In "Save the Park Buffalo," *Forest and Stream* asked "that every reader who is interested in the Park or in natural history, or in things pertaining to America, should write to his Senator and Representative in Congress asking them to take an active interest in the protection of the Park."[28] Another editorial dramatically underscored its point with three photographs of slain bison in the snow.[29]

The American people answered Grinnell's call. Eight years earlier, a railroad spokesman's rhetorical question—"Is it true that the . . .

demands of commerce [meaning a right-of-way through the park] . . .
are to yield to . . . a few sportsmen bent only on the protection of
a few buffalo?"[30]—had gone almost unchallenged. Now, those few
sportsmen were joined by a significant percentage of the articulate
and conservation-minded public. For the first time a bill to protect Yellowstone, introduced by Iowa Congressman John F. Lacey,
a Boone and Crockett member, faced little opposition in either
house, and the "Act to Protect the Birds and Animals in Yellowstone National Park" was signed by President Cleveland on May 7,
1894. It incorporated the park within the United States judicial district of Wyoming, making the laws of that state applicable except
when federal law took precedence. Killing animals, except to protect human life or property, was forbidden. All traffic in wildlife,
alive or dead; removal of mineral deposits; and timber destruction
were also forbidden.[31]

Despite the satisfaction that the passage of this legislation brought
the Boone and Crockett guardians of the park, they worried that
the clause allowing the killing of animals that endangered life or
property might be misused in the future. Still, the act was as close
to ideal as could be had at that time. Although "the . . . bill is not
perfect," Grinnell wrote Roosevelt, "with a good man at the head
of the Interior Department, and a good [park] superintendent,
it will prove effective." Despite Grinnell's central role in the campaign to protect the park, which he had initiated years earlier, he
chose to give most of the credit to other club members. While he
felt that Phillips "has of late years done more than anyone else for
the Park," he was well aware of Roosevelt's contributions, writing
his friend: "You personally have done a great deal and ought to be
'blown off' for your help."[32]

In founding a policy and administration for the nation's first
national park based on continuous, apolitical, scientifically based
management, Grinnell and his colleagues had established precedents that would be followed in the operation of all later national
parks. As one historian has observed, "the provisions of the Lacey
Act . . . formed the basis for the present law and policy under which

the National Park Service has administered the natural treasures of the United States since 1916,"[33] the year that agency came into existence. The earlier creation of the U.S. Forest Service (1905) and the national forest system was due in part to this energetic campaign in defense of Yellowstone, Grinnell noted in *A Brief History of the Boone and Crockett Club* (1910). In it he argued that "the attempt to exploit the Yellowstone National Park for private gain in a way led up to the United States forest reserve [national forest] system as it stands today," because "as a natural sequence to the work" the club's leaders had been doing in regard to Yellowstone Park "came the impulse to attempt to preserve western forests generally."[34]

As in the case of Yellowstone, Grinnell had led the club on the forestry issue. In 1882, the same year he began his drive to protect the park, he launched an editorial campaign to transform the nation's orientation to its timberlands—a campaign that would continue unabated throughout the decade.[35] What was needed in America, Grinnell argued, was the European attitude toward its woodlands. In an 1883 editorial, "Forestry," he reported that "in parts of Europe forestry is a science, and officers are appointed by the governments to supervise the forests, and only judicious thinning of young trees and cutting of those which [have] attained their growth is allowed."[36] To make his point, Grinnell contrasted the European emphasis on continuous, scientific resource management with the situation existing in America, where the sovereignty of private ownership allowed an individual to "buy a tract of land in the great water producing region of the State, and for his own pecuniary benefit, render it forever sterile."[37] He demanded that laws like those already existing in Europe, regulating forest use, be immediately passed in the United States. As in the case of fish and game legislation, he believed that statutes designed to scientifically manage the forests would have democratic results and "work well for the people at large."[38] After all, as all hunters and fishermen should know, "No woods, no game; no woods, no water; and no water, no fish."[39]

Since their original concern had been the park, it may seem strange at first that Grinnell and the other club members who had joined his campaign for forests would achieve concrete results on this issue three years before the passage of the 1894 Lacey Act. The reason for this was simply that the battle over the park took place in a public arena against determined Western opposition, while the results in forest conservation were achieved by circumventing the public forum. The event that gave Boone and Crockett leaders their opportunity was President Benjamin Harrison's appointment in 1889 of John W. Noble as secretary of the interior. Like his predecessors Noble received special attention from the club as soon as he entered office, which consisted of visits by Phillips, Hague, and Roosevelt, and invitations to the Boone and Crockett dinners. Adopting the position held by *Forest and Stream*,[40] he agreed that the first step in saving the timberlands was to give the president the power to withdraw them from the public domain. As soon as this goal of revising the land laws of the United States had been accomplished, Hague, representing the club, "saw Secretary Noble and [suggested] . . . the setting aside of the Yellowstone Park Forest Reserve adjoining the Park."[41] After Supreme Court lawyer Phillips, his close friend and adviser, assured Noble that there were no legal pitfalls involved, he took the plan to President Harrison, who proclaimed the Yellowstone National Park Timberland Reserve on March 30, 1891.[42] It contained 1,239,040 acres, all in Wyoming, and its establishment inaugurated the national forest system, which today totals more than 190 million acres.

Shortly after the creation of the Yellowstone Reserve, Roosevelt, representing the Boone and Crockett Club, endorsed the action and commended Harrison and Noble. Grinnell also expressed the club's gratitude to them in *Forest and Stream* and urged the public to accept the reserve and the policy it represented. Some years later Noble would gratefully acknowledge the aid Grinnell and "his very popular and influential paper" had given him, before and after the forest reserve system was initiated.[43]

In these early years of the conservation movement, when the Boone and Crockett Club played a pivotal role in establishing the laws and precedents that would govern future national parks and

19. An elderly George Bird Grinnell in his duck blind on Currituck Sound, North Carolina. Like Theodore Roosevelt, he was an avid hunter his entire life. John Reiger Collection.

national forests, George Bird Grinnell led the way. His importance as Theodore Roosevelt's chief conservation adviser would continue apace while they coedited the club's book series on hunting, natural history, and conservation, and during Roosevelt's brief tenure as governor of New York (1899–1900).[44] After 1901, however, when Roosevelt ascended to the presidency, Grinnell would be replaced, with his blessings, by Gifford Pinchot, the "trained professional" Grinnell had first called for in 1884 to lead the nation in the "inauguration of a system of forest conservancy."[45] Despite President Roosevelt's later emphasis on preserving and managing American forests, he got his start as an active conservationist on the national stage by answering Grinnell's call to save the threatened wildlife of Yellowstone Park, for generations yet unborn.

Notes

1. *Forest and Stream*, July 2, 1885.

2. John F. Reiger, ed., *The Passing of the Great West: Selected Papers of George Bird Grinnell* (Norman: University of Oklahoma Press, 1985).

3. *New York Times*, April 12, 1938, https://www.nytimes.com/1938/04/12/archives/dr-g-b-grinnell-naturalist-dead-founder-of-the-first-audubon.html.

4. William Ludlow, *Report of a Reconnaissance from Carroll, Montana Territory, on the Upper Missouri, to the Yellowstone National Park, and Return, Made in the Summer of 1875* (Washington DC: U.S. Government Printing Office, 1876), 61; Reiger, *The Passing of the Great West*, 117–19.

5. Reiger, *The Passing of the Great West*, 142–44.

6. For my articulation of the sportsman's code, see John F. Reiger, *American Sportsmen and the Origins of Conservation*, 3rd ed. (Corvallis: Oregon State University Press, 2001), 45–52, 182–83.

7. *Forest and Stream*, December 14, 1882.

8. The Roosevelt Memorial Association to Grinnell, January 23, 1923, George Bird Grinnell Papers, Yale University. Hereafter cited as "GBG Papers."

9. George Bird Grinnell, "Introduction," *The Works of Theodore Roosevelt*, vol. 1 (New York: Charles Scribner's Sons, 1926), xiv.

10. Grinnell, "Introduction," xv–xvi.

11. Edward N. Saveth, "The American Patrician Class: A Field for Research," *American Quarterly* 15 (Summer 1963): 235–52.

12. Grinnell to T. E. Hofer, January 15, 1919, Letter Book (hereinafter cited as LB), 269, GBG Papers.

13. Grinnell to Cromwell Childe, March 24, 1899, LB, 215, GBG Papers.

14. "The Boone and Crockett Club," *Forest and Stream*, March 8, 1888.

15. Because of Grinnell's influence, Hague and Phillips, in fact, became regular members, but they seem to have been the only nonhunters to receive that honor.

16. Grinnell, "Introduction," xxiii.

17. Grinnell to Lyman, April 23, 1890, LB, 289, GBG Papers.

18. Grinnell to Captain F. A. Boutelle, December 9, 1890, LB, 80–81; Grinnell to Archibald Rogers, December 19, 1890, LB, 129.

19. Grinnell to Arnold Hague, December 1, 1890, LB, 64–65.

20. Grinnell to Archibald Rogers, December 24, 1890, LB, 133.

21. Grinnell to Arnold Hague, January 13, 1891, LB, 183.

22. "Boone and Crockett Club Meeting," *Forest and Stream*, January 22, 1891.

23. Grinnell to Archibald Rogers, January 17, 1891, LB, 186–87.

24. "Dangers of Segregation," *Forest and Stream*, March 31, 1894.

25. Roosevelt, Letter to the Editor, *Forest and Stream*, December 15, 1892.

26. "The Account of Howell's Capture," *Forest and Stream*, May 5, 1894

27. "A Premium on Crime," *Forest and Stream*, March 24, 1894.

28. "Save the Park Buffalo," *Forest and Stream*, April 14, 1894.

29. "The Account of Howell's Capture," *Forest and Stream*, May 5, 1894.

30. Roderick Nash, *Wilderness and the American Mind*, 5th ed. (New Haven: Yale University Press, 2014), 114. Nash is quoting the *Congressional Record*.

31. "Act to Protect the Birds and Animals in Yellowstone National Park," Code of the Laws of the United States, 28 Stat., 73, May 17, 1894.

32. Grinnell to Theodore Roosevelt, May 8, 1894, LB, 57–58.

33. James B. Trefethen, *Crusade for Wildlife: Highlights in Conservation Progress* (Harrisburg PA: Stackpole, 1961), 42.

34. George Bird Grinnell, "A Brief History of the Boone and Crockett Club," in *Hunting at High Altitudes*, ed. George Bird Grinnell (New York: Harper & Brothers, 1913), 453, 455.

35. Reiger, *American Sportsmen and the Origins of Conservation*, 112–20, 166–68, 289n123.

36. *Forest and Stream*, July 19, 1883.

37. *Forest and Stream*, July 19, 1883.

38. *Forest and Stream*, July 19, 1883.

39. *Forest and Stream*, July 19, 1883; see also *Forest and Stream*, April 13, 1882.

40. "Forests of the Rocky Mountains III," *Forest and Stream*, November 8, 1888.

41. Arnold Hague to Grinnell, April 11, 1910, GBG Papers.

42. Arnold Hague to Grinnell, April 11, 1910, GBG Papers.

43. Reiger, *American Sportsmen and the Origins of Conservation*, 170; *Forest and Stream*, April 9, 1891; October 22, 1891; and December 3, 1891; quotation from Noble to Grinnell, March 11, 1910, and March 15, 1910, GBG Papers.

44. Reiger, *American Sportsmen and the Origins of Conservation*, 175–81.

45. *Forest and Stream*, May 15, 1884.

6

Play, Work, and Politics

The Remarkable Partnership of Theodore Roosevelt and Gifford Pinchot

CHAR MILLER

Theodore Roosevelt spared no words in praise of Gifford Pinchot, with whom the president worked closely and formatively in advancing the nation's environmental protections. Pinchot, the nation's first chief forester, "is the man to whom the nation owes most for what has been accomplished as regards the preservation of natural resources of our country," Roosevelt asserted in his autobiography. As the "foremost leader in the great struggle to coordinate all our social and governmental forces in the effort to secure the adoption of a rational and farseeing policy for securing the conservation of all our natural resources," Pinchot was not just the "moving spirit" behind the administration's remarkable record, but also the epitome of a self-sacrificing public servant:

> Taking into account the varied nature of the work he did, its vital importance to the nation and the fact that in regards to much of it he was practically breaking new ground, and taking into account also his tireless energy and activity, his fearlessness, his complete disinterestedness, his single-minded devotion to the interests of the plain people, and his extraordinary efficiency, I believe it is but just to say that among the many, many public officials who under my administration rendered literally invaluable service to the people of the United States, he, on the whole, stood first.[1]

Roosevelt's effusive praise was what any doting mother especially would love to hear about her offspring. Mary Eno Pinchot indeed

20. Mary, Gifford, and James Pinchot. U.S. Forestry Service (USFS).

took considerable pride in the president's evaluation of her son's manifold contributions to the administration and nation. Not just because of what Roosevelt wrote, but the fact that he written those generous words at all. Their presence on the page signaled that the twenty-sixth president had taken her seriously when she had chastised him for failing to acknowledge Gifford's efforts in the penultimate draft of his account of his years in the White House. Like Roosevelt she was a force of nature.

In the summer of 1913, Mary Pinchot's nearly forty-eight-year-old son Gifford appeared to suffer a blow probably only this mother could (and would) correct: Theodore Roosevelt had gone back on his word, withholding much-promised praise from his autobiography for the outstanding work Pinchot had done during his administration. The mother and son had discovered the disturbing omission while sitting together in the library of Grey Towers, the family's mansion in Milford, Pennsylvania. On that warm June evening, Gifford was reading aloud the page proofs of the manuscript for his mother's amusement—only she was not amused. To his diary, the slighted Pinchot confided that his mother "was indignant at the scant mention of me," and confessed to sharing some of his mother's anger, "especially in view of his declarations that he would give me much credit, several times repeated."[2]

Pinchot deserved the credit he craved. No one had been more intimately involved with the president's thinking on conservation matters; no one had worked as hard to turn those thoughts into political reality. Pinchot had been among a coterie of federal scientists and bureaucrats devising and implementing the aggressive conservationist agenda that has defined Roosevelt's continuing legacy in environmental politics: the number of national parks doubled from five to ten; the first eighteen national monuments were set aside, many located within Forest Service lands; and more than fifty bird sanctuaries were established. Roosevelt also signed off on the creation of the U.S. Forest Service and its jurisdiction over a rapidly expanding National Forest system, with Pinchot as its first head. Designating these forests and developing the agency to manage them occupied the lion's share of Pinchot's time and energy, but not exclusively. He also was centrally involved in the organization of countless national and regional conferences, among them the National Governor's Conference on the Conservation of Natural Resources in May 1908. From these podiums Roosevelt proclaimed his administration's allegiance to the conservation movement, proclamations Pinchot often ghostwrote. The men's close relationship had been one reason why Roosevelt asked Pinchot to draft an earlier version of the autobiography's chapter on conservation; once the chapter was drafted, TR was to have inserted the words that honored his valued colleague.[3] When Roosevelt failed to keep his side of the bargain, counseling his disappointed friend that "he had intended to treat me as he did himself (in his autobiography) by merely reciting facts," Pinchot felt boxed in, unable to respond. Those in the know, Roosevelt implied, would know the significance of Pinchot's many contributions.[4]

Mary Pinchot would have none of this heroic, masculine reticence.

As soon as her son had finished reading the chapter, she walked to her writing desk, picked up a pen, and, with her "right hand stiff with rheumatism," a painful fact she just happened to convey to her correspondent, wrote a scathing rebuke. "We have been reading tonight this chapter on Conservation for the 'Autobiography'—I am wondering if you know how little importance is given there to Gifford," she began. Warming to her task, Mary Pinchot wrote that she could not imagine how it was possible that "he who was the soul and fount of Forestry is scarcely mentioned by name," leaving the impression, which she knew Roosevelt knew to be false, that her son "was only incidentally connected" with the great policies of his administration. Gifford would not ask that the president correct the record—"His own modesty and generous way of regarding what others do, always prevents his taking credit for what is justly his due." Mary Pinchot was under no such restraint. This is "history you are writing," she counseled, "and so far as I know, there is little record of him except the shameful treatment of the last [Taft] administration and the vituperation of those who, being envious of righteousness and truth, hate him." Her son's intense devotion to Roosevelt's conservation ideals, which in 1910 had led William Howard Taft to sack him from his position as chief of the Forest Service for insubordination, should have impelled the former president to reestablish Gifford's reputation. Since it had not, she was reminding him of his duty: "It is for future generations that I wish [his] name to be vindicated and his services honored."[5]

Her angry words hit home not least because Mary Pinchot made it clear to the legacy-minded Roosevelt that her claims for her son were cut from the same cloth as *his* autobiographical ambitions, ambitions that had driven the former president "to seek the publication to the world of the truth" of his many accomplishments in office. Boosting Gifford would help elevate TR.[6] The former president rose to the challenge, revising the relevant chapter so that it contained the flattering words the Pinchots, mother and son, longed to read. "Gifford Pinchot is the man to whom the nation owes most for what has been accomplished as regards to the preservation of the natural resources of our country," Roosevelt now declared. As the "moving and directing spirit in most of the conservation work," the nation's chief forester "was practically breaking new ground."[7] For the restoration of her son's standing, Mary Eno Pinchot was grateful: "You told me I would be satisfied with your chapter on Conservation, and so I am," she responded after reading the published version. "I thank you for your admirable tribute to Gifford."[8]

Play Time

That the two men admired one another had much to do with their shared recreational interests, which in turn dovetailed with their commitments to the natural world and to its protection and conservation. An early expression of this emerged in Roosevelt's 1897 nomination of Pinchot to the Boone and Crockett Club, an organization of elite hunters and anglers whose proficiency with gun and rod was critical to the nomination process. This was not just a chummy club—it had a political mission. Roosevelt was one of its founding members, and helped make it the "first private organization to deal effectively with conservation issues on a national scope," historian John Reiger has observed. One mark of its effectiveness was the club's "all-important role in the creation and administration of the first national parks, forest reserves, and wildlife refuges." These were matters close to TR's and Pinchot's hearts, so it is not a surprise that the Rough Rider tapped the forester for membership.[9]

Nor that two years later, in February 1899, the two men indulged their joy in roughhousing. The occasion was Pinchot's first visit to the then-governor of New York. "We arrived just as the Executive Mansion [in Albany] was under ferocious attack from a band of invisible Indians," Pinchot later recalled, "and the Governor of the Empire State was helping a handful of children escape by lowering them out of a second story window on a rope." That night Roosevelt and Pinchot indulged in a few games of their own. The taller Pinchot used his long reach to good effect in a round of boxing: "I had the honor of knocking the future President of the United States off his very solid pins," he would boast. Bragging rights were not his alone. The smaller, albeit more powerfully built Roosevelt came back to overwhelm his lanky guest in a wrestling match.[10]

Tales of rugged outdoor adventures rounded out the evening. Pinchot and Grant LaFarge, son of the painter John LaFarge, had stopped off to see Roosevelt on their way to examine a forested tract the Adirondack League Club owned in the North Woods. The club had requested help from the U.S. Bureau of Forestry in establishing a plan to manage the lands; Pinchot and LaFarge hoped that making the trip would also help them sketch out their plans for a coauthored book on the region (the volume was never written). They had another reason for heading north, they confessed to Roosevelt. They wanted to make a winter ascent of Mount Marcy, which at 5,344 feet was the highest elevation in New York State. Their plan met with Roosevelt's robust support—"that was exactly in his line."[11]

What sounded so exciting in the cosseted warmth of the executive mansion turned brutal in reality. After completing their forest survey work for the Adirondack Club, Pinchot and LaFarge snowshoed with two guides through glistening white woods, every tree of which "was a monument of snow." The temperature had fallen to well below zero—Pinchot guessed it was anywhere between minus twenty-five and minus forty degrees outdoors—and the frigid air easily penetrated his light clothing. "I was wearing just what I wore in the woods in the summer, plus sweater, cap and mittens," the underdressed climber acknowledged. The next morning the foursome left base camp and slogged their way uphill, as heavy snow fell. Before they reached the timberline, the two guides turned back. Pinchot and LaFarge pressed on, struggling against a furious blizzard, which, though they did not know it, was battering the entire Eastern Seaboard; hundreds of miles to the south more than thirty inches of snow fell on Washington DC. On Mount Marcy the gale-force winds were so powerful that they forced LaFarge to stop, leaving Pinchot to crawl on his hands and knees, breaking handholds in the ice, "holding my head down in the squalls, and stopping every minute or two to rub my face against freezing." He stayed on the summit only long enough to snap photographs of the mountain's signal pole, then "thankfully crawled down again."[12]

Theirs had been a "foolish" ordeal, Pinchot admitted. One of the guides suffered a severe case of frostbite, as did LaFarge. Pinchot's ears and neck were also frostbitten, though he was not as badly off as his fellow climbers. There was this compensation—Pinchot and LaFarge, on their way back to New York City, spent the night in a snow-snarled Albany, regaling an envious Roosevelt with tales of their exploits.[13]

Like Roosevelt and Pinchot's earlier and sweaty embrace in sport, this incident was not simply an example of male posing and bonding (though it was surely that, too). It revealed, even as it helped to launch, an intellectual closeness between the future president and forester that henceforth would characterize their personal relationship and public careers. Just how far did this meeting of body and soul go? Their friendship clearly deepened during Roosevelt's tenure in the White House. Pinchot, who served first as head of the USDA Bureau of Forestry and later as chief of the new Forest Service, founded in 1905, reported that he visited the White House on an almost daily basis, "sometimes several times a day." The great outdoors continued to be the context for their evolving relationship. Together they would chop wood for exercise and practice jujitsu (a rigorous regimen that left Pinchot exhausted: "I often came back too tired to eat," he related abashedly). On weekends they would set off on extended tramps through Washington's Rock Creek Park, ride horses out into the fields surrounding the city, or swim the cool Potomac River in late fall. Not all of the swims were planned, as Robert Bacon discovered one November. Invited to the White House shortly after being appointed the assistant secretary of state, Bacon came dressed for the occasion, wearing "a cutaway coat, striped trousers, patent leather shoes, an expensive silk necktie, and carried in his hand a beautifully rolled silk umbrella." Pinchot knew better, wearing a set of old clothes, as did the president, who then set a blistering pace for the closest swamp. "After sloshing through mud and water for the better part of an hour,

21. Photograph of President Roosevelt and Gifford Pinchot on the river steamer *Mississippi*, taken on the trip of the Inland Waterways Commission down the Mississippi River in October 1907. Library of Congress Prints and Photographs Division. https://www.theodorerooseveltcenter.org/Research /Digital-Library/Record?libID=0291075. Theodore Roosevelt Digital Library. Dickinson State University.

we reached the bank of an inlet. . . . There T.R. expected to find a boat. But the boat was on the other shore." Undaunted the president took off his hat, "reached into his pocket, put his watch and other contents into his hat and carefully set it back carefully on his head. Bacon and I, watching him, did the same." The three of them plunged into the freezing waters. When the sodden Pinchot finally returned home, his childhood nurse, Mary McFadden, took one look at him, "pointed her finger in reproof, and exclaimed, 'You've been out with the President!'"[14]

These rugged excursions posed two kinds of tests. "On his walks and rides T.R. was supposed to be followed by two Secret Service men," Pinchot noted, but the president delighted in trying to outdistance his protectors, leaving the forester to act in their stead: "After my responsibility came home to me," Pinchot, a superb shot, took to carrying a gun. "Thank Heaven, I never had to use it." Far more enjoyable were the physical challenges Roosevelt threw his way and that of countless others, like Robert Bacon. "When a new man came to Washington as a member of the Administration inner circle," Pinchot remembered, "it was T.R.'s habit take the new man, as he took me, along what he called The Crack, a sloping fissure in the vertical rock wall of a quarry, on the west bank of Rock Creek, just below the [national] zoo. If you fell off," Pinchot recounted, "you would not be hurt. It was only a few feet above the ground. If you made it, you belonged."[15]

Pinchot belonged, a fact to which Roosevelt attested in a March 1909 letter he wrote to the charismatic forester just before Roosevelt relinquished the White House to the incoming William Howard Taft. "For seven and a half years we have worked together, and now and then played together—and have been altogether better able to work because we have played." Those years in the arena, whether in nature or indoors, were as significant for Pinchot, not least because of Roosevelt's astonishing energy. "I have seen many men who could keep pace with [T.R.] physically, and a few who could endure as much high pressure mental strain," Pinchot later wrote. "But I have never seen another man who could combine as much mental and physical exertion day after day as he could." By sharing in and contributing to this strenuous life, this active engagement, Pinchot had earned his stripes, becoming one of the president's "faithful bodyguard."[16]

Office Hours

A significant part of Pinchot's job was to advance, explain, and defend the president's conservation agenda. That was easy, given that he and Roosevelt were of like mind on the need to create what would become the U.S. Forest Service. Their goals were multiple and interconnected: to transfer millions of acres of public land to the new agency, located in Department of Agriculture, from the General Land Office, sited in the Department of the Interior, and to secure managerial authority to protect these lands, including the right to charge fees for logging, mining, and grazing on the national forests. The latter task was the most contested; here, too, Pinchot proved a formidable advocate. Consider the role he played at the June 1907 Denver Public Lands Convention. It drew an estimated four thousand delegates from around the West, each of whom appeared incensed by the Forest Service's regulatory mission and, by extension, the administration's assertion of executive power. One of these was Oregon senator Charles Fulton, who routinely denounced the administration's highbrow activism. "While these chiefs of the Bureau of Forestry sit in their marble halls and theorize and dream of waters conserved, forests and streams protected and preserved through the ages and the ages," he once asserted, "the lowly pioneer is climbing the mountain side, where he will erect his humble cabin and within the shadow of the whispering pines and the lofty firs of the western forest and engage in the laborious work of carving out for himself and his loved ones a home and a dwelling place."[17]

The Colorado state legislature shared Fulton's anger, calling the Denver convention "for the purpose of discussing the relation of the states to public lands, and, if possible, [to] agree upon some policy in regards these lands to be urged upon the general government." The conference's timing fed off an upsurge in western frustration with

22. Gifford Pinchot, first chief of the U.S. Forest Service, seated at his desk. Library of Congress, Prints and Photographs Division.

Roosevelt's conservation agenda. During the preceding six months western congressional representatives had beaten back attempts to institute grazing regulations on the public domain and vigorously attacked but failed to derail increases in the Forest Service's budgetary appropriations. Senator Fulton struck the most significant blow by inserting an amendment to the appropriations section of the agricultural bill of 1907; it included language prohibiting the president from creating or expanding forest reserves within Oregon, Washington, Idaho, Montana, Colorado, and Wyoming.[18] Roosevelt had to sign the bill by March 4, 1907, a week after its passage, but in the intervening seven days he unleashed Pinchot and his staff to prepare the necessary paperwork authorizing him to withdraw more than sixteen million acres of public land. The acreage helped establish sixteen new or previously designated national forests located in the six western states cited in Fulton's amendment. "We knew precisely what we wanted," Pinchot wrote. "Our field force had already gathered practically all the facts. Speedily it supplied the rest. Our office force worked straight through, some of them for thirty-six and even forty-eight hours on end, to finish the job." For his part Pinchot walked each completed proclamation over to the White House, watched as "T.R. signed them and sent them to the State Department for safekeeping," and later noted that "when the job was done some sixteen million acres . . . were rescued from passing into the hands of private corporations."[19]

The president's congressional opponents were livid and, in Roosevelt's felicitous phrase, "turned handsprings in their wrath." Pinchot was in the room when a delegation of angered western representatives met with the president, a "meeting [that] ended in a highly temporary era of good feelings."[20] Within two weeks Colorado legislators issued their call for the Denver meetings that they billed as a showdown with the federal government, a rebuke of the administration's usurpation of "the rights of the states and its citizens to develop and acquire title to these public lands and to utilize [their] resources." At Denver, then, the question of whose lands these were would be thoroughly debated: at stake was whether the states or the federal government had ultimate sovereignty over public lands.

Defusing the charged atmosphere was one of the reasons Roosevelt sent Pinchot to the 1907 Public Lands Convention in Denver. The nation's forester was also to assess the political damage that would come from continued implementation of federal regulation. "We must be careful that we do not invite a reaction by going too far in the creation of the new reserves," the president had noted in early February 1907. "We have gone ahead very fast indeed, and I think it extremely important that we should not do more than we can stand."[21] To judge from the conference's first two days, Pinchot's work in Denver was complicated. Each speaker seemed to feed off his predecessor's animosity; speech after speech lacerated the Roosevelt administration and Pinchot in particular. Senator Henry Teller of Colorado was among those who blasted the concept of federal sovereignty: "We cannot remain barbarians to save timber. I do not contend that the government has the right to seize land, but I do contend that we have the right to put it to the use that Almighty God intended." Such blunt and contentious language emboldened the audience, so that when on the afternoon of the convention's third day Pinchot finally strode to the elevated podium at Denver's Brown Theater, a cacophony of catcalls and jeers cascaded down.[22]

A light retort—"If you fellows can stand me, I can stand you"— seemed to quiet the hecklers. Pinchot then delivered a much-practiced speech about the critical relationship between national forests, watershed protection, economic growth, and political equity. Creating the vast national forests had had a series of beneficial effects, he declared: "government-regulated timber auctions prevented monopoly and the consequent excessive price of lumber" and they stabilized markets and ensured that there was "no question of favoritism or graft." Pinchot emphasized what he considered to be a critical connection between woods and water: forested lands protected "streams used for irrigation, for domestic water and manufacturing supply, and for transportation." He declared that, taken by itself, the "protection of irrigation throughout the west would justify the president's forest policy."[23] He must have been convincing because, at the conclusion of his address, surprised reporters noted that Pinchot was cheered "lustfully." Not everyone in the audience had been persuaded, but by the end of the conference its resolutions were decidedly more temperate than the anger that had brought the many delegates to Denver.[24] That Pinchot was willing to stand before his detractors helped his cause. So, too, did his argument that every legitimate interest must be acknowledged and negotiated. Take grazing. It was "primarily a local issue and should always be dealt with on local grounds. Wise administration of grazing in the reserves is impossible under general rules based upon theoretical considerations." Being sensitive to different landscapes meant that "local rules must be framed to meet local conditions, and they must be modified from time to time as local needs may require."[25] Citizen participation restrained federal power.

Pinchot made this case even more directly in "The Use of the National Forests," a Department of Agriculture pamphlet released

23. Forester Pinchot, center, with rangers in Yellowstone Forest Reserve, 1907. Kenneth D. Swan, U.S. Forest Service, Forest History Society Photograph Collection.

in June 1907 to coincide with the Denver meetings. In it he asserted that public lands "exist to-day because the people want them. To make them accomplish the most good the people themselves must make clear how they want them run." No single interest would be allowed to dominate Forest Service policy. "There are many great interests on the National Forests," and of necessity these "sometimes will conflict a little." Securing necessary consensus would ensure a rational use of the land; there "must be hearty cooperation from everyone."[26] Nature would compel them to do so in any event, Pinchot had warned the Denver conferees: "The protection of the forest and the protection of the range by wise use are two divisions of a problem vastly larger and more important than either." This is "the problem of the conservation of all our natural resources. If we destroy them, no amount of success in any other direction will keep us prosperous." Private interests and short-term thinking must give way to the long-term interests of the public good.[27]

Subordinated, too, were the interests of Native American tribes.

Reflective of this was the designation of the so-called midnight forests themselves. The thirteen proclamations that Pinchot and his staff had scrambled to produce, and that the president signed, historian Theodore Catton has observed, "targeted tribal lands for transfer to the U.S. Forest Service," conveying "seven tribal forests to adjacent national forests" for a period of twenty-five years. This process stripped the tribes of their authority over these acres and authorized the secretary of the interior and the head of the Bureau of Indian Affairs to oversee the management of any relevant resources—mostly timber and grasslands—and to disburse funds that any leases might generate. It crucially set in motion the allotment of land to individual Indians, as sanctioned under the terms of the General Allotment Act of 1887. The act's intent was to destroy tribal sovereignty and replace it with "the white man's values of private property ownership." Those acres not so allotted at the end of the twenty-five-year period would formally become part of the national forest system.[28]

No administration was keener on pressing forward on allotments than was Theodore Roosevelt's. In 1900, when Roosevelt entered the White House, the total number of allotments over the previous thirteen years had been 56,000; in 1909, when the twenty-sixth president stepped down, the figure had soared in excess of 190,000. The Forest Service was the prime beneficiary of this aggressive policy of land transfer, Catton argues: "At the same time that Roosevelt and Pinchot built up the National Forest System, they also played a major role in shrinking the Indian estate." Between 1905 and 1909, for example, the national forests "increased in size by around 97 million acres, while allotment led in fairly short order to Indians' loss of around 86 million acres. The rise of conservation dovetailed with a national closeout sale on the Indians' landed heritage."[29]

That Roosevelt and Pinchot operated in lockstep to accelerate this damaging dispossession is linked to their shared values as conservationists, at home and abroad. Yet, however conjoined they were, Pinchot did not forget his place. When he spoke or acted, he did so on behalf of the president. This latter point is crucial, for as much as Pinchot was a friend and confidant of Roosevelt's, and notwithstanding their shared familial privilege and position, and the like-minded character of their ideas and instincts, Pinchot knew that he was an agency chief, not the chief executive. He manifested his understanding of this difference in stature and significance every time he went on the road on behalf of Roosevelt. Serving as Roosevelt's "lightning rod," he absorbed the opposition's blows and shielded his boss from whatever political heat opponents hurled in his direction, just as he had done at the Denver Public Lands Conference. Strikingly, Pinchot never chafed at his role, but rather took advantage of this unparalleled opportunity. As an administrative spokesman, he proved dynamic. As an executive, he gained seasoning every time Roosevelt tasked him with extra responsibilities outside his daily work for the Forest Service (which happened frequently). And Pinchot learned by observing: "When I could," he wrote, "I loved to come before the morning rush [at the White House] was quite over and sit in the Cabinet room watching T.R. deal with problems and people."[30] Later Pinchot would put many of these newfound skills to work during his two terms as governor of Pennsylvania.

At the time he reveled in his full-bore role as a member of Roosevelt's team. For his part Roosevelt saw in Pinchot his own high-voltage approach to life, telling one correspondent that Pinchot "loved to spend his whole strength, with lavish indifference to any effect on himself, in battling for a high ideal." Gifford's self-sacrificing tendencies concerned his parents. They insisted that Roosevelt was a "vampire," drawing off Gifford's energy to such a degree that their forty-two-year-old son would "soon be a used up man—old and worn-out." Pinchot had no such worries. He welcomed the demands of the symbiotic relationship he and the president had developed, and promoted and benefitted from a very similar reciprocity within the Forest Service. Many of the rangers, lookouts, and staff whom he hired called themselves "G.P.'s Boys." One of them, Elers Koch, met Pinchot in a Washington State logging camp in 1899, was drawn to the chief forester's "magnetic personality and enthusiasm," and within a couple of years was studying for a master's in forestry at the Yale Forest School, which Pinchot and his family underwrote.

Shortly after graduating in 1902 Koch joined the Bureau of Forestry, the start of his forty-year career in the agency. He wrote: "I have always been proud of being one of Gifford Pinchot's young men. It was as fine, enthusiastic, and inspired a group of public employees as was ever assembled."[31]

Natural Outgrowth

These heady times did not last. On March 4, 1909, William Howard Taft was inaugurated president, ending Roosevelt's action-packed seven and a half years in the White House. Within ten months Taft would fire Pinchot for insubordination. The two events are linked. Pinchot had objected strenuously to the Interior Department's leasing of coalfields in the Chugach National Forest in Alaska, a public disagreement that reached such a pitch that President Taft had no choice but to fire the nation's chief forester. Pinchot's dismissal was a critical factor in Theodore Roosevelt's decision to seek the Republican Party's presidential nomination in 1912, and, when that failed, to run for president under the banner of the newly formed Progressive Party. Although Roosevelt threw himself into the two campaigns, with Pinchot serving as a key strategist, fundraiser, and speechwriter, Woodrow Wilson prevailed. Not all was lost: Roosevelt introduced Pinchot to another campaigner, feminist Cornelia Bryce, whose family's Long Island estate was near Roosevelt's beloved Sagamore Hill. A regular at Roosevelt's political roundtables, Bryce was every bit as shrewd, competitive, and energetic as her future husband. Among the handful of celebrants at the Bryce-Pinchot wedding in late August 1914 were Theodore and Edith Roosevelt.

Five years later, Roosevelt died. His death rocked Pinchot but also galvanized him. In 1920 Gifford and Cornelia Pinchot began to take the steps necessary to build support for their runs for office. Over the next two decades Gifford would serve two terms as governor of Pennsylvania, losing a number of other attempts to secure a seat in the U.S. Senate; Cornelia tried three times to win a seat in the U.S. House, but came up short. Win or lose, Gifford especially committed himself to upholding Roosevelt's legacy. "I was a follower of Roosevelt while he was living," Pinchot declared in his 1923 inaugural address as a first-term governor. "I am a follower no less today, and his great soul still leads this people on the road to better things." Progress required that the "public good comes first"; Pinchot promised that his new administration, like Roosevelt's, would "erect a structure of honest and effective service to all the people, without distinction of race, creed, sex, or political complexion." In Pennsylvania, a devoted Pinchot revived the Square Deal.[32]

Mary Eno Pinchot, who had died in 1914, would have been proud of her son's political success. She might have taken pride, too, in his enduring devotion to Rooseveltian ideals. After all, Gifford's deep commitment to TR, which the former president had not acknowledged in the first draft of his autobiography, had led her in 1913 to rebuke Roosevelt for not enumerating her son's substantial contributions in his administration. He complied not simply because she had admonished him, but also perhaps in acknowledgment of their tête-à-tête at Washington DC's Union Station immediately following Taft's inauguration. She, along with Gifford and a host of friends and dignitaries, had assembled there to wish the twenty-sixth president Godspeed. An observant *New York Times* reporter watched as Roosevelt chatted with Pinchot's "snow-haired mother," noting that "Roosevelt lingered talking with her longer than to any of the others. He repeated to her over and over again how loyal Mr. Pinchot had stood by him, and when she finally left, accompanied by the President's naval aide, who went to get her carriage, Mr. Roosevelt told her goodbye with apparent regret."[33]

Notes

1. Theodore Roosevelt, *An Autobiography* (New York: Macmillan, 1913), 411.

2. Gifford Pinchot, Diary, June 13, 1913, Gifford Pinchot Papers, Library of Congress (hereafter, GP); M. Nelson McGeary, *Gifford Pinchot: Forester-Politician* (Princeton: Princeton University Press, 1960), 240–41.

3. Gifford Pinchot, Diary, April 15, 1913, GP; portions of this chapter draw on Char Miller, *Gifford Pinchot and the Making of Modern Environmentalism* (Washington DC: Island Press, 2001), 147–77; McGeary, *Pinchot*, 94–100; Roosevelt, *Autobiography*, 428–61.

4. Pinchot, Diary, July 2, 1913, GP.

5. Mary Eno Pinchot to Theodore Roosevelt, June 13, 1913, Series 1, Reel 176, Theodore Roosevelt Papers, Library of Congress (hereafter, TR).

6. Mary Eno Pinchot to Theodore Roosevelt, June 13, 1913, Series 1, Reel 176, TR.

7. Roosevelt, *Autobiography*, 429; Mary Pinchot to Theodore Roosevelt, June 13, 1913; June 20, 1913, TR.

8. Mary Pinchot to Theodore Roosevelt, June 13, 1913; June 20, 1913, TR.

9. John F. Reiger, *American Sportsmen and the Origins of Conservation*, 3rd ed. (Corvallis: Oregon State University Press, 2001), 4.

10. Gifford Pinchot, *Breaking New Ground* (Washington DC: Island Press, 1998), 144–46.

11. Pinchot, Diary, December 26, 1898; February 4–10, 1899, GP; Pinchot, *Breaking New Ground*, 144–46.

12. Pinchot, Diary, December 26, 1898; February 4–10, 1899, GP; Pinchot, *Breaking New Ground*, 144–46.

13. Pinchot, Diary, December 26, 1898; February 4–10, 1899, GP; Pinchot, *Breaking New Ground*, 144–46. Nineteen months later, in September 1901, Roosevelt hiked up Mount Marcy; after descending he learned that President McKinley was dying and that soon he would become the president; Douglas Brinkley, *The Wilderness Warrior: Theodore Roosevelt and The Crusade for America* (New York: Harper, 2009), 392–95.

14. Pinchot, *Breaking New Ground*, 317–18.

15. Pinchot, *Breaking New Ground*, 314–15.

16. Kathleen Dalton, "Why America Loved Teddy Roosevelt: Or, Charisma is in the Eyes of the Beholders," in *Our Selves/Our Past: Psychological Approaches to American History*, ed. Robert J. Brugger (Baltimore: Johns Hopkins University Press, 1981), 269–91; Roosevelt to Pinchot, 2 March 1909, in *The Letters of Theodore Roosevelt*, ed. Elting Morison (Cambridge MA: Harvard University Press, 1954), 6:1541 (hereafter cited as *Letters*); Roosevelt to Kermit Roosevelt, 10 February 1904, in *Letters*, 4:724; McGeary, *Pinchot*, 65–67.

17. Fulton, quoted in Pinchot, *Breaking New Ground*, 299–300.

18. G. Michael McCarthy, *Hour of Trial: The Conservation Conflict in Colorado and the West, 1891–1907* (Norman: University of Oklahoma Press, 1977), 200–210, offers the fullest account of the ensuing battle between regional interests and federal power.

19. Pinchot, *Breaking New Ground*, 299–300.

20. Pinchot, *Breaking New Ground*, 299–302; McCarthy, *Hour of Trial*, 200–210.

21. Theodore Roosevelt to Gifford Pinchot, February 9, 1907, TR.

22. Pinchot, Diary, March-July, 1907, GP, tracks his interviews with various western leaders and his evaluation of the relative seriousness of their protests; McCarthy, *Hour of Trial*, 221–26.

23. Pinchot's speech appears in Char Miller, ed., *Gifford Pinchot: Selected Writings* (University Park: Penn State University Press, 2017), 51–53.

24. Quoted in Elmo R. Richardson, *The Politics of Conservation: Crusades and Controversies, 1897–1913* (Millwood NY: Krause, 1980), 39.

25. Miller, *Gifford Pinchot: Selected Writings*, 51–53; Pinchot, "Grazing in the Forest Reserves, *The Forester*, November 1901, 276.

26. Pinchot, *The Use of the National Forests*, (Washington DC: USDA-Forest Service, 1907), 25.

27. Miller, *Gifford Pinchot: Selected Writings*, 51–53; many of these same ideas are articulated in Theodore Roosevelt to Gifford Pinchot, August 24, 1906, quoted in Brinkley, *The Wilderness Warrior*, 664–65; Pinchot's earlier article, "Grazing in the Forest Reserves," *The Forester*, November 1901, 276–280, argued that the deep-seated antagonisms between interest groups vying for limited grazing land on public lands forced the federal government to mediate between these competing interests. To facilitate the resolution of these vexing disputes, Pinchot advocated a policy of consensus-building in which all groups and interests recognized at the outset that they would not—because the conditions of the land would not enable them to—obtain all that they wanted.

28. Theodore Catton, *American Indians and National Forests*, (Tucson: University of Arizona Press, 2016), 36–37.

29. Catton, *American Indians and National Forests*, 40.

30. Miller, *Gifford Pinchot and the Making of Modern Environmentalism*, 173–74; Pinchot, *Breaking New Ground*, 316: a partial list of the extracurricular work that Roosevelt tapped Pinchot to help organize and serve on includes the Keep Commission, the Inland Waterways Commission, the National Conference of Governors, and the Commission on Country Life.

31. Roosevelt to Henry Cabot Lodge, March 1, 1910, in *Selections from the Correspondence of Theodore Roosevelt and Henry Cabot Lodge, 1884–1918*, , ed. Henry Cabot Lodge and Charles F. Redmond (New York: Charles Scribner's Sons, 1925), 2:361; James Pinchot to Gifford Pinchot, April 9, 1907, GP; Bibi Gaston, *Gifford Pinchot and the First Foresters: The Untold Story of the Brave Men and Women Who Launched the American Conservation Movement* (New Milford CT: Baked Apple Club Productions, 2016); Elers Koch, *Forty Years a Forester,* ed. Char Miller (Lincoln NE: Bison Books, 2019), 34, 42.

32. Miller, *Gifford Pinchot and the Making of Modern Environmentalism*, 177–81; 249–89; 295–96; Miller, ed., *Gifford Pinchot: Selected Writings*, 133.

33. "Roosevelt Says Good-bye," *New York Times*, March 5, 1909, 3.

7

Friendship under Five Inches of Snow

Theodore Roosevelt and John Muir in Yosemite

BARB ROSENSTOCK

This is the story of how Theodore Roosevelt's 1903 camping trip with John Muir changed my life. Ten years ago, despite way too many viewings of the movie *Night at the Museum*, I'd have been hard-pressed to tell you anything about Theodore Roosevelt other than that (1) he hunted big game, (2) he had a mustache, and (3) he hunted big game. About John Muir I knew nothing.

I was a corporate marketing executive raising two sons with my husband in the suburbs. My boys didn't happen to like children's books that rhymed or featured talking bunnies. They tended to like stories about real people. Back then it was a challenge to find history-related children's stories that did not read like date-heavy fourth-grade textbooks. So, when we read together, I began making up stories to go with the pictures. Fast forward a few years and I was actively writing and submitting children's books that ironically featured rhymes *and* talking bunnies. I wrote what I saw promoted in bookstores, not what I found interesting. I was, as John Muir once wrote in his journal, "*on* the world, but not *in* it."[1] Not one manuscript sold.

That changed with a single line in a review of a book on Theodore Roosevelt. The book reviewer mentioned a time when Roosevelt had "left the presidency" to camp in Yosemite. I wondered, "How could a president just leave and go camping?"

An internet search of "Roosevelt camping" found the famous photograph of TR standing above Half Dome in Yosemite National

Park. The photo resulted in more questions: Who's that old, scrawny guy standing next to the president? How could any sitting president be allowed to be that much alone? Could the idea of a president and a camping trip make a decent children's book? How would I make young readers relate to the challenges faced by two men over one hundred years ago? That last question would take up the next two years of my life.

My local librarian found almost nothing specific to the camping trip, so I read multiple biographies on Roosevelt and Muir. Here were the three things I knew about their trip:

1. Roosevelt wrote a letter, March 14, 1903, asking Muir to guide him through Yosemite. The letter reads in part, "I do not want anyone with me but you, and I want to drop politics absolutely for four days and just be out in the open with you."[2] Those words struck me as poetic. Perhaps there *was* more to Theodore Roosevelt than the stereotypes I had learned.

2. In May 1903, Roosevelt traveled to Raymond, California, where he first met Muir, who had a home and farm about a hundred miles away in Martinez. There were lots of events planned, but Roosevelt nixed a number of them, irritating some of his hosts. They were not any happier to be left behind when TR and Muir went off into the wild to camp for three days.

3. By 1906 Roosevelt had signed a bill that put the Yosemite Valley and Mariposa Grove under federal protection as part of Yosemite National Park, eventually also adding almost 150 million acres to the national forests, and a host of wildlife sanctuaries, national monuments, and parks.

These three facts and a bunch of random biographical details were worked into a confusing picture-book manuscript that I sent off to publishers called *Teedie & Johnnie, the Wild Boys that Saved America's Wild Places.* This masterpiece was also rejected at least ten times, with comments like "Great idea on that camping trip part, but good luck with the rest."

Shoring up my confidence with Roosevelt's quotation, "There is no effort without error,"[3] I started over, tracing the story back to the essential question that any author should address—what is this story really about? A camping trip, yes. But what made it important? Through trial and error I studied the events through its main characters' letters, places, and objects—hunting for the story's heart. That heart turned out to be the friendship between John Muir and Theodore Roosevelt.

One would have a hard time inventing, let alone finding, two men more opposite in character. Roosevelt was stocky and prosperously fashionable. Muir was very thin and often disheveled at best. They were roughly a generation apart in age. At the time of the camping trip, Muir was sixty-five years old to Roosevelt's forty-four. They grew up in different worlds. Roosevelt was the pampered son of a prominent New York City business family, with mostly loving family relationships. Muir was the impoverished, immigrant son of a harsh, religious Scotsman who farmed in rural Wisconsin and believed much too strongly in "spare the rod, spoil the child." Roosevelt graduated Phi Beta Kappa from the exclusive Harvard; Muir dropped out of a public institution, the University of Wisconsin in Madison. Roosevelt loved a crowd; Muir preferred long periods of solitude. John Muir, averse to violence of any kind, had dodged serving in the Civil War by moving to Canada. He fasted often, ate meat irregularly, and called hunting animals "the murder business." Theodore Roosevelt's famous military legacy as a Rough Rider is well known. He enjoyed hunting (and eating!) game. Roosevelt was first married at twenty-two; had six children, five of them in a relatively short time frame; and his adult life was centered on the East Coast. Muir first married only at forty-two years of age, had just two daughters more than five years apart, and his adult life was centered on the West Coast.

After looking at these opposite lives side by side, I wondered, "Why *camp* for three nights with a stranger with whom you had nothing in common?" That's the definition of a terrible plan. So, either they weren't strangers or the time together was crucially important—or maybe they had more in common than first appears.

It is true that Muir and Roosevelt had never met in person before the start of the camping trip on May 15, 1903. However, Roosevelt may have felt he knew Muir because of one of the things they had in common—the great pleasure they took in books and storytelling. Both were avid readers and writers. Muir penned twelve books and hundreds of articles and essays; Roosevelt eventually authored approximately forty books. Douglas Brinkley's *Wilderness Warrior* states that Roosevelt had read all of the books Muir wrote. Given Roosevelt's lifelong fascination with natural history, that is not too surprising; yet, considering his busy life, TR obviously thought Muir's writings were worth his time. Though they had never met, Roosevelt, along with many other readers at that time, probably felt he knew Muir's life and thoughts from his writings.

For Muir was quite famous: "John of the Mountains," a globally known, traveling preservationist, a leading nature scientist, and an acknowledged sage. He was also a brilliant prose writer, engaging city people with new ideas about experiencing wilderness—as in this beginning paragraph on the birds of the Yosemite from his 1901 book, *Our National Parks*:

> Travelers in the Sierra forests usually complain of the want of life. 'The trees,' they say, 'are fine, but the empty stillness is deadly; there are no animals to be seen, no birds. We have not heard a song in all the woods.' And no wonder! They go in large parties with mules and horses; they make a great noise; they are dressed in outlandish unnatural colors; every animal shuns them. Even the frightened pines would run away if they could. But Nature-lovers, devout, silent, open-eyed, looking and listening with love, find no lack of inhabitants in these mountain mansions, and they come to them gladly.[4]

An astute politician, Roosevelt and his staff certainly could not resist keeping track of Muir's efforts to save California's (in fact, the nation's) wilderness. His successes included protecting parts of Yosemite as a national park in 1890 and the 1892 founding of the Sierra Club, with its ongoing political efforts, including protecting Mount Rainier as a national park in 1899.

Knowing Roosevelt's naturalist leanings, I am not sure he could have resisted Muir's scientific study of nature. Muir's theories on glaciation and his first-person encounter stories starring squirrels, snakes, and bears were regular parts of his writings. So, when in 1901 Muir wrote a book calling on the federal government to "save the trees," TR answered. It suited Roosevelt's vision for a country then controlled by unbridled capitalism *and* it dovetailed with his vision for how to promote the conservation of America's natural resources.

For Theodore Roosevelt loved the natural world. The idea that guns, hunters, and saving wilderness ever went together was new to me. The Boone and Crockett Club that TR founded with George Bird Grinnell in 1887, to save big game? I'd never heard of it. Roosevelt was as romantic an advocate for wilderness as Muir, but with a much more human-use-oriented bent. He believed both approaches—the utilitarian and preservationist—were necessary. We are still not sure today if this is possible. Although Muir initially shared this dual perspective, in time he would come to argue that the preservation of nature and the use of natural resources was a contradiction in terms.

Despite these differences and to his everlasting credit, even before 1903 Roosevelt had put political muscle behind preserving national forests; beginning in 1903 he began to set aside our earliest game and bird preserves. He saw the mountains, the bears, the deer, and the trees, especially those in the "Wild West," as America's most important heritage—essential things that could not disappear without diminishing the nation itself. And it was all disappearing fast, much faster than anyone expected.

What would the country have looked like without forceful advocates like Muir and Roosevelt, among so many others, saving what they could, when they could? Well, the norm was men like Frederick Weyerhaeuser, who bought, cut, and abandoned millions of acres of old-growth forests across the country. Sheep were grazing totally bare the lands supposedly protected by state or federal law; resource-extraction companies regularly invaded national forests and parks. There was no regular security force, so who would stop them?

24. Theodore Roosevelt and John Muir standing on Glacier Point, Yosemite National Park, 1903. Theodore Roosevelt Birthplace National Historic Site. https://www.theodorerooseveltcenter.org/Research/Digital-Library /Record?libID=0283095. Theodore Roosevelt Digital Library. Dickinson State University.

The buffalo were gone—conservatively, an estimated fifty million buffalo had been slaughtered in the final decades of the nineteenth century, leaving less than a thousand on the Great Plains. Grizzlies were on their last legs; many species of elk, wolves, foxes, and birds were either at or over the brink of extinction. Even with the president's blend of human use and preservation, nature faced powerful opponents—those who thought the wilderness would recover or didn't care because of the immense amounts of money involved in railroads, mining companies, and big timber. To make his case Theodore Roosevelt needed the public on his side; with his big bully pulpit, he went out to get them.

Roosevelt left Washington for the longest, most publicized cross-country trip by any president up to that point at nine o'clock in the morning on April 1, 1903. The camping trip was part of a much wider effort called the Great Loop tour, a campaign for reelection that included preaching about America's natural heritage to her citizens. It was a grueling schedule for Theodore Roosevelt and his staff—a fourteen-thousand-mile, sixty-six-day journey through states and territories in the Midwest and West. Before he toured Yosemite with Muir, he whistle-stopped, waved, and speechified his way through hundreds of small towns and big cities. He also camped in Yellowstone with John Burroughs, whom he knew well.[5]

I realized there was no way to get the trip right without seeing Yosemite in person. I traveled there in September 2007 at its least impressive, low-water time. I did not camp but stayed in a park service cabin, sticking mostly to the main roads and tourist areas.

But still, and always, the place speaks for itself.

It turns out that John Muir was right: the farther you go from the crowds the louder Yosemite speaks. I could only imagine what it had been like in 1903; but could I do more than imagine?

I learned that some of our national parks have actual libraries in them. There is a Yosemite Research Library, upstairs in the museum that contained half a shelf of materials on the camping trip, including period photos, illustrations, and news articles. I read a then-unpublished version of the only first-person account of the trip, by

Charlie Leidig, who was there as a guide.[6] Others along on the trip with Muir and Roosevelt were another guide named Archie Leonard and an army packer named Jack Alder. There was also a big official entourage with the president, including four Secret Service men; William Loeb Jr., Roosevelt's secretary; Nicholas Murray Butler, Columbia University president; Dr. Presley Marion Rixey, the surgeon general; George Pardee, governor of California; William Moody, secretary of the navy; and Benjamin Wheeler, president of the University of California. Various people wrote the letters that helped Muir and Roosevelt get together, but Wheeler made the final arrangements.

Muir had plans to leave on a world tour in May. At first he did not want to take the president camping—he was tired of politicians and had many preparations to make before his trip. Wheeler basically ordered Muir to change his tour dates and take Roosevelt camping with a stern note: "You surely ought not to let [this opportunity] fail." It was so important; those who cared about conservation knew Muir's potential persuasive power once he had the president in Yosemite's gorgeous grip.

The morning of May 15, 1903, Roosevelt arrived in Raymond on the presidential *Special*. Muir was on the train already, but they had not met. The day before, Roosevelt had had a speaking engagement at the University of California. Muir was invited to sit on the dais but had said he was too busy with his cherry crop, so, never being very concerned with proprieties, he sent his seventeen-year-old daughter, Helen, as his stand-in. After Muir finished with the cherries at home, he had supper then took the ferry over to Oakland. It was almost ten o'clock at night when he found the presidential *Special* waiting on a siding. Muir simply climbed on the train, located a porter, and asked to be shown to bed. The porter told him it was not proper to retire before the president returned to the train. Muir apparently replied, "But it's my bedtime," and went right to sleep without meeting Theodore Roosevelt! TR got back to the train about 1:00 a.m., when Muir was out like a light. Through the night, the presidential train, with both men on board, made its way toward Yosemite itself.[7]

Because of his taxing schedule, Roosevelt had hoped to rest a bit in the wilderness. Instead, at seven thirty in the morning on May 15, the train pulled into Raymond, the last real town before Yosemite, population less than five hundred people. There Roosevelt was surprised to find essentially the whole town waiting for him. He was not prepared at all, so he spoke quickly off the cuff about seeing Yosemite with Muir, whom he must have met at some point that morning, though no one knows when or how. At this point, as far as we can tell, as in their letters, they were "Mr. President" and "Mr. Muir" to each other.

In addition to missing pieces of the historical record, even the best accounts of the trip start to differ a bit. The president's whole party, which included Muir at this point, got into one or two eleven-passenger coaches. The president was driven either by a man named Tom Gordon or a man named Bright Gillespie, while the entourage received a military escort under the command of U.S. Army Lieutenant Mays and thirty cavalrymen. They either went first to Sell's Ahwahnee Tavern (which was more typical) and then to the Mariposa Grove or, alternatively, according to Leidig, directly to the Grizzly Giant in Mariposa Grove. The photographers Underwood and Underwood took formal pictures. Then Roosevelt dismissed the troops, and the stagecoach took all the members of his party to the Wawona Hotel, except for Muir, Roosevelt, Charlie Leidig, Archie Leonard, Jack Alder, four horses for the men, and four mules that hauled equipment.

In an unprecedented move the Secret Service did not accompany Roosevelt; the press was not allowed on most of the trip either. Roosevelt made a huge effort to be alone in the wilderness with Muir. As an example, according to the official schedule, Roosevelt was supposed to have dinner at the hotel, where there were fireworks and speeches planned. Instead the officials stayed at the hotel, while Roosevelt and Muir stayed far away from them under the giant sequoias. Leidig cooked beefsteak, fried chicken, and strong coffee over the fire. They camped right under the Grizzly Giant. Roosevelt slept under a "shelter half" (like a half pup tent), with forty blankets piled up for warmth. Muir rolled up in his own blanket on a bed of branches, as he often did when outdoors.

But what did the two speak about that entire day? As with their historic introduction, no one thought to note their interactions down.

On Day Two, May 16, they broke camp at Mariposa Grove and were on horses by six thirty in the morning. Roosevelt asked the guides, Charlie and Archie, to "keep away from civilization," so they didn't go anywhere near the hotel. Instead they went down Lightning Trail and crossed the South Fork Merced River to Empire Meadows Trail, where they ate a cold lunch. They climbed toward Sentinel Dome. The *San Francisco Chronicle* describes their day like this: "The President rode through the deep snow, accompanied by John Muir and Guides Leonard and Leidig, stopping now and then to allow their fatigued horses to rest before plunging through another snowdrift." Perhaps some press did follow at a distance.

In Bridalview Meadows the snow was almost five feet deep. Roosevelt's horse got stuck, so Charlie Leidig used a log to get them out. Muir wanted to camp right behind Sentinel Dome but Charlie won out, so they camped at Glacier Point, where fresh water was more readily available.

Charlie heard Muir and Roosevelt talking around the campfire far into the night about many topics: Muir's glacial theory of Yosemite's formation, the conservation of the country's forests in general and of Yosemite's big trees in particular. They discussed setting aside other areas in the United States for national parks. They seemed to have problems conversing at times, not because they ran out of things to say as you would with a stranger, but because "both men wanted to do the talking." They were trading stories and stepping on each other's words—they were becoming friends.

This time they both rolled up in tarps and blankets and woke up on Day Three, May 17, covered in five inches of snow. As TR related later that day, "We slept in a snowstorm last night! This has been the grandest day of my life."

They traveled down to Glacier Point for prearranged pictures.

25. Roosevelt seated at Glacier Point, 1903. Library of Congress Prints and Photographs Division. https://www.theodorerooseveltcenter.org/Research /Digital-Library/Record?libID=0275141. Theodore Roosevelt Digital Library. Dickinson State University.

There were at least five professional photographers on hand, including press and some of the official party who had come by stage to meet the president along the way. Afterward, Roosevelt, Muir, Charlie, Archie and Jack left everyone else at Glacier Point and continued their rambles. Muir picked twigs to place in Roosevelt's buttonhole, which seemed to irritate the president—a sure sign they were dropping pretenses and really getting to know each other.[8] They spent a lot of time quizzing each other on birds they heard along the way. Roosevelt won. He seemed to know the songs of every bird they encountered, whistled in reply, and, to Muir's astonishment, often got an answer.

Muir and Roosevelt went for lunch to Little Yosemite Valley, where a huge crowd had gathered. Roosevelt requested they be kept at a distance so he could continue to "rough it." At two o'clock in the afternoon, they reached Camp Curry, where a crowd of women blocked the way. They wanted to shake hands with the president. Roosevelt was very annoyed and asked Charlie to "do something!" Charlie Leidig reared up on his already half-wild horse. The women backed off, the president gaily waved his hat, shouted his apologies to the ladies about the horse's behavior, and followed Charlie right on past.

When they reached Sentinel Bridge, officials were there to meet him. The president was tired, but the whole party went to artist Chris Jorgenson's studio and had a glass of champagne. Jorgenson lived and painted in Yosemite. He and his wife offered a room for the president to spend the night indoors. Roosevelt politely refused, wishing to continue camping. Always the politician, he hugged and blessed a little girl, then gave a hearty scolding to a boy who made the mistake of yelling out to the president of the United States, "Hi Teddy!"

The small party of five then left the officials and continued down the valley to pick a campsite near Bridalveil Falls, which is where Muir wanted to spend their last night.

As they traveled down the south side of the river, a crowd of people followed them and started filling in Bridalveil Meadows. TR said, "Leidig, these people annoy me. Can you get rid of them?" Charlie told the crowd that the president was very tired and asked them to leave. Every single person did, some of them walking away on tiptoe so as not to disturb President Roosevelt.

"Charlie," Roosevelt then said, "I am hungry as Hell. Cook any damn thing you wish. How long will it take?" Leidig said he needed thirty minutes, so TR fell fast asleep on a blanket. He snored, loudly. He woke up for dinner with Muir and the two then went away from everyone out in the meadow until way after dark, talking, talking, and talking. Again, no one recorded any specifics.

When they returned, they sat around the campfire and the president told stories, including some about past hunting trips. Some accounts say this is when Muir asked Roosevelt, "When are you going to get beyond the boyishness of killing things? Are you not getting far enough along to leave that off?" If these stories are to be believed, TR supposedly looked around for a moment and thoughtfully replied, "Muir, I guess you are right." The friends slept their last night together under the trees.

Before dawn on Day Four, May 18, crowds of people started returning to the meadow and could be spotted through the brush. Charlie kept them away until after breakfast. Then the stage came down with the official party and TR said to goodbye to his guides. The stage driver, Tom Gordon, covered the sixty-nine-mile trip back to Raymond with TR, Muir, and the officials in about ten hours. No one knows exactly when Muir left the president, but it could have been Lathrope, the nearest station to transfer back home to Martinez. Years later, in an appreciation of Muir he wrote in *Outlook*, Roosevelt told a version of what happened as they said their camping trip goodbyes.[9]

It seems a scientific colleague wrote Muir requesting an introduction by letter from President Roosevelt to Russia's czar and China's emperor. This way, the scientist could study trees in Siberia and Manchuria uninhibited by local officials. Roosevelt explained to Muir that he could not introduce random people directly to heads of state. Muir, thinking that Roosevelt had not understood what his colleague had asked for, simply handed Roosevelt the original letter and said, "Read it yourself."

Roosevelt started reading, then laughed and laughed: "John [for it was now "John," not "Mr. Muir"], do you remember exactly the words in which this letter was couched?" Muir looked startled and said, "Good gracious! There was something unpleasant about you in it, wasn't there? I had forgotten." At the beginning of the letter were these words: "[Roosevelt] takes a sloppy, unintelligent interest in forests," as well as a few other choice comments about TR and his immediate staff. Roosevelt so admired Muir's honest innocence, or by this point felt so close to him, that he sent along the diplomatic introduction letters the very next day, in spite of the insults.

Almost two years into my research, through diaries and newspaper accounts, I discovered that Muir and Roosevelt seem to have briefly attended the same public function about seven years later in Los Angeles. However, the two men never spent any length of time together again. Two days after they parted company, on May 19, Roosevelt wrote Muir from Sacramento:

> How happy were the three days in Yosemite I owed to you, and how greatly I appreciated them. I shall never forget our three camps; the first in the solemn temple of the giant sequoias, the next in the snow

storm among the silver firs near the brink of the cliff; and the third on the floor of the Yosemite, in the open valley fronting the stupendous rocky mass of El Capitan, with the falls thundering in the distance on either hand.[10]

In total there are only nine letters from Muir to Roosevelt and ten from Roosevelt to Muir. In their correspondence they talk of policy, often disagreeing, sometimes vehemently so. Among those points of disagreement was the damming, for use as a reservoir for San Francisco, of the Tuolumne River inside Yosemite National Park that led to the 1913 inundation of the fabled Hetch Hetchy Valley. The failure to prevent it, some people believe, hastened Muir's death in 1914. But most of their letters still include tender phrases. From Theodore to John, "I wish I could see you in person"; and from John to Theodore, after his final term ended in 1909, "somehow the whole country seems lonesome to me since you left Washington." Their friendship shines through in one special letter from Roosevelt (a man who had early on lost a young and beloved wife), sent in condolence to Muir upon his wife's death in 1905. "Get out among the mountains and trees, friend, as soon as you can," Roosevelt wrote. "They will do more for you than either man or woman could."[11]

Right after the camping trip, Muir had told his wife, Louie, that he "fairly fell in love" with Roosevelt. Roosevelt many years later called his time with Muir "the one day of my life . . . that I will always remember with pleasure." The camping trip bonded these two mostly opposite personalities. And Muir certainly did his job on a president who was already primed to care for nature. John Muir proudly wrote that he had "stuffed him pretty well regarding the timber thieves, and the destructive work of the lumbermen and other spoilers of the forest." Roosevelt, who shared Muir's anger and who, prior to his visit to Yosemite, had already designated a number of new forest reserves, used his campfire conversations with Muir to further their shared cause.[12]

Starting right after their journey, Roosevelt employed Muir-like phrases in a speech he delivered in Sacramento just two days after decamping from Yosemite:

> As regards some of the trees, I want them preserved because they are the only things of their kind in the world. . . . I hope for the preservation of the groves of giant trees simply because it would be a shame to our civilization to let them disappear. . . . We are not building this country of ours for a day. It is to last throughout the ages.[13]

What exactly did these two men have in common? A passion for the importance of story, a deep respect for nature, a love of country, and, later, a great affection for each other as fellow human beings. That was enough to build a friendship and help change a country. But they were also two fathers—men who hoped to leave the world in better shape for their children.

About two years into my primary research, with a deep knowledge about the feelings Yosemite inspires, I became convinced that modern children could relate to Muir and Roosevelt's camping trip. Happily it turned into my first picture book, *The Camping Trip that Changed America*, illustrated by Caldecott medalist Mordicai Gerstein.[14]

As corny as it may sound, Muir's passion and Roosevelt's determination turned me into a children's author. Without working through their challenges, learning how to track down the truth, and "fairly falling in love" with both men, I would not have discovered my own life's work—telling history's stories to today's children. We also need children to learn about Roosevelt and Muir, who as kids fell in love with nature, and as adults were not afraid to stick their necks out to say what they believed, argue, organize, volunteer, read, and write about the enduring need to save the planet for future generations. I write history so that my young readers know they are not alone, so they know they can make a difference, so they know that Roosevelt and Muir, like all of history's giants, have *always* struggled and failed, then struggled and succeeded. Roosevelt and Muir started out as ordinary children, yet changed the nation. Today's ordinary children start out with everything they need—curiosity, motivation, and open hearts—to change America for the better, too.

Notes

1. Linnie Marsh Wolfe, ed., *John of the Mountains: The Unpublished Journals of John Muir* (Boston: Houghton Mifflin Company, 1938), 230.

2. TR to John Muir, March 14, 1903, quoted in Frederick Turner, *John Muir: Rediscovering America* (New York: Da Capo Press, 2000), 325–26.

3. TR, "Citizenship in the Republic," speech delivered at the Sorbonne, in Paris, France, on April 23, 1910.

4. John Muir, *Our National Parks* (Boston: Houghton Mifflin Company, 1901), 213.

5. Douglas Brinkley, *The Wilderness Warrior: Theodore Roosevelt and the Crusade for America* (New York: HarperCollins, 2009), 536–47.

6. Charlie Leidig's Report of President Roosevelt's Visit to Yosemite in May 1903, Yosemite Research Library, Yosemite National Park, typescript, 1–4.

7. The following paragraphs are drawn from William F. Kimes, "With Theodore Roosevelt and John Muir in Yosemite," in *The Westerners Brand Book No. 14*, ed. Doyce Nunis (Los Angeles: Los Angeles Corral of the Westerners, 1974), 189–204; Brinkley, *The Wilderness Warrior*, 536–47.

8. Brinkley, *The Wilderness Warrior*, 546.

9. The following paragraphs are drawn from TR, "John Muir: An Appreciation," *Outlook* 109, January 16, 1915, 27–28, https://vault.sierraclub.org/john_muir_exhibit/life/appreciation_by_roosevelt.aspx.

10. TR to John Muir, May 19, 1903, Online Archive of California, http://www.oac.cdlib.org/ark:/13030/kt3199r8rw/?order=2&brand=oac4.

11. TR to John Muir, August 17, 1905, https://scholarlycommons.pacific.edu/jmcl/3507/.

12. W. H. Trout, "Reminiscence of John Muir," Holt-Atherton Special Collections, University of the Pacific, https://scholarlycommons.pacific.edu/jmr-all/98/.

13. TR, Address at the Capitol Building in Sacramento, California, May 19, 1903, http://www.presidency.ucsb.edu/ws/?pid=97748.

14. Barb Rosenstock, *The Camping Trip that Changed America: Theodore Roosevelt, John Muir, and Our National Parks* (New York: Dial Books, 2012).

8

The Cowboy, the Crusader, and the Salvation of the American Buffalo

CLAY S. JENKINSON

My policy is no quarter to the destroyers of wildlife.
—WILLIAM T. HORNADAY, 1913

Two of America's great conservationists, Theodore Roosevelt (1858–1919) and William Temple Hornaday (1854–1937), traveled west in the 1880s for the purpose of killing buffalo. Roosevelt rode the just-completed Northern Pacific Railroad in September 1883 to the badlands of the Little Missouri River valley in Dakota Territory.[1] He got his buffalo, fell in love with the stark landscape, established two ranches in what is now southwestern North Dakota, and gave a significant portion of the next four years (1883–87) to Dakota frontier adventures. He later told New Mexico senator Albert Fall that his time in the Little Missouri River valley was the single greatest experience of his life, for which he was prepared to erase all other memories, if necessary. Hornaday traveled west in May 1886 to kill buffalo to mount and display at the National Museum in Washington DC. Like Roosevelt, who had said he wanted to get his trophy "while there were still buffalo to shoot,"[2] Hornaday was racing against time. By the spring of 1886 there were not more than one thousand buffalo left in North America.

For the rest of his life Hornaday was troubled by the paradox of being a serious conservationist and wildlife advocate who had killed several dozen of the last buffalo on the continent. He worked hard to atone for what he regarded as the necessary but problematic killing of the approximately thirty buffalo he gathered for the National Museum. Years later he wrote, "To all of us the idea of killing a score or more of the last survivors of the bison millions was exceedingly unpleasant, but we believed that our refraining from collecting the specimens we imperatively needed would not prolong the existence of the bison species by a single day."[3] If Roosevelt felt that paradox, he never wrote about it. Hornaday did: "Not since Juan Cabeza de Vaca killed the first buffalo on the Texas plains did any man ever set forth bison hunting with a heart as heavy, or as much oppressed by doubt, as that carried westward by the writer in 1886."[4]

The Northern Pacific Railroad delivered Roosevelt and Hornaday to what was left of buffalo country. The railroad also transported the buffalo they killed east, to Oyster Bay on Long Island and to the National Museum in Washington DC. There is substantial irony here. It was the penetration of the transcontinental railroads (the Union Pacific in Nebraska and the Northern Pacific in Dakota and Montana) that did more than any other single factor to break the resistance of the Native Americans of the West and to thrust the great bison herds toward the brink of extinction. George Bird Grinnell understood the paradox. "Up to within a few years the valley of the Yellowstone River has been a magnificent hunting ground," he wrote. "The progress of the Northern Pacific Railroad, however, has changed all this. The Indians have been run out and the white men have had a chance to do what they could toward killing off the game."[5]

William Temple Hornaday was born in Indiana on December 1, 1854, to dissenting stock. Theodore Roosevelt was born on October 27, 1858, in New York City to a wealthy and distinguished Dutch-American family. Hornaday had to struggle to attend college, beginning at Oskaloosa College in Oskaloosa, Iowa, because he did not have the money to attend the University of Iowa at Ames. The only barrier to Roosevelt's university expectations was his precarious health. He was almost entirely home-tutored until he entered Harvard in 1876. Despite the differences in their backgrounds, Hornaday and Roosevelt were destined to become friends, partners in

26. William T. Hornaday with bison calf he named Sandy, which he may
have brought back to Washington from his 1885 field in Montana.
Unknown, 1886. Smithsonian Institution Archives, Image # 74–12338.

conservation, and two of the most significant figures in the saving of the buffalo from extinction. They were easterners who were drawn to the West, who returned to the East to become champions of the West.

No precise figures exist for the number of buffalo in North America at the time of the Lewis and Clark Expedition (1804–6), but the best estimates put the number somewhere between thirty-five million and sixty-five million.[6] Meriwether Lewis reckoned he saw at least ten thousand buffalo in a single grass landscape under the Montana sky near today's Great Falls in late July 1806. Orthographically challenged William Clark, reconnoitering the Yellowstone River at the same time, reported what he called "gangues" of buffalo so overwhelming that he finally declared that "for me to mention or give an estimate of the different Spcies [sic, throughout] of wild anbimals on this river particularly Buffalow . . . would be creditable. I shall therefore be silent on the Subject further."[7]

By the time Theodore Roosevelt killed his first buffalo on the Montana-Dakota line on September 20, 1883, there were fewer than two thousand buffalo (*Bison bison*) left on earth. The number may actually have been even smaller than that. In 1889 William Hornaday added up the numbers in Yellowstone National Park, private commercial and hobby herds, Wild West shows, Indian reservations, circuses, zoos, and Canada, and estimated the number of living buffalo at 1,100.

In less than a single century, the advance of Euro-American civilization had brought the extermination of tens of millions of buffalo. Some were hunted for food, often just for hump meat, tongues, and ribs. Some were hunted as trophies to adorn the studies of big-game hunters. Some were hunted for their robes, particularly after 1871–72, when tanners in Britain and the United States developed new methods that made buffalo leather ideal for use in industrial machinery. Some were hunted just for the pleasure of killing North America's most magnificent and iconic quadruped. Many were killed to fulfill the de facto United States government "Indian policy"—on the principle that the best way to quell Indian unrest and extinguish independent tribal sovereignty was to destroy, as far as possible, their food supply.

It was never the official policy of the United States government or the U.S. Army to subjugate Native Americans by destroying the buffalo herds on which their economies depended, but it was a widely understood, tacit strategy. General William Tecumseh Sherman unofficially declared, "Let them kill, skin, and sell until the buffalo is exterminated, as it is the only way to bring lasting peace and allow civilization to advance."[8] Buffalo hunter Frank Mayer said, "Don't understand that any official action was taken in Washington and directives sent out to kill all the buff on the plains. Nothing like that happened. What did happen was that army officers in charge of the plains operations encouraged the slaughter of buffalo in every possible way."[9] Texas buffalo hunter J. Wright Mooar summed up the triumphalism of the late nineteenth century with brutal candor: "I want to state that any one of the families killed and homes destroyed by the Indians would have been worth more to Texas and to civilization than all the millions of buffalo that ever roamed from the Pecos River on the south to the Platte River on the north."[10]

Conversion Experiences

Hornaday and Roosevelt both had conversion experiences in the northern Great Plains. Roosevelt's conversion was broader and more gradual and—since he said in 1910 that he would never have become president of the United States had it not been for his experiences in North Dakota—much more consequential. Hornaday's conversion was sharper, more immediately dramatic, and it led to a lifetime of professional conservation activity. Hornaday later confessed, "It came like a thief in the night, when I was satisfied with life and not in the least looking for something new to conquer."[11] When he observed hundreds, even thousands, of rotting buffalo carcasses on the barren plains northwest of Miles City, Hornaday was "shocked and outraged that such a strong and virile beast numbering in the tens of millions could be hunted out of existence in two decades." He wrote about the moment as if it were his road to Damascus:

"Just as a care-free and joyous swimmer for pleasure suddenly is drawn into a whirlpool—in which he can swim but from which he cannot escape—so in 1886 was I drawn into the maelstrom of wild life protection."[12]

Roosevelt's transformation was more gradual and has a strongly mythological feel, the stuff of what Joseph Campbell called a "hero story." Roosevelt had come to the badlands of the Dakota Territory a wealthy, highly educated, physically fragile, somewhat snobbish New York "dude." Like so many other wealthy men from eastern American cities and Great Britain who ventured out to play in the American West, Roosevelt did not at first seem authentic to frontier denizens. His thick spectacles, designer buckskin suits, personalized silver spurs, belt buckle, and knife hand-carved by Tiffany's, evoked skepticism and at times derision among the hardscrabble population of the Dakota badlands.

Thanks to his unquenchable thirst to be "in the arena" and his desire to be accepted by people for whom the frontier was not a vacation but a way of life, Roosevelt managed to overcome many of his physical issues during his four years in the badlands. His body became thicker, better muscled, stronger, and more ostensibly virile than before. He learned a range of practical frontier skills in the badlands, from saddling his own horse to helping build his ranch headquarters. He developed a sincere respect for average Americans who did not share his wealth, education, social status, or linguistic capacities. In some sense he became a small *d* democrat in the Dakota badlands. Indeed, he was, as his new Dakota friends Victor Hugo Stickney and A. T. Packard immediately suggested, well on his way to becoming America's first cowboy president. Stefan Bechtel concludes, "In a sprawling country famous for transformations, and out of the bottomless grief of all his losses, Theodore Roosevelt began undergoing one of the most remarkable transfigurations in American history."[13]

Roosevelt undertook his four-year sojourn in the Dakota badlands for a number of reasons. His immediate purpose in September 1883 was to kill a buffalo, because he reckoned that the buffalo

27. Roosevelt in cowboy garb, 1910. Library of Congress Prints and Photographs Division. LC-DIG-ppmsca-35864.

would go extinct and he wanted to get his first. Not only was the buffalo a great trophy for a young man who envisioned himself as a big-game hunter and as a hero in a buckskin tunic; it was also the quintessential symbol of the passing frontier. Like his friend Frederick Jackson Turner, Roosevelt believed that the frontier experience had been one of the most important forces that shaped the American character.[14] While Turner famously wondered what the post-frontier era would mean to American identity, Roosevelt was certain that something essential in the American character would be lost. He fretted endlessly that the American people, especially white males, would grow soft and "effeminate," that these men were losing the sometimes-violent resourcefulness that had domesticated the continent and made the American people the most enterprising and dynamic in the world. In his first badlands book, Roosevelt summed up his theory of the frontier with particular respect to cowboys and ranchers, among whom he counted himself: "I suppose it is right and for the best that the great cattle country, with its broad extent of fenceless land, over which the ranchman rides as free as the game that he follows or the horned herds that he guards, should be in the end broken up into small patches of fenced farm land and grazing land; but I hope against hope that I myself shall not live to see this take place, for when it does one of the pleasantest and freest phases of western American life will have come to an end."[15]

Although saddened by this climax, he was not altogether sorry. In the third installment of his badlands trilogy, *The Wilderness Hunter* (1893), Roosevelt wrote, "The seething myriads of shaggy-maned wild cattle vanished with remarkable and melancholy rapidity before the inroads of the white hunters, and the steady march of the oncoming settlers. Now they are on the point of extinction. Two or three hundred are left in that great national game preserve, the Yellowstone Park; and it is said that others still remain in the wintry desolation of Athabasca."[16] Roosevelt acknowledged that "the extermination of the buffalo has been a veritable tragedy of the animal world."[17] In *Hunting Trips of a Ranchman*, published in 1885, Roosevelt wrote words that might have convinced Hornaday not to make his quixotic journey to Miles City, Montana, one year later, had he read them. "A ranchman," Roosevelt reported, "who at the same time had made a journey of a thousand miles across Northern Montana, along the Milk River, told me that, to use his own expression, during the whole distance he was never out of sight of a dead buffalo, and never in sight of a live one."[18] A relict of a primordial America that must now yield to family farms and industrial civilization, "the slaughter of the buffalo has been in places needless and brutal," he wrote,

> and while it is to be greatly regretted that the species is likely to become extinct, and while, moreover, from a purely selfish standpoint many, including myself, would rather see it continue to exist as the chief feature in the unchanged life of the Western wilderness; yet, on the other hand, it must be remembered that its continued existence in any numbers was absolutely incompatible with any thing but a very sparse settlement of the country, and that its destruction was the condition precedent upon the advance of white civilization in the West, and was a positive boon to the more thrifty and industrious frontiersmen.[19]

With some wistfulness Roosevelt acknowledged that he approved of America's tacit Indian policy:

> Above all, the extermination of the buffalo was the only way of solving the Indian question. As long as this large animal of the chase existed, the Indians simply could not be kept on reservations, and always had an ample supply of meat on hand to support them in the event of war; and its disappearance was the only method of forcing them to at least partially abandon their savage mode of life. From the standpoint of humanity at large, the extermination of the buffalo has been a blessing. The many have been benefited by it; and I suppose the comparatively few of us who would have preferred the continuance of the old order of things, merely for the sake of our own selfish enjoyment, have no right to complain."[20]

Hornaday's introduction to the extermination of the buffalo came from a March 1886 newspaper article that changed the trajectory of his life and eventually helped to save the buffalo from extinction. For him the article's description of the collapse of the buffalo population was a "severe shock, as if by a blow on the head from a well-directed mallet."[21] Hornaday immediately conducted an inventory of bison materials at the National Museum of Natural History, where he served as the chief taxidermist. He discovered that the museum did not possess a single decent buffalo specimen. He found only two "sadly dilapidated" hides and a hodgepodge of skulls and bones. The "Museum was actually without presentable specimens of this most important and interesting animal," he wrote.[22] When he presented his report, the secretary of the Smithsonian, Spencer Baird, advised Hornaday to "go west as soon as possible" to obtain buffalo specimens before it was too late. At about the same time an army captain visited the museum. When he heard of Hornaday's plans, he was openly skeptical: "Well, I hear that you are going to Montana to hunt buffalo, and I would like to bet you a hundred dollars that you don't find even one wild buffalo."[23]

Within two months Hornaday was in Montana, the first of two trips that year. Between mid-May and mid-June he conducted a reconnaissance of the region, and learned from Henry R. Philips of the LU-bar Ranch that he might find some stray buffalo thirty miles northwest of Miles City. Philips was partly right. In the country north of the Yellowstone River, Hornaday entered Montana's killing fields. "Go wherever we might," he wrote, "on divides, into badlands, creek-bottoms, or on the highest plateaus, we always found the inevitable and omnipresent grim and ghastly skeleton."[24] Somehow, amid all that senseless carnage, Hornaday and his crew managed to kill two buffalo that were shedding their winter coats; they also captured a live buffalo calf, dubbed Sandy, that Hornaday brought back to Washington DC. Before he returned to the nation's capital, Hornaday begged local ranchers, cowboys, hunters, and army personnel not to kill any more buffalo before he returned. He would return in the fall when the buffalo's coats were in full luxuriance.

Over that summer Hornaday improved his accuracy with the rifle and fed the buffalo calf on cow's milk, but after it consumed a large quantity of damp clover in July, Sandy died. The calf would later be immortalized in Hornaday's glass-box bison display at the Smithsonian. Hornaday returned to Miles City on September 24, 1886.

Meanwhile, in the late spring of 1886, Roosevelt was participating in the last great cattle roundup of his life. During a cold spell he went hunting with William Sewall and W. J. Tompkins in the high country between the Little Missouri and the Yellowstone rivers. During that interlude he would have been no more than a hundred miles from Hornaday's buffalo camps. They did not know each other, or perhaps even *of* each other. Roosevelt spent most of the spring and summer of 1886 in the Dakota badlands, a three-and-one-half-month period constituting "Roosevelt's longest unbroken visit to Dakota Territory."[25] It was a time of strenuous and transformative activity for the twenty-seven-year-old widower, whose wife and mother had died two years previously on the same day, Valentine's Day 1884, but whose approach to sorrow was to declare that "black care seldom sits behind a rider whose pace is fast enough."[26] He had by now emerged from the depths of his sorrow and was engaged to his childhood sweetheart Edith Carow, whom he was scheduled to marry at the end of the year. Before then he had to finish his contract biography of Missouri senator Thomas Hart Benton and, though he did not know it yet, run unsuccessfully for mayor of New York.

Roosevelt arrived in Medora on March 18, 1886, spent the night in the village, then made his way directly to the Elkhorn Ranch the following day. Less than a week later one of the great adventures of his life began, when he and his ranch hands discovered that his boat had been stolen from the banks of the Little Missouri River by a ne'er-do-well by the name of Red Headed Mike Finnegan and two accomplices. The boat thieves adventure lasted until April 11, when a footsore, weary, but nevertheless giddy Roosevelt deposited the desperadoes with the local sheriff in the frontier town of Dickinson (population ca. 500) and sought a doctor to look after his badly damaged feet. Dickinson's sole physician, Dr. Victor Hugo Stickney, did what he could for the remarkable and grimy stranger. His after-action description of Roosevelt is priceless: "His fringed buckskin jacket and chaps were covered with sticky gumbo mud. He was all teeth and eyes. His clothes were in rags. He was scratched, bruised and hungry, but gritty and determined as bull dog."[27]

Roosevelt spent the next four weeks participating in the annual Little Missouri spring roundup. It was a massive undertaking, involving more than five thousand cattle and five hundred horses. Roosevelt slept little, seldom took breakfast after 4 a.m., rode hard and long, wore out his horses, shirked no difficult work, and wrote self-congratulatory letters home. With his characteristic sense of the heroic, Roosevelt wrote his closest friend Henry Cabot Lodge, "When we started there were 60 men in the saddle who splashed the shallow ford of the river, every one a bold rider, and every one on a good horse."[28] His were words that Owen Wister or Zane Grey might have used to begin a novel.

To cap off this magical interlude in the West, Roosevelt delivered what some regard as his first great national speech at the first-ever Fourth of July festival in Dickinson, Dakota Territory, on July 5, 1886. After declaring how much he liked "big things, big prairies, big forests and mountains, big wheat fields, railroads," Roosevelt announced, more to the point, "I am myself at heart as much a westerner as an easterner; I am proud indeed to be considered one of yourselves."[29] Returning on the train to Medora later that day, Roosevelt spoke with such deep conviction about America's civic ideals that his traveling companion, A. T. Packard, the editor of the *Bad Lands Cow Boy*, became one of the first individuals to predict that Roosevelt would someday become the president of the United States. "If your prophecy comes true," Roosevelt replied, "I will do my part to make a good one."[30]

While Roosevelt spent that September in New York, mounting a quixotic campaign for mayor and battling for civic righteousness in the sullied arena of New York politics—a race in which he came third—Hornaday was back in Montana Territory earnestly collecting his buffalo specimens. He had returned to Miles City on September 24, 1886; after collecting horses, supplies, and a support crew, the expedition left Fort Keogh. A rough terrain awaited: "The whole of the country bordering Sand Creek," Hornaday later wrote, "quite up to its source, consists of rugged hills and ridges, which sometimes rise to considerable height, cut between by great yawning ravines and hollows, such as persecuted game loves to seek shelter in."[31] The Hornaday party did not see its first buffalo until October 13, after three fruitless and frustrating weeks in the field. The next day they brought down their first specimens: a fine old bull, a two-year-old "spike" bull, a cow, and finally another old bull. Hornaday was trying to work fast, "before the terrors of a Montana winter should catch us afield."[32] It was hard, cold, tedious, exhausting, and sometimes dangerous work. "Brown and I worked all day on the buffalo skins, fleshing, washing out blood, etc.," Hornaday wrote in his journal on October 20. "It is a fearful job, freezing to the hands, breaking to the back. Worked all day on 2 skins."[33] At times the exhilaration of hunting buffalo on the wild plains of Montana caused the Smithsonian party to forget the fact that they were collecting specimens for science and—they all knew—killing some of the last wild buffalo in North America. "In our eagerness to succeed in our task, the sad fact that we were hunting the last representa-tives of a mighty race was for the time being lost sight of," Horna-day confessed.[34] By November 1, they had killed a dozen buffalo. It was the night before Roosevelt's election debacle in New York City.

On November 20 the Hornaday expedition killed its twentieth buffalo. Five days later the party was overwhelmed by a ferocious Montana blizzard. They holed up in a makeshift cabin along Por-cupine Creek, waiting out the first wave of the infamous "winter of blue snow," the worst recorded Great Plains winter of the nineteenth century. For ten days the party hunkered down amid temperatures that plummeted to sixteen degrees below zero. After the storm sub-sided Hornaday (with help from others of the party) killed the great buffalo bull that eventually took pride of place in the Smithsonian glass display box: "He seemed to me then, ay, and he did later on, the grandest quadruped I ever beheld, lions, tigers, and elephants not excepted. His huge bulk loomed up like a colossus."[35] Horna-day estimated that the great bull weighed 1,600 pounds. When the hunting party dressed the buffalo out, they found four old bullets embedded in the carcass. Hornaday wrote, "Nearly every adult bull we took carried old bullets in his body, and from this one we took four of various sizes that had been fired into him on various occa-sions. One was sticking fast in one of the lumbar vertebrae."[36] This was also the buffalo bull that became the image on the ten-dollar bill, first printed in 1901 during the initial year of Roosevelt's presi-dency. In his own way Hornaday believed he was immortalizing the buffalo. "Perhaps you think a wild animal has no soul, but let me tell you it has. Its skin is its soul," he insisted, "and when mounted by skillful hands, it becomes comparatively immortal."[37]

Wagons arrived at Hornaday's camp on December 13 just as the hunting party used the last of its provisions. Two days later the whole party, with all of its specimens in tow, began the long return jour-ney that would end, weeks later, at the Smithsonian. Totaling up the number of specimens collected during his fall 1886 hunt, Hor-naday provided the following summary: ten old bulls, one young bull, seven old cows, four young cows, two yearling calves, and one three-month-old calf that was "caught alive, but died in captivity July 26, 1886, and now in the mounted group."[38] The total number of specimens came to twenty-five: "Our total catch of buffalo . . . constituted as complete and fine a series as could be wished for. I am inclined to believe that in size and general quality of pelage the adult bull and cow selected and mounted for our Museum group are not to be surpassed, even if they are ever equaled, by others of their kind."[39]

From Miles City Hornaday wrote a triumphant letter to his boss, Spencer Baird: "I think we can say without boasting that we have by long odds the finest and most complete series of buffalo skins ever collected for a museum, and also the richest collection of skeletons and skulls. Of skins we have enough to make four sets, with several skins to spare." Then, in a more melancholy spirit, he wrote, "We killed very nearly all we saw and I am confident there are not over thirty-head remaining in Montana, all told. By this time next year the cowboys will have destroyed about all of this remnant. We got in our Exploration just in the nick of time,—the last day in the evening, so to speak, and I do not hesitate to say that I am really rejoiced over the fact that we have been successful in securing the specimens we needed so urgently."[40]

Once back in Washington DC, Hornaday began work on what he regarded as "about the biggest thing ever attempted by a taxidermist."[41] He created his sixteen-by-twelve-foot, ten-foot-high glass bison display for several reasons. He wanted to establish himself as the finest taxidermist in the United States, if not the world. He wanted to fill a void in the National Museum's large-animal collection. He wanted to give the American public the opportunity to see bison in a simulacrum of their natural habitat. His assumption was that the overwhelming majority of Americans would never have the chance to see buffalo in an actual western landscape, and he hoped to call attention to the plight of the bison and other American fauna in danger of extinction.

Hornaday's glass-box display of six Montana buffalo, including Sandy, generated a good deal of press. Harry P. Godwin of the *Wash-*

28. William T. Hornaday, center, in his taxidermy studio at the Smithsonian
Institution. Smithsonian Institution Archives, Record Unit 95,
Box 28, Folder: 31A, 6071 and NHB-6071, siris_sic_9561.

ington Star wrote, "This case and the space about it, at the south end
of the south hall, has been enclosed by high screens for many days
while the taxidermist and his assistants have been at work."[42] Hornaday used the multistage "clay manikin process" that he had developed—a great improvement, he declared, over the "rag-and-stuff
method" that was still the industry standard. According to writer
Stefan Bechtel, "Essentially, he had created a life-size statue of a buffalo, over which the preserved skin, head, hooves, and other parts
were stretched."[43] In keeping with his philosophy of not just plop-
ping down stuffed specimens on a flat museum surface, Hornaday
attempted to place the bison in the museum-equivalent of their natural habitat. In the finished display his six bison stood near a faux
pool of alkali water, a grassy mound, fossil bones protruding from
an outcropping, a buffalo trail, two bleaching buffalo skulls, buffalo
grass, bunchgrass, and sagebrush. Hornaday actually collected all of

these "ambience" materials on site in eastern Montana and transported them to his studio in Washington DC. His goal was total integration of creature and environment. "Even seeing live animals in a zoo did not really convey what the animals looked like in their natural habitat," Bechtel writes. In Hornaday's mind, "animals were so embedded in their habitats, having actually been created by their surroundings, that the two could not really be separated."[44] One of the journalists who reviewed the finished display wrote, "The homesick Montana cowboy, far from his wild haunts, can here gaze upon his native sod again; for the sod, the earth that forms the face of the bank, the sage-brush, and all were brought from Montana."[45] The Hornaday bison group was on display at the Smithsonian for sixty-nine years, from the spring of 1888 until 1957.

Enter Roosevelt, Talking

Theodore Roosevelt and William Hornaday finally met in March 1888 at the National Museum in Washington DC. Roosevelt was visiting the national capital to begin research for what he would regard as his magnum opus, *The Winning of the West*, his four-volume study of the westering movement in American history (1774–1836). Hornaday's taxidermy project and his widely reprinted eight-part newspaper series, "The Last Buffalo Hunt," were attracting a good deal of attention. Curiosity seekers turned up at the National Museum in hopes of getting a glimpse of Hornaday's bold and innovative experiment in museum design. Most visitors were turned away. Few were permitted to peek behind a protective curtain. Roosevelt observed that nicety and then ignored its implication by calling out questions to the beleaguered Hornaday *through* the curtain. Such details as we have of this historic encounter come from Hornaday's unpublished autobiography, *Eighty Fascinating Years*.[46] At first annoyed by the stranger's boisterousness, overfamiliarity, and clipped falsetto voice, soon enough Hornaday recognized that the loud stranger understood firearms, knew how to kill a buffalo, and even knew the Sunday Creek Trail northwest of Miles City, way out in Montana Territory. The curtain opened on what turned out to be a remarkable and historically important collaboration.

In spite of the awkward beginning, "these two fierce and ambitious young men forged a bond that was to last for the rest of their lives."[47] Hornaday later wrote, a little breathlessly: "In our first hour ... [Roosevelt] told me a serious secret, and we dealt in secrets forever after. I think I proved that I knew how to keep things that should not be told—and he told me many mighty interesting things that, while new, never appeared in print."[48] Although they were never close friends, Roosevelt was determined to serve as Hornaday's informal patron and protector. "Whenever you really, really need me," Roosevelt wrote, "when you can't get further, call me."[49] The offer was generous, considering that Hornaday was, as historian Douglas Brinkley observes, "obsessive, unbuckling, and stubborn beyond words," a man with "a cultivated crudeness to his manners."[50] According to Brinkley Roosevelt generally held the volatile and sometimes obnoxious Hornaday at arm's length.

However ambitious and driven Hornaday was, Roosevelt operated in a much larger arena. He was on his way to becoming the twenty-sixth president of the United States. His achievements were global in reach and scope, including his expansion of U.S. military might via the Panama Canal and the Great White Fleet, and he was committed to a range of domestic conservation initiatives, such as the establishment of the U.S. Bureau of Reclamation (1902) and the U.S. Forest Service (1905). Saving the buffalo was just one relatively minor initiative.

Roosevelt and Hornaday returned as changed men from their sojourns in the American West in late 1886. Revisiting Medora in the badlands during the presidential campaign of 1900, Roosevelt said, "It was here that the romance of my life began." Hornaday immediately sat down to write a book, a cri de coeur that Bechtel says he "wrote like a man on fire, convinced that this could be the last written record of a species that soon would vanish from the earth."[51] In an essential way these talented young men were formed (or re-formed) out among the endless grasslands, the breaks, coulees, the buttes, and the cottonwoods—what Roosevelt called "a land of vast silent spaces, of lonely rivers, and of plains where the wild game stared at the passing horseman."[52]

Roosevelt hunted his first bison for personal, not scientific reasons. He wanted to kill the largest of North America's quadrupeds. He wanted to catch up with his brother Elliott, who had hunted bison on the Staked Plains of Texas in 1877. He wanted to bring home a trophy for his new home on Long Island, then still known as Leeholm (later, Sagamore Hill). If he was then aware that he was helping to bring the bison to the brink of actual extinction, he made no reference to it in his letters and accounts of the hunt. In fact TR danced "an Indian war dance" around his first bison carcass on the Montana-Dakota line in the upper reaches of Little Cannonball Creek, not far from today's Marmarth, North Dakota. At this point, in 1883, he was constructing himself more in the template of Daniel Boone or Davy Crockett than of George Bird Grinnell or John Muir. He was not yet thinking about larger habitat and ecosystem questions that would become a driving force during his seven years and 171 days as president of the United States. That is when Roosevelt magnified the arena, setting aside almost a quarter of a billion acres for conservation purposes. He doubled the number of America's national parks from five to ten; added 150 million acres to the National Forest System; signed the Antiquities Act (1906), using it to designate the first eighteen national monuments, including the Grand Canyon; and created the National Wildlife Refuge System (then called the Federal Bird Sanctuaries), naming the first fifty-one sites.

Hornaday came away from his time in Montana with four tasks in mind. First, he began work on his six-figure bison display for the National Museum. Second, he wrote an angry book, *The Extermination of the Buffalo*, published in 1887. Third, he took the first steps toward the creation of a national zoological park in Washington DC, founded in 1889. Fourth, he began to lay the groundwork for a political organization to help protect and revive the buffalo. That initiative bore fruit in 1905 with the creation of a conservation organization dedicated specifically to the salvation of the buffalo.

By the beginning of Roosevelt's second term as president, the two men's ambitions converged. The American Bison Society (ABS) was born in the Lion House at the New York Zoological Society (the Bronx Zoo) in December 1905. Roosevelt was named honorary president and Hornaday himself agreed to serve as acting president. On behalf of the ABS Hornaday lobbied Congress to create the National Bison Range in Montana, agreeing, as a condition of the legislation, to raise the money needed to purchase the animals for the herd. In 1909 more than a dozen bison were introduced to the National Bison Range, carved out of Native American land reclassified as "surplus" by the application of the General Allotment Act (the Dawes Act) of 1887. Once Indian families had the chance to file "homestead" claims for 80 or 160 acres on their ancestral homelands, the remaining "unclaimed" reservation lands were made available to non-Indian homesteaders or repurposed by the U.S. government. In other words the 13,000-acre National Bison Range was carved out of a portion of the Flathead Indian Reservation. The ABS raised $10,000 to purchase the first thirty-four buffalo for the reserve. Hornaday did much of this work himself.

Although Roosevelt and Hornaday played pivotal roles, the salvation of the buffalo resulted from the confluence of a number of dynamics, institutions, and individuals. Perhaps most importantly the establishment of Yellowstone National Park in 1872 created a sanctuary for the few hundred buffalo living within its boundaries. They were protected in large part because there was no competition for their habitat within the park from white ranchers, farmers, loggers, and miners. In 1894 Congress passed the Lacey Act, which among other things outlawed buffalo hunting in Yellowstone National Park. Pressed by a growing cadre of dedicated and ardent conservationists, including Hornaday and George Bird Grinnell, the U.S. government stocked buffalo in Yellowstone National Park in 1892 and Wind Cave National Park in 1913 and 1914. It established buffalo preserves at the Wichita Mountains National Wildlife Refuge in Oklahoma in 1907, the National Bison Range at Moiese in northwestern Montana (1909), and Fort Niobrara National Wildlife Refuge in Nebraska in 1913.

Dedicated individuals contributed to this belated preservationist impulse. Texas ranchers Mary Ann and Charles Goodnight were responsible for saving a remnant of the great southern buffalo herd.[53] South Dakota rancher James "Scotty" Philip developed a significant herd from an initial purchase of seventy-four survivors. Meanwhile William F. Cody's Wild West helped to create a curious and sympathetic national and international buffalo constituency; more Americans saw buffalo in Cody's Wild West than in the Smithsonian and other museums.[54] Other ranchers and entrepreneurs realized that public appetite to see buffalo away from their natural habitat could bring significant profits. They raised buffalo for mostly commercial reasons, but the fact that such ranches were scattered across the entire Great Plains helped to preserve some of the genetic diversity of the species, ensuring that the future of the species was not dependent on a single node.

In this long and complicated process Hornaday played a more important role than Roosevelt. For one thing, he could devote more of his life's energy to the project than Roosevelt possibly could. For another, he was not ideologically constrained like Roosevelt by a stage-theory frontier thesis, which argued that the passing of the buffalo was probably inevitable and almost certainly good, at least from a macro-civilizational perspective: "Hornaday never blithely dismissed the demise of the buffalo or any other species as simply a consequence of the 'advance of civilization' as did some other conservationists."[55]

Hornaday's activism bore fruit. "I regard the American bison species as now reasonably secure against extermination," he wrote in 1913.[56] Six years later, at the time of Theodore Roosevelt's death in early January 1919, there were an estimated 12,521 buffalo in North America, according to a census conducted by the American Bison Society. By the time Hornaday died in 1937 the ABS had actually been disbanded because by then it was clear that the buffalo was no longer in danger of extinction: "The numbers continued to rise through the twentieth century and, at the turn of the twenty-first century, the U.S. Fish and Wildlife Service estimated that the buffalo population in the United States had surpassed a sustainable population of 200,000, with their numbers increasing rapidly." [57]

Thanks to the passion of men like Hornaday and Grinnell, and the political power and determination of Roosevelt, the buffalo did not—as virtually everyone had predicted—become extinct. Their salvation came at a price, however. "Today, the vast majority of buffalo are in private herds," Bill Yenne notes, "and buffalo meat is once again on the menu, widely enjoyed by Indians and non-Indians alike throughout the northern Plains, the Mountain West, and elsewhere. However, even as the buffalo population approaches a half million, the days of them being the cornerstone of a way of life for the inhabitants of an area the size of Western Europe ended within Sitting Bull's lifetime and will never return." [58]

In 1957 when the staff of the Smithsonian finally dismantled Hornaday's bison display, they found a small metal box embedded in the floorboards of the exhibit. It had been placed at the foot of the great bull. When they opened the box they found a handwritten note:

> To my illustrious successor. The old bull, the young cow, and the yearling calf you find here were killed by yours truly. When I am dust and ashes, I beg you to protect these specimens from deterioration and destruction as they are among the last of their kind. Of course they are crude productions in comparison with what you may now produce, but you must remember that at this time, The American School of Taxidermy had only just been recognized. Therefore give the devil his due and revile not Wm T. Hornaday.

The note was dated March 7, 1888.

These specimens were not, in fact, *the last of their kind*. By the time the glass box was dismantled, there were nearly a hundred thousand buffalo in America, thanks in no small part to the man who took time to address the future before he put finishing touches on his masterpiece. Although William Hornaday was determined to do whatever it took to save the buffalo, he needed the help of men in positions of power to achieve his goals: Spencer Baird of the Smithsonian; the officers and enlisted men at Fort Keogh in Montana Territory; a small number of hospitable ranchers and cowboys along Big Dry Creek in eastern Montana; wealthy and enlightened individuals in Washington DC, New York City, and the Bronx; and perhaps, in particular, the friendly and respectful patronage of Theodore Roosevelt. Their meeting in March 1888 is one of the great (and amusing) moments in the natural history of America. Their coincidental but separate adventures in Medora–Miles City corridor in the spring, summer, and fall of 1886 is one of the intriguing "near misses" in the history of the buffalo, the history of conservation, the history of the badlands, and the history of the northern Great Plains.

In a certain sense, of course, they did not just miss each other at all.

Notes

Epigraph: Quoted in Gregory J. Dehler, *The Most Defiant Devil: William Temple Hornaday and His Controversial Crusade to Save American Wildlife*, (Charlottesville: University of Virginia Press, 2013), 3.

1. The Northern Pacific Railroad, authorized in 1864, reached Bismarck, Dakota Territory, in 1873, the badlands in 1880, Miles City in 1881, and was completed in September 1883. For Roosevelt and Hornaday, it was "just in time" technology. Some of the railroad's impact along its route is explored in Hiram M. Drache, "The Economic Aspects of the Northern Pacific Railroad in North Dakota," *North Dakota History* 34, no. 4 (Fall 1967): 320–72.

2. Rolf Sletten, *Roosevelt's Ranches: The Maltese Cross and Elkhorn* (Badlands ND: Theodore Roosevelt Medora Foundation, 2015), 28.

3. Quoted in Stefan Bechtel, *Mr. Hornaday's War: How a Peculiar Victorian Zookeeper Waged a Lonely Crusade for Wildlife That Changed the World* (Boston: Beacon Press, 2013), 61.

4. Bechtel, *Mr. Hornaday's War*, 36.

5. Michael Punke, *Last Stand: George Bird Grinnell, the Battle to Save the Buffalo, and the Birth of the New West* (Lincoln NE: Bison Books, 2009), 127.

6. Punke, *Last Stand*, 33.

7. Gary E. Moulton, ed., *The Journals of the Lewis & Clark Expedition* (Lincoln: University of Nebraska Press, 2002), see entries for July 11, 1806; July 24, 1806, at 8:176–77 and 8:217–19.

8. James Welch with Paul Jeffrey Stekler, *Killing Custer: The Battle of Little Bighorn and the Fate of the Plains Indians* (New York: W. W. Norton, 1994), 67.

9. Quoted in Punke, *Last Stand*, 89; Frank H. Mayer and Charles B. Roth, *The Buffalo Harvest* (New York: Sage Books, 1958).

10. Quoted in Punke, *Last Stand*, 91. It is important to remember that for the Native Americans of the Great Plains the buffalo represented far more than food. Buffalo were systematically harvested to extract hides for clothing and lodging and, at times, trade; to make hoes and rakes from buffalo bones; to fashion luggage (parfleches) out of stiffened hides from which the hair had been removed; to serve as sacred and ceremonial objects; to manufacture water-carrying vessels and cooking pots from hardened buffalo stomachs; to make sinew for use in sewing tents, clothing, and other utensils; to build round boats of buffalo hides stretched over a willow frame; to make flyswatters from tails; to stoke fires by way of dung. There is no analogy in Euro-American culture, no single resource from which food, clothing, shelter, fuel, and a range of tools and implements could be fashioned. The buffalo was also one of the principal sources of spirit medicine, *wakan,* in Plains cultures. It would, in short, be difficult to exaggerate the place of the buffalo in Plains Indian culture and harder still to exaggerate how profound a crisis the systematic extermination of the buffalo precipitated among tribal nations between the Mississippi River and the Rocky Mountains.

11. Quoted in Dehler, *The Most Defiant Devil*, 66.

12. Quoted in Dehler, *The Most Defiant Devil*, 64.

13. Bechtel, *Mr. Hornaday's War*, 54.

14. Frederick Jackson Turner, *The Frontier in American History* (New York: Henry Holt and Company, 1920), 1–38.

15. Theodore Roosevelt, *Hunting Trips of a Ranchman: Sketches of Sport on the Northern Cattle Plains* (New York: G. P. Putnam's Sons, 1885), 37–38.

16. Theodore Roosevelt, *The Wilderness Hunter* (New York: The Review of Reviews Company, 1922), 343.

17. Roosevelt, *Hunting Trips of a Ranchman*, 75.

18. Roosevelt, *Hunting Trips of a Ranchman*, 237.

19. Roosevelt, *Hunting Trips of a Ranchman*, 242–43.

20. Roosevelt, *Hunting Trips of a Ranchman*, 243.

21. Quoted in Dehler, *The Most Defiant Devil*, 60.

22. Quoted in Punke, *Last Stand*, 136.

23. Quoted in Dehler, *The Most Defiant Devil*, 60–61.

24. Quoted in Punke, *Last Stand*, 185

25. Roger L. DiSilvestro, *Theodore Roosevelt in the Badlands: A Young Politician's Quest for Recovery in the American West* (New York: Bloomsbury, 2012), 198.

26. David McCullough, *Mornings on Horseback: The Story of an Extraordinary Family, a Vanished Way of Life and the Unique Child Who Became Theodore Roosevelt* (New York: Simon & Shuster, 1982), attributes this quotation to Roosevelt, frontispiece.

27. Quoted in Carleton Putnam, *Theodore Roosevelt: The Formative Years, 1858–1886* (New York: Charles Scribner's Sons, 1958), 568.

28. Sletten, *Roosevelt's Ranches*, 163.

29. Theodore Roosevelt, "Address to Citizens of Dickson, Dakota Territory," July 5, 1886, Theodore Roosevelt National Park, http://www.theodorerooseveltcenter.org /Research/Digital-Library/Record?libID=0273668, Theodore Roosevelt Digital Library, Dickinson State University.

30. Quoted in Putnam, *Theodore Roosevelt*, 583.

31. William T. Hornaday, *The Extermination of the American Bison* (Washington DC: Government Printing Office, 1889), 535, 545.

32. Quoted in Bechtel, *Mr. Hornaday's War*, 35.

33. Quoted in Bechtel, *Mr. Hornaday's War*, 39.

34. Quoted in Bechtel, *Mr. Hornaday's War*, 36.

35. Quoted in Bechtel, *Mr. Hornaday's War*, 43.

36. Punke, *Last Stand*, 137.

37. Quoted in Punke, *Last Stand*, 137.

38. Hornaday, *The Extermination of the American Bison*, 545.

39. Hornaday, *The Extermination of the American Bison*, 545.

40. William T. Hornaday to Spencer Baird, December 21, 1886, Smithsonian Institution, https://siarchives.si.edu/history/featured-topics/stories/letter-dated-december-21-1886-professor-spencer-f-baird-secretary-smithsoni.

41. Quoted in Dehler, *The Most Defiant Devil*, 64.

42. Quoted in Hornaday, *The Extermination of the American Bison*, 546.

43. Quoted in Bechtel, *Mr. Hornaday's War*, 55.

44. Bechtel, *Mr. Hornaday's War*, 56.

45. Quoted in Hornaday, *The Extermination of the American Bison*, 547.

46. William T. Hornaday, "Eighty Fascinating Years," unpublished manuscript, William T. Hornaday Papers, Wildlife Conservation Society Archives, Chapter 11:18, 19.

47. Bechtel, *Mr. Hornaday's War*, 51.

48. Hornaday, "Eighty Fascinating Years," quoted in Bechtel, *Mr. Hornaday's War*, 50.

49. Hornaday, "Eighty Fascinating Years," quoted in Bechtel, *Mr. Hornaday's War*, 58.

50. Douglas Brinkley, *The Wilderness Warrior: Theodore Roosevelt and the Crusade for America* (New York: HarperCollins, 2009), 281.

51. Bechtel, *Mr. Hornaday's War*, 60–74.

52. Theodore Roosevelt, *An Autobiography* (New York: Macmillan, 1916), 94.

53. The Goodnights' efforts are discussed in R. D. Rosen, *A Buffalo in the House: The True Story of a Man, An Animal, and the American West* (New York: Free Press, 2007), 145–46.

54. David Nesheim, "How William F. Cody Helped Save the Buffalo without Really Trying," *Great Plains Quarterly* 27, no. 3 (Summer 2007): 163–75.

55. Dehler, *The Most Defiant Devil*, 7.

56. Dehler, *The Most Defiant Devil*, 106.

57. Bill Yenne, *Sitting Bull* (Yardley PA: Westholme Publishing, 2008), 162.

58. Yenne, *Sitting Bull*, 162.

PART 3
Natural Politics

9

Theodore Roosevelt, the West, and the New America

ELLIOTT WEST

The story of Theodore Roosevelt and the West has extraordinary appeal. It has a mythic rhythm to it. It begins following his first hunting trip on the Great Plains, then proceeds through profound tragedy and adventure and some comedy. It is a kind of odyssey, a time of trial and personal search that ends with Roosevelt's return to New York. It is a story of redemption and, in political terms, something of a resurrection. We find ourselves especially caught up in the story's drama because we know where Roosevelt eventually goes. Returning east still a young man, he goes on to become arguably the most significant, and certainly the most revelatory, political figure in the United States of his time. His story is so human and so classic in its themes that it is easy to overlook its larger context. That is unfortunate, because the odyssey of that remarkable man can tell us plenty about the equally remarkable course of American history.

In the 1880s, when Theodore Roosevelt was out in North Dakota, the United States was well on its way to becoming a transformed nation. By the opening of the twentieth century, it was a different country from what it had been even fifty years before. It was different physically as, starting in the 1840s with expansion to the Pacific coast, the country had added 1.2 million square miles to its land base. It was different in its economic arrangements, in its economic landscape, and contours. It was different in its human makeup—in who Americans were—and in its definitions of citizenship. It was different in the power of the federal government and in its relations to the regions, the states, and the individuals in the country. More and more of its people were moving from villages and the countryside to cities, where more and more of them were laboring in industrial pursuits. It was a new nation, a new America.

The American West that Roosevelt visited was itself coming into focus as a distinctive part of this country; as it did, the West played an absolutely critical part in the transformation of America. As part of that process, the West became something that no other region had ever been, a playground of popular fantasy. Something about the West caught the imaginations of the people of this country and of countless others. We talk about westerns, but nobody talks about southerns or midwesterns. Westerns and the detective story are the two of the prime cultural exports from America to the rest of the world.

Then there was Theodore Roosevelt himself. He had an uncanny knack for somehow sensing what a considerable portion of his nation was feeling, what its aspirations, anxieties, and fears were. He was in touch with the American public in a way that very few people, certainly very few politicians, ever are, and, in politics, that ability is the ultimate coin of the realm. There have been plenty of presidents who did little during their administrations and ended up well liked. There have been plenty of others who did a lot and ended up greatly disliked. How many, however, have been extraordinarily active and then left office as popular, or more so, than when they came in? You can count them on three or four fingers—Andrew Jackson, Theodore's cousin Franklin, and most recently probably Ronald Reagan. Certainly that short list includes Theodore Roosevelt. He must be the only national politician who ever had to actively quash an effort to nominate him for president, as he did in 1908.

There is something to be learned by bringing together those three stories—the nation in transformation, the emergence of the West as a force and as imagined theater, and the maturing of that era's leading political figure as he felt his way toward the values, beliefs, attitudes, and perspectives that would guide him when he became the president of the new America. We might weave them together by looking at two areas not usually associated with the West of that time.

29. Roosevelt as a cowboy, 1883, one year before he headed for Dakota to start ranching. The photograph suggests his romanticized image of ranching on the eve of his taking it up. Theodore Roosevelt Birthplace National Historic Site. https://www.theodorerooseveltcenter.org/Research/Digital-Library /Record?libID=0284914. Theodore Roosevelt Digital Library. Dickinson State University.

The two topics were of great concern to many people during those years and, interestingly, to the American people today. The first, to use a shorthand from those days, was big business—the economic contours of the nation that were developing in such a remarkable way, specifically with the rise of giant corporations, those powerful concentrations of capital that were so important and would become such an important focus of Roosevelt's presidential years. The second topic is race, or, to use another bit of shorthand, ethnicity, the changing nature of the American people in their racial and their ethnic makeup. More specifically we might look at the question of immigration, the great influx of new people into this country—into areas urban and rural—and the challenges it posed during those years.

The years from the 1880s to the turn of the century saw extraordinary economic change in this country. The United States was well on its way to becoming the powerhouse it remains today, the eight-hundred-pound gorilla of the global economy. These were remarkably prosperous years. Many enjoyed greater buying power as well as a far wider range of things to buy. Others, however, were left out and lived at a level of poverty deeper than at any time before it. Among the many questions and alarms raised by these changes was a heightening concern over new concentrations of capital and the power they exerted over everything from high politics to the price of beefsteak. That power impacted people's everyday lives in ways immediate and intimate, yet that power was far beyond the control or even the understanding of most individuals.

Roosevelt, as president, would address those issues, which raises the question of what he was thinking about them during his Dakota sojourn in the 1880s. The first place to look would be his wonderful book, *Ranch Life and the Hunting Trail*. In its stories and distinctive writing style, we can feel the energy of a young man having a fine time, getting his legs back under him after the same-day deaths of his wife and mother in February 1884. We do not have to look too far or peel away too much to see Roosevelt as a man much in tune with the people of his time. He was more than a bit in love with the idea that in the American West one would find an earlier, less bewildering way of life. In ranching, specifically, he saw a life and a way of making a living that was under siege, about to be overwhelmed by the disturbing changes that were afoot back east. His treatment of ranching is full of stories about cowboys and what he calls "frontier types." Ranching here is not just something he took part in. It epitomized a passing age of American development:

> The great free ranches with their barbarous, picturesque, and curiously fascinating surroundings, mark a primitive stage of existence as surely as do the great tracts of primeval forests and, like the latter, must pass away before the onward march of our people; and we who have felt the charm of the life, and have exulted in its abounding vigor and its bold, restless freedom, will not only regret its passing for our own sakes, but must also feel real sorrow that those who come after us are not to see, as we have seen, what is perhaps the pleasantest, healthiest, and most exciting phase of American existence.[1]

He describes the ranchers themselves, not the cowboys but the ranch owners like himself, in this way: "Ranching is an occupation like those of vigorous, primitive pastoral peoples, having little in common with the hum-drum workaday business world of the nineteenth century; and the free ranchman in his manner of life shows more kinship to an Arab sheik than to a sleek city merchant or tradesman."[2] To Roosevelt, then, a western ranch was among the last holdouts of an older way of life just on the edge of being overwhelmed by the concentration of great economic power that then was looming in the urbanized East and looking westward to extract meat and other resources critical to its growth and development.

In the day-to-day lives of ranchers and of cowboys, there was still plenty of the boldness and freedom that Roosevelt found so alluring. This is still true today. There are ranchers and ranching families who stay in the business out of a sense of freedom and individuality, of being part of an uncommon way of life. If we step back and look at ranching in the years that Roosevelt was experiencing it, however, we will see that it was not a life that stood apart from the new economic order. It was a prime example of it. Ranching was

30. Cattle branding at ranch of Marquis de Mores illustrates how behind popular image were entrepreneurs with considerable capital bringing innovative business to plains. Theodore Roosevelt National Park. https://www .theodorerooseveltcenter.org/Research/Digital-Library /Record?libID=0279927. Theodore Roosevelt Digital Library. Dickinson State University.

one of many examples of local enterprises giving way to national and international systems. Neighborhood cobblers were giving way to shoe factories in Maine; local millers and mills were giving way to enterprises like Pillsbury's chilled roller flour factories; thousands of local breweries were giving way to the giants like Schlitz and Pabst and Anheuser Busch. The local butcher was also giving way to this same nationalizing impulse, as mega-meatpackers such as Gustavus Swift and Philip Armour began to dominate the emerging industry.

A rapidly developing system of transport and production brought a supply of cattle in southern Texas together with consumer demand in the Northeast by the revolutionary technology of the railroad. Texas cattle, driven first to the central Great Plains, were carried by rail to be first fattened and then disassembled in what were essentially beef factories in Chicago, Cincinnati, and Kansas City. Then their various parts were dispersed, again by rail, across a regional market. It all was coordinated by the most important breakthrough in the history of human communication, the telegraph, which tied the whole system together and allowed it to operate on a national and, eventually, an international scale.[3]

This was modernity defined. Ranching was an industry, a nationalized arrangement of regional specialization, modern transport, and noisome factories. A ranch in the Dakotas or Wyoming was one part of a far larger system that in turn was part of the very economic order that Roosevelt and others found so alien and threatening to the life they imagined themselves living out in the West.

There was, to be sure, a distinctive western tone to this way of life. In *Ranch Life and the Hunting Trail*, Roosevelt wrote with great affection of his modest ranch house.[4] He would sit on its lovely veranda and daydream, watching the wind blow through the trees. He seems to picture the place as a physical manifestation of that older, simpler, more elemental order he sets against the new one in the East, as expressed by the elaborate lodgings like The Breakers of Cornelius Vanderbilt in Rhode Island, Andrew Carnegie's mansion in Manhattan, or J. P. Morgan's New York City brownstone.

But looks can be deceiving. One such seemingly small and simple ranch house in Wyoming was the headquarters of the Swan Land and Cattle Company, organized in 1883, the year of Roosevelt's first exposure to western North Dakota. Its original investment was about $3.75 million, and a few years later it was capitalized at $50 million. In time Swan would be the largest ranch in Wyoming, with about 600,000 acres there and in Nebraska. Controlled by Scottish investors, it was one of many gigantic international ranching corporations. The Matador Land and Cattle Company, founded in Texas before spreading up into Colorado, the Dakotas, and Wyoming, was also financed by Scottish capitalists. It was managed by Roosevelt's good friend Murdo Mackenzie, a legendary figure on the northern plains who eventually left the Matador to manage a Brazilian ranch larger than any in the United States.[5] By 1886 four states and territories—Montana, Wyoming, Colorado, and New Mexico—alone hosted 439 corporate ranches capitalized at nearly $170 million.[6]

Ranching reflected the new economic order in one more way. Elsewhere the great concentrations of corporate power were often in partnership with the federal government. So it could be with western ranches. Owners of larger ranches would often buy and fence off land along the streams to deny access to competitors, then they would turn their own cattle loose on the public domain. In the semiarid West, whoever controlled the water controlled everything, so by sealing off ranching's essential resource from everyone but themselves, they were indirectly reserving for themselves what was outside their fences—the vast government lands and, on them, the fundamental fuel of ranching: grass. In effect they were using their capital to privatize the commons.

The partnership appeared even more dramatically in the coming of the lifelines of the ranching industry, the railroads. To build the transcontinentals that allowed ranches to operate, Washington provided almost unimaginable amounts of land to some of the nation's largest corporations. The Homestead Act of 1862 hearkens to that older, individualistic economic life that Roosevelt thought epitomized the West. Between 1862 and 1880, 19,265,000 acres were "proved up" under the law. In that same period acreage granted to the railroads was nearly seven times that, around 127 million acres. The total eventually rose to more than 180 million acres. The extreme example was the Northern Pacific, the primary artery for Roosevelt's North Dakota. The amount of land Congress provided along its full route was more than the size of New England. It would cover almost the entire state of North Dakota. Richard White recently pointed out that if all land given to fund the transcontinentals had been brought together it would be the third largest state in the union. There would be Alaska, Texas, and then what he calls Railroadiana.[7]

Ranching—and much of the West brought into the nation by this system of railroads—showed every one of the characteristics that we normally associate with the new American economic landscape. Ranching was not just one of the best examples. It was also one of the first. The other industries that we normally associate with this new economy—iron and steel and petroleum, for instance—came later. The ranching industry, emerging right after the Civil War in the earliest moments of the Gilded Age, paved the way. By the 1880s it had matured into one of the prime exhibits of corporate America, even as Roosevelt celebrated it as a brave but doomed survivor of a vanishing age.

The second area worth critical reexamination is race, the term used to describe the evolving human makeup of the United States on its way to becoming the new, transformed America. During the half-century from 1860 to 1910, the United States changed its human composition more than in any other comparable time in its history. This began with emancipation. African Americans had been in what would become the United States for three hundred years, but in 1865 four million persons of color, former slaves, were introduced into American citizenship. By that time the United States had expanded to the Pacific, which meant that the American embrace included more than a hundred thousand Hispanos, formerly citizens of Mexico, as well as tens of thousands of Native Americans. These Indians in the West were not like those of the East, such as the Cherokees, Delawares, and others with generations of contact with white society. Most Native peoples beyond the Missouri River never had had the slightest exposure to national institutions. Then the gold rush of 1848–49 made California the most polyglot collection of humanity on earth. There was, besides, a surge of the so-called new immigration into ports of the Atlantic coast, newcomers increasingly from southern and eastern Europe rather than from the British Isles and northern Europe, which had been the largest source of earlier waves of migrants.

The human face of the nation was being radically transformed. This was part of the new America and, like questions surrounding big business, it preyed on the thinking of much of the public. It bothered a lot of them. It bothered Theodore Roosevelt.

To look for Roosevelt's view on race, specifically in the West, an obvious place to start is with Native Americans.[8] He did not write a lot about them, but a chapter in *Ranch Life and the Hunting Trail* focused on Indian-White relations and on Indians in general. As anyone who has read much of his writing will likely agree, Roosevelt presents himself as something of an authority on whatever subject is under his pen, and Indians are no exception. He divides them into broad (if crude) categories of good and bad. "The Nez Perces differ from the Apaches as much as a Scotch laird does from a Calabrian Bandit," he writes, although at this point he almost certainly had never seen either a Nez Perce or an Apache (or a Calabrian bandit, for that matter).[9] Undeterred, the young Roosevelt simply repeated a cliché of the day, as he did by portraying the better sorts of American Indians, like the Nez Perces, Pueblos, and Cherokees, as nonetheless backward peoples with no inherent right to land they had not yet learned to use properly. Even the best of them were destined to give way to a new order of civilization. Roosevelt continued to speak of Indians in that way, even as president. He would often refer to the insurrectionists in the Philippines as Apaches and Comanches. He sometimes gives the impression that he was so irritated the western Indians surrendered before he could get out there to fight them that he projected them across the Pacific.

Good and bad, Roosevelt believed, Indians were bound for defeat; those who resisted should quite properly pay a price for standing in the way of progress. In a frequently quoted letter from his time in North Dakota, he wrote: "I don't go so far as to think that the only good Indians are dead Indians, but I believe nine out of ten are, and I shouldn't like to inquire too closely into the case of the tenth."[10] In his biography of Thomas Hart Benton, Roosevelt wrote similarly about Colorado's Sand Creek Massacre in November 1864: "In spite of certain objectionable details . . . on the whole it was as righteous and beneficial a deed as ever took place on the frontier."[11] The "objectionable details" to which Roosevelt referred were the cold-blooded murder of those Cheyennes in the camp who had surrendered, among them scores of children and women, as well as the mutilation of their bodies, with the taking of female genitals as trophies, later displayed to standing ovations in the Denver Opera House.[12]

The main cause of public concern over the changing face of the new America, however, had not to do with Indians but with the millions of new immigrants pouring into the United States from countries like Russia, Poland, Italy, and Sicily. Especially disturbed were many of the "old stock" Americans who had been here for many generations, those long-tailed families of the East like those of Roosevelt's lineage and social class who were alarmed by people that spoke strange languages, practiced questionable religions, lived by strange and exotic customs, and often smelled strongly of garlic. Once again the young Roosevelt was no exception in his concern over the issues and questions that bothered people of his particular background.[13]

Best known among Roosevelt's attitudes and writings were those on what he called "race suicide."[14] He believed that it was the responsibility of every proper old stock American family to produce as many children as possible, while the duty of every American male was to work, fight, and breed. Roosevelt talked about the "warfare of the cradle," how the old stock Americans must keep up with the newer folks who were coming in and producing so many children. In his annual address to Congress in 1906 President Roosevelt proposed an amendment to bring under federal control marriage and divorce in the United States. Later Roosevelt made two additional proposals. One envisioned the federal government providing incentives to parents with three or more children. Another proposed that the salaries of public officials be tied to how many children they produced; a public official who failed to produce children would never get above the lowest pay level. (Proposals like these inspired Roosevelt's daughter Alice to establish the "Race Suicide Club," which she designed to ridicule her father's extreme views.)[15]

Then there was the case of Roosevelt's friendships. There were those in his time who took concern over the new immigration to remarkable extremes. In a part of our history that makes many of us uncomfortable, there were prominent and respectable figures espousing racial theories of Aryan supremacy that were disconcertingly suggestive of others with hideous consequences a few decades later. They called themselves race scientists, and they were in favor of eugenics, breeding rules in this country to make sure that the right sorts of Americans were born.[16] Madison Grant was probably the best known of these. Two others were Henry Fairfield Osborn, director of the New York Museum of Natural History, and John C. Merriam. Together they were the big three of the American eugenics movement. Grant and Osborn were close friends and lifetime correspondents with Roosevelt.

Grant, the most prominent of them, was the author of the book that was the bible of this movement, *The Passing of the Great Race*.[17] Upon its publication in 1916 Roosevelt immediately ordered a copy and read it at Sagamore Hill, writing to his friend Grant: "This is a capital book in purpose and vision and grasp of the facts that our people most need to realize . . . Americans should be sincerely grateful to you for writing it."[18] Roosevelt's words were emblazoned on the back of the book for future editions.

It is worth emphasizing that these ideas, ones we find disturbing and in some cases bizarre, were in the cultural air that many people were breathing at the time. Certainly they were common in Roosevelt's world. His opinions would evolve in interesting and admirable ways in the years ahead, and his thoughts and actions as president and afterwards provide a fascinating and contrasting perspective on what he would say and write in those early years. Still, he would never abandon those attitudes entirely; it is certainly no surprise that he shared them in his years out west.

Especially interesting is that those who had such unnerving concerns over race and immigration found the West so powerfully appealing. They saw the West as the last bastion of the true Americans, the old stock Americans, just as they saw the West as the last stand against the economic changes of the time. They put their faith in the left-hand side of the national map and wrote off the East, the Atlantic coast, as hopelessly overwhelmed by calamitous changes, demographic, economic, and cultural.

Roosevelt himself did not write much along these lines, but others very close to him did. Two close friends, Frederic Remington and the aforementioned Madison Grant, were, like Roosevelt, in love with the West and doing much to create the image of the West that was emerging in the later part of the nineteenth century. Remington wrote in the early 1890s that in its racial composition the West was the true America's last stand and that when the time came he would take his Winchester down from over the mantle and proceed to kill the Italians, Jews, and others in the foreign swarms coming in from the Atlantic coast. Owen Wister, another of Roosevelt's close friends, was caught up in the same idea. Wister's *The Virginian*, a book dedicated to Theodore Roosevelt, has often been read as kind of a hymn to the best of the East that saves itself by heading west— the Virginian, a southern gentleman turned cowboy, and Mollie, his schoolmarm bride from the Northeast. It was, they believed, the best of those two older worlds coming together to save the white elite.

William Jackson Palmer, the railroad magnate and founder of Colorado Springs, summarized this way of thinking in a letter to his wife back east:

> We shall have a new and better civilization in the far West; only may the people never get to be as thick as on the Eastern seaboard. We will surrender the briny border as a sort of extensive Castle Garden to receive and filter the foreign swarms and prepare them by a gradual process for coming to the inner temple of Americanism out in Colorado.[19]

Wister later would write much the same in an article in *American Magazine* titled "Shall We Let the Cuckoos Crowd Us Out of Our Nests?":

> Alien eggs are being laid in our American nest … Our native spirit is being diluted and polluted by organized minorities every hour of the day … It might actually come to pass some day that the American Eagle simply to be able to call his soul his own would have to deal emphatically with all the cuckoos.[20]

To these folks the West was the last stand of this older ethnic order. It had to be saved; it had to be protected.

For western historians, such notions have some fascinating and ironic wrinkles. Consider, for instance, Roosevelt as conservationist. Conservation is one firm connection between Roosevelt and the West. We properly praise him for helping save the national forests. The Boone and Crockett Club, organized immediately after his time in North Dakota, was dedicated to saving the dwindling populations of large game animals. Roosevelt was its first president. Similarly, the American Bison Society, an organization created to save that animal from extermination, named him as its first honorary president. The National Wildlife Refuge System was established under his presidency, as were organizations like the Save the Redwoods League. We associate all of these things with Roosevelt, and we applaud them as great and beneficial accomplishments.

Yet conservation is a topic that can surprise us when we put it into the larger intellectual context of the era. It has an intriguing connection to those questions around race and immigration so prominent at the time.[21] If you visit Redwood State Park in California, you might encounter the Founders Tree, a 325-foot giant dedicated to the three founders of the Save the Redwoods League—Madison Grant, Henry Fairfield Osborn, and John C. Merriam. All three, Grant in particular, were best known in their early careers not as eugenicists but as conservationists. Grant in particular saw himself throughout his career essentially as a conservationist. He saw a direct connection between conserving the dwindling resources out west, whether redwoods or bison or eagles or other wildlife, and what he considered the other essential elements of the true America—the people of his particular ethnic background.

Once Roosevelt stepped down from leading the Boone and Crockett Club, Madison Grant became its longest running president. He was also one of the founding spirits behind the American Bison Society, though its president was the much better known William Hornaday. The nation's first bison refuge, located in Wichita Mountains in Oklahoma, grew out of a previously established forest. This site was also the brainchild of Madison Grant, the Aryan supremacist who saw saving the bison as related to his racial concerns. And the first bison taken out to what is now known as the Wichita Mountains Wildlife Refuge were from the Bronx Zoo of the New York Zoological Society, founded by among others Madison Grant, Henry Fairfield Osborn, and Theodore Roosevelt.[22]

From the perspective of these leading conservationists, the West was a beleaguered refuge, not only for magnificent species of plants and animals, but also for their human equivalents, the so-called true Americans born of the first European pioneers. In both cases the contrast was with the East, that "briny border" that was written off as a lost cause. Once again, as with their impressions of the new economic order, they got it just about exactly backwards.

Consider the ethnic makeup of states along the Atlantic coast, ranked by the highest percentage of foreign-born persons:

Percentage of Foreign-Born in 1880: Atlantic Coast

Massachusetts	25%
New York	24%
Connecticut	21%
Virginia	15%
Pennsylvania	14%
Maryland	9%

Now compare those numbers with those from the states and territories out west:

Percentage of Foreign-Born in 1880: American West

Nevada	41%
Arizona	40%
Dakota	38%
California	34%

Idaho	31%
Utah	31%
Montana	29%
Wyoming	28%

Merge the two lists into a national ranking, and the two states on the "briny border" of the Atlantic with the highest concentration of those born outside the United States would rank ninth and tenth overall. Of all states and territories in American history, the one with the highest percentage of first- or second-generation immigrants—those persons either born outside the country or who had one or both parents born outside the country—was Roosevelt's North Dakota. At the opening of the twentieth century, seventy percent of its people met that criterion. In other words, if people like William Jackson Palmer and Frederic Remington wanted to escape the foreign swarms, they should have left Colorado and Montana and headed back for Massachusetts.

Putting Theodore Roosevelt in these varied contexts can help situate him within the culture of his time and his class as well as the American West that was itself coming into focus as a distinctive part of the nation. From one angle this shows us that the man, so remarkable in traits he displayed even at that age, was in other ways quite unremarkable. He shared with many Americans, especially those of his social status, a cultural alarm at the direction the nation was taking. He held to a nostalgic view of a passing age, even while taking part in a business that in many ways epitomized the changes he was mourning. He flirted strongly with a racial stereotyping common to the time, one that relegated Native peoples to, at best, a lower rung on the cultural ladder and looked on the swelling numbers of "new" immigrants as something like an invasive species threatening to overwhelm the "real" America. To be sure, he expressed these common views in uncommon ways, with that characteristic Rooseveltian élan, engaging style, and unquestioning self-assurance. We see much the same themes in his *The Winning of the West*, published not long after his return from the Dakotas: the rightful mastery of Anglo pioneers, the equally proper eclipse of Indian power, the forging of an individualistic American character and ethic through the westering experience.[23] The book's style and vigor are distinctively Roosevelt's own, but the views and attitudes in this book, now likely to make present-day readers wince, are well within the boundaries of his time and his place in it.

That, of course, is not the end of Roosevelt's story. Those early years, when he bought so lovingly into an imagined West, have such an appeal to us because we know what lies ahead. They allow us a fascinating perspective on his life's trajectory over the next thirty years when he returned to the East, reengaged in politics, and moved through that extraordinary succession of events—failures and successes, war and assassination, diplomatic confrontations and maneuvering, and battle after battle—as he matured into the dominant political figure of his age. The theme of that stage of his story is the evolution of his ideas, a widening awareness of modern realities, and the transcendence of the limits of the young master of Elkhorn Ranch.

By the opening of the twentieth century there was a growing public awareness that the expanding power of corporate wealth and influence had brought with it a dangerous imbalance to the nation's politics, its economy, and its social relations. With that came a range of growing and increasingly organized movements to redress that imbalance. Roosevelt as president became the dominant voice in one of those movements, coined the New Nationalism, dedicated to matching and checking the concentration of corporate influence with an expanded regulatory role for the federal government. A special target in his presidency were the railroads, the very institutions that had provided the essential means for ranching as an early model of corporate power. Through legislation like the Elkins and Hepburn acts, he worked to trim back the power and advantages of corporations that earlier legislation had graced with tens of millions of acres of the public domain, much of it across the ranching country that the young Roosevelt had looked upon as the heart-land of individual enterprise.

It is natural to wonder whether President Roosevelt, looking back from the White House, ever experienced at least a slight shock of recognition that in his younger years he had been squarely in the middle of the process producing the very conditions he was now confronting. (Interestingly, he would praise railroad workers for the virtues he had found in the ranching life. Speaking to the Brotherhood of Locomotive Firemen in 1902, he commended them for exercising the "old, old qualities of courage and daring resolution, and unflinching willingness to meet danger." In workers of the rails, he found industrial equivalents of his ranchers and cowboys.)[24]

As for Roosevelt's ideas on race and "real" Americans, we do not have to wonder quite so much. He left some of his thoughts in the archival record.[25] Take, for instance, an exchange of letters between him and his friend Henry Fairfield Osborn. Osborn wrote along the familiar lines of his thinking, in this case lamenting the hopeless situation of Indians, specifically those in Oklahoma. Roosevelt answered that his views had changed: "Sir, in my regiment at Cuba there were fifty men of Indian blood . . . They behaved exactly like the whites, and their careers since then have been exactly like the white men." He went on to say that he had received many delegations from Oklahoma, and that these people were perfectly civilized.[26]

The tone is still patronizing and condescending by our standards, but the opinion is quite a ways from that of a couple of decades earlier.[27] The maturing Roosevelt was moving toward a faith in a common American identity, forged as people of varied racial, ethnic, and cultural origins lived together within the same nation and under the same institutions. To be sure, Roosevelt never surrendered wholly his belief in white superiority, nor his suspicion of immigrants of lineage different from his own. His praise for Grant's *The Passing of the Great Race* as a "capital book" with ideas "our people most need to realize" came in 1916, just three years before his death. Yet the maturing Roosevelt clearly moved toward a greater acceptance of diversity and came to embrace the creation of a unified national community—a point of view in many ways starkly different from that of the younger man. Roosevelt's views here seem closely related to his approach to natural history. In his understanding of evolution, he had been a devotee of the French theorist Jean-Baptiste Lamarck, who argued before Darwin for the inheritance of acquired characteristics. If one of a species changed fundamentally during its lifetime, Lamarck argued, future generations would inherit those changes. Similarly, immigrants who embraced and shared an American experience would forge a common national identity and pass it along to those who followed them.[28] In this there was yet another connection to the West. That American experience, he thought, had worked its greatest transformations on the frontier, that advancing line of Euro-American settlement that in his younger years was playing out in the Dakotas of the Elkhorn Ranch.[29]

In that process and its mechanics, he found a beneficial aspect that is especially striking. When he wrote Osborn of those Indian men who had fought with him in Cuba—who were now all but indistinguishable from the most upright citizenry—"almost all of them [were] of mixt blood."[30] Native peoples, he came to believe, would come to behave "exactly like the white men" in part through intermarriage. In his first annual address as president Roosevelt called for governing marriage practices among American Indians to be identical to those observed among whites; the next year he declared the goal of Indian policy to be their "ultimate absorption into the body of our people."[31]

That was the ultimate nightmare among eugenicists like Osborn and Grant; it lay behind the fear of "race suicide" that was so troubling to the younger Roosevelt when he was calling for families of the correct background to reproduce prolifically, with their own kind, of course, to keep pace in the racial competition. The change in his thinking is striking, and there is further indication of how far he seems to have come.

The familiar term for the making of a unified national people through the mixing of blood and cultures was the "melting pot." Its image is of disparate elements melding through the heat of intermingling and work and ambition into a common alloy. The term was coined as the title of a popular play written by Israel Zangwill and first performed in 1908, the final year of Roosevelt's presidency.[32] The play's central figure, David Quixano, is a Russian Jew whose family had died in a pogrom. He escapes to New York, falls in love with a Christian Russian, Vera, and composes a symphony inspired by his vision of America as a grand meeting ground "where all races and nations come to labour and look forward!" The concept of the melting pot quickly became American vernacular for the belief that immigration and the mixing of peoples was not a prime threat to America but the source of its strength and vitality. The notion could not have been more opposed to the views of some of Roosevelt's friends, views he had earlier found congenial.

A few years after the play opened, Zangwill published it—and dedicated it to a former president: "To Theodore Roosevelt in respectful recognition of his strenuous struggle against the forces that threaten to shipwreck the great republic which carries mankind and its fortunes, this play is, by his kind permission, cordially dedicated."[33] Roosevelt had attended the opening night and recalled: "I do not know when I have seen a play that stirred me as much."[34] When Zangwill wrote later to ask whether the president ever thought about the play, he responded: "Sir, indeed I do." It was a play "that was among the very strong and real influences upon my thought and my life. It expresses the great ideals which are just as essential for the native born as for the foreign born if this nation is to make its rightful contribution to the sum total of human achievement."[35]

When we can pull two books from library shelves, both dedicated to Roosevelt, one by Owen Wister, who wrote elsewhere of the danger of "alien eggs being laid in our American nest," and the other celebrating the nesting of "Celt and Latin, Slav and Teuton, Greek and Syrian" as the source of national greatness, something interesting is going on. We are invited to think of the twin contexts of Roosevelt and his life: that of America and the American West at the time of his sojourn in the 1880s, and that of his path from rancher to president and political force over the next quarter-century.

31. Owen Wister. Author of a novel (*The Virginian*) that was dedicated to TR. Wister wrote of the dangers of immigration and race-mixing. *Little Pilgrimages*, published by L. C. Page and Company, Boston, 1903. Wikimedia Commons.

32. Israel Zangwill. Author of a play (*The Melting Pot*) that was dedicated to TR. Zangwill celebrated both immigration and race-mixing. Library of Congress Prints and Photographs division, LC-USZ62–63569.

The dating of *The Virginian* (1902) and the first performance of *The Melting Pot* (1908) suggest that during his presidential years Theodore Roosevelt came to see the changing face of the nation and the role of immigration in national life in a different and certainly a more nuanced light. The West was no longer simply the refuge of an older, racially unpolluted America but also, and more accurately, a new polyglot reality.[36] Similarly, in his presidential years Roosevelt faced off against centers of corporate power, the "malefactors of great wealth" that had been so well exemplified in the ranching from which he returned to the East revitalized for the extraordinary political course he would take.

To watch Roosevelt in his early years on the Elkhorn Ranch and then to follow him to the White House and beyond is to see the leader evolving as he moved with the nation whose public affairs he would come to dominate as no other figure of his day. In Dakota Roosevelt venerated as a model of individualism a business that in fact was among the earliest examples of the domination of capital and the expanding role of corporations in American life. Then we follow him to his presidency and see him confronting such concentrations of power, in particular the railroads, which more than any other industry was responsible for the rise of corporate ranching. In Roosevelt the rancher we see a champion of a racial order whose opinions jibed with those of leading advocates of eugenics and race warfare. Then we see the maturing Roosevelt rising mostly above such leanings, leaving his youthful flirtations, and embracing a vision of a common national identity made from a global gathering of peoples and cultures. His is quite an American story with plenty to teach us.

As always the maturing Roosevelt was also sensing the popular pulse at a time when America itself was evolving in its attitudes, concerns, and anxieties—he was something of a mirror to the nation. From that perspective Roosevelt's West and Roosevelt himself have at least a few things in common. Both are easily misunderstood and easily underestimated. Both are far too easily given to caricatures. Both are far more complex and nuanced in their natures than we give them credit for. When we begin to understand and appreciate those complexities, then we will have learned something about that new America, and about our own America, which the West and Roosevelt shaped so profoundly.

Notes

1. Theodore Roosevelt, *Ranch Life and Hunting Trail* (Mineola NY: Dover Publications, 2009), 24.

2. Roosevelt, *Ranch Life*, 6.

3. Terry G. Jordan, *North American Cattle-Ranching Frontiers: Origins, Diffusion, and Differentiation* (Albuquerque: University of New Mexico Press, 1993); Ernest Staples Osgood, *The Day of the Cattleman* (Minneapolis: University of Minnesota Press, 1929); Edward Everett Dale, *The Range Cattle Industry: Ranching on the Great Plains from 1865 to 1925* (Norman: University of Oklahoma Press, 1960).

4. Roosevelt, *Ranch Life*, 25.

5. Harmon Ross Mothershead, *The Swan Land and Cattle Company, Ltd.* (Norman: University of Oklahoma Press, 1971); William Martin Pearce, *The Matador Land and Cattle Company* (Norman: University of Oklahoma Press, 1964).

6. Gene M. Gressley, *Bankers and Cattlemen* (Lincoln: University of Nebraska Press, 1966), 109; the amount represented money pledged, not truly invested.

7. Thomas Donaldson, *The Public Domain* (Washington DC: U.S. Government Printing Office, 1884), 350; Richard White, *Railroaded: The Transcontinentals and the Making of Modern America* (New York: W. W. Norton, 2011), 24–25.

8. For a summary of Roosevelt on American Indians, see Thomas G. Dyer, *Theodore Roosevelt and the Idea of Race* (Baton Rouge: Louisiana State University Press, 1980), 69–88.

9. Roosevelt, *Ranch Life*, 107.

10. Hermann Hagedorn, *Roosevelt in the Bad Lands* (New York: Houghton Mifflin, 1921), 355.

11. Herman Hagedorn, ed., *The Works of Theodore Roosevelt, Memorial Edition* (New York: Charles Scribner's Sons, 1924), 8:157.

12. Ari Kelman, *A Misplace Massacre: Struggling over the Memory of Sand Creek* (Cambridge MA: Harvard University Press, 2015).

13. Carol Chin and Hans Krabbendam, "'True Americanism': The Role of Race and Class in Theodore Roosevelt's Immigration Policy and Its Effect on U.S.-European Relations," in eds., *America's Transatlantic Turn: Theodore Roosevelt and the Discovery of Europe*, ed. Hans Krabbendam and John M. Thompson (New York: Palgrave Macmillan, 2012), 65–82.

14. Dyer, *Theodore Roosevelt*, 143–67.

15. Stacy Cordery, *Alice: Alice Roosevelt Longworth, From White House Princess to Washington Power Broker* (New York: Penguin Books, 2007), 77–78.

16. Alexandra Stern, *Eugenic Nation: Faults and Frontiers of Better Breeding in America* (Oakland: University of California Press, 2016); Stephan Kuhl, *The Nazi Connection: Eugenics, American Racism, and German National Socialism* (New York: Oxford University Press, 1994); Paul A. Lombardo, *A Century of Eugenics in America: From the Indiana Experiment to the Human Genome Era* (Bloomington: Indiana University Press, 2010).

17. Madison Grant, *The Passing of the Great Race, Or the Racial Basis of European History* (New York: Charles Scribner's Sons, 1916).

18. Jonathan Peter Spiro, *Defending the Master Race: Conservation, Eugenics, and the Legacy of Madison Grant* (Burlington: University of Vermont Press, 2009), 158.

19. John S. Fisher, *A Builder of the West: The Life of General William Jackson Palmer* (Caldwell ID: Caxton Printers, 1939), 202–3.

20. Anders Breidlid et al., eds., *American Culture: An Anthology of Civilization Texts* (London: Routledge, 1996), 39.

21. Spiro, *Defending the Master Race.*

22. "History of the Bison Herd," Wichita Mountains Wildlife Refuge, https://www.fws.gov/refuge/Wichita_Mountains/wildlife/bison/history.html.

23. Theodore Roosevelt, *The Winning of the West*, 4 vols. (New York: Putnam's, 1889–99).

24. Paul Michel Taillon, "'To Make Men out of Crude Material': Work Culture, Manhood, and Unionism in the Railroad Running Trades, c.1870–1900," in *Boys and Their Toys? Masculinity, Technology, and Class in America*, ed. Roger Horowitz (New York: Routledge, 2001) 33.

25. The Theodore Roosevelt Center at Dickinson State University (ND) is systematically digitizing Roosevelt's writings, correspondence, and other texts: http://www.theodorerooseveltcenter.org/Research/Digital-Library.

26. Elting E. Morison, ed., *The Letters of Theodore Roosevelt* (Cambridge MA: Harvard University Press, 1952), 6:1434–35.

27. On the influence of advocates for Native Americans on Roosevelt during his presidency, see William T. Hagan, *Theodore Roosevelt and Six Friends of the Indians* (Norman: University of Oklahoma Press, 1997).

28. Chin and Krabbendam, "'True Americanism,'" 33–34; Dyer, *Theodore Roosevelt,* 37–44.

29. The theme of the frontier in Roosevelt's thinking is a key point in Leroy G. Dorsey, *We Are All Americans, Pure and Simple: Theodore Roosevelt and the Myth of Americanism* (Tuscaloosa: University of Alabama Press, 2007).

30. Morison, ed., *Letters of Theodore Roosevelt*, 6:1435.

31. Hagedorn, ed., *The Works of Theodore Roosevelt*, 15:130 and 15:163–64.

32. On Zangwill, see Joseph H. Udelson, *Dreamer of the Ghetto: The Life and Works of Israel Zangwill* (Tuscaloosa: University of Alabama Press, 1990).

33. Israel Zangwill, *The Melting-Pot: Drama in Four Acts* (New York: Macmillan, 1916).

34. Morison, ed., *The Letters of Theodore Roosevelt*, 6:1289.

35. Dyer, *Roosevelt,* 131.

36. Two studies in particular stress the dualism of Roosevelt's views on ethnicity and national identity, elaborating on how, as president, he walked a line between his attitudes on racial superiority, expressed from early in his life, and the need for and value of a common American community: Dorsey, *We Are All Americans*, and Gary Gerstle, "Theodore Roosevelt and the Divided Character of American Nationalism," *Journal of American History* 86, no. 3 (December 1999): 1280–1307.

10

Theodore Roosevelt and Conservation
Looking Abroad

IAN TYRRELL

When Theodore Roosevelt left the presidency on March 4, 1909, the event was widely reported around the world. Journalists typically gave their summaries of Roosevelt's two terms and his character. Not all international reports were favorable, of course, but, as at home, TR was almost impossible to ignore. The press coverage was strong in the British Empire, especially Australia and New Zealand, boosted by the practice of republishing items of likely interest from major European and American publications. The spread of wire services enabled readers in many countries to follow Roosevelt's postpresidential exploits. Roosevelt's gift for publicity and manipulating the media did not stop at national boundaries. His overseas visits and tours, especially the trip to Africa and Europe in 1909–10, and the visit to South America in 1913–14, extended his global reputation and reach. Equally important, his specifically international initiatives while president—and just after—served the same purpose. The calling of the North American Conservation Conference for February 1909 was one of the earliest international conferences on the subject. His plans for a World Congress on Conservation likewise revealed the extent, and limits, of his international influence.

It is impossible to state definitively the impact of the press coverage that TR received. On the one hand, it can be argued that local papers in other countries used such material as filler but, on the other, that readers were genuinely interested in the exploits of the American president; otherwise such material would not be persistently included. Certainly there are independent indications of his popularity abroad. When Roosevelt traveled to Europe and South America in the post-presidential years, he was typically greeted by large and enthusiastic audiences. An estimated quarter of a million people cheered him in Buenos Aires in November 1913.[1] Though Roosevelt never made it to Australia or New Zealand, the visit there of the Great White Fleet in 1908 was in some measure a surrogate, since the circumnavigation was widely understood as his pet project—the publicity received and the crowds present were immense.[2] As a result, a New Zealand paper could suggest that TR had ceased being merely a president for the United States, becoming a world leader in a way that no other U.S. president to that time could claim. He was "America's strongman."[3] As the positive assessment of the Great White Fleet indicates, by no means all of the material about him concerned "nature" or "conservation," but much did.

The dissemination of knowledge about Roosevelt can be illustrated through a single but significant example. Published in the prominent *Daily Mail* of London, the article identified Roosevelt as the "man of action."[4] This was a commonplace idea that rested on TR's reputation for vigor and masculinity. But the article in the *Daily Mail* was not commonplace. It was written by an astute person who displayed intimate knowledge of the White House, and it circulated around the globe. The impact was boosted many times over across the British Empire. It was reprinted in the *Times of India*, and picked up in newspapers in Australia and New Zealand. The unsigned piece was written by a Briton watching the Washington scene. Coyly presented not as a regular correspondent but an "occasional" one, the writer was most likely none other than Alfred Harmsworth, the great British newspaper baron, a shrewd observer of the United States and a man who had visited the White House during Roosevelt's presidency and corresponded with the president. He was in the United States in the autumn of 1908 and again in 1909, the period in which the item appeared.

This piece drew upon the idea of TR as the frontiersman par excellence. He was depicted as a force of nature. His other achievements were elaborated in terms of this force and consequently as a breath of fresh air in the world of global as well as Washington politics. Roosevelt had "never lost the whiff of the prairie, the primitive, wholesome ways and instincts of the outdoor life." These frontier circumstances had "coloured his thoughts and actions, his speech and habits." It was not simply that "Mr Roosevelt has kept himself as physically fit as President as he ever was as cowboy," the *Daily Mail* went on. The "distinctive force of the man, his methods of taking and handling things, his whole personality and attitude towards life and affairs, seem to have derived direct from the air and soil of the Western plains." Whether viewed from the White House or from afar, one could not do so "without thinking of the cabins, camp fires, and open, breezy spaces" of western America.[5] This was history as myth, manufactured not in the United States but abroad.

Roosevelt translated this set of character traits into policy, the "occasional correspondent" went on. Under TR's leadership the United States had "in the last decade" been boosted by a "reversion to the robust buoyancies and simplicities of Nature, a harking back to the original sources of life and vigour." Here nature and nation were elided; Roosevelt's personality became equated with the nation itself. This conception was another, more democratic version of *L'état, c'est moi*, projected upon Roosevelt. Roosevelt "planned and originated the great movement for the protection and conservation of the natural resources of the land," proclaimed the *Daily Mail* correspondent. He had "more than embodied the movement" to assert "nature" in his own person; he had been "the first to apply it to the direction of affairs of State." Roosevelt's ideas of nature and nation were reproduced word for word in the *Times of India*, in at least eleven Australian papers, and still others in New Zealand, reinforcing Roosevelt's global image.[6]

Partly the attention to Roosevelt in 1909 reflected the fact that he embarked that year on his celebrated hunting trip to Africa, a highly newsworthy event. Thus, the *West Australian* (Perth) wrote of "Mr Roosevelt's Prowess," telling how five lions had been "bagged" by mid-July, 1909.[7] The hunt stimulated much interest afterward, thanks to

33. Roosevelt's reputation as a hunter preceded him to South America.
The cartoonist shows wildlife fleeing in fear, though in reality it was
Roosevelt who should have been fearful of what he would encounter.
Theodore Roosevelt Birthplace National Historic Site. https://www
.theodorerooseveltcenter.org/Research/Digital-Library
/Record?libID=o284969. Theodore Roosevelt Digital Library.
Dickinson State University.

the publishing juggernaut that reports of the trip became through the serialization and then book publication of *African Game Trails*. It was widely noted in Australia and published in London as well as New York; the *Geelong Advertiser* reviewed it as "Ex-President Roosevelt's Adventures."[8]

International interest was not limited to TR's hunting exploits. There was also widespread discussion of his plans for the conservation of nature through efficient management. The issues of hunting and conservation were intertwined. Roosevelt, for one, had long evidenced this connection since cocreating the Boone and Crockett Club for the control of hunting to prevent, among other things, the extermination of the American bison. The Society for the Preservation of the Wild Fauna of the Empire (SPWFE), established in London in 1903, was partly inspired by protests over the near-extinction of the bison in North America. Because of his outspoken attitude and personal ties to British conservationists, Roosevelt had already won kudos, having been made an honorary vice president of that British society. The *Journal of the Society for the Preservation of the Wild Fauna of the Empire* carried an endorsement from Roosevelt on his "hearty sympathy with all that is being accomplished."[9]

But TR's efforts went beyond conserving animals for gentlemanly hunting or opposing the extinction of the world's megafauna. The role of Roosevelt alongside his able adviser Gifford Pinchot in making Americans aware of the necessary limits of resource exploitation is well told by others.[10] Less well known is the international reception of Roosevelt's efforts. Two of his late presidential and post-presidency initiatives contributed to a global interest in his conservation work. This work was manifest in the North American Conservation Conference and the World Congress on Conservation, which he proposed for The Hague in 1909.

In the waning days of his presidency TR resolved to do what he had begun to plan since mid-1908, and take the conservation crusade to the international stage. For this reason he pushed beyond the National Conservation Commission of 1908, and its inventory of resources, to hold a North American Conservation Conference in February 1909. Though pitched as cooperation with Canada, Newfoundland, and Mexico, the Declaration of Principles asserted a sweeping program framed in "the interest of mankind." It made central the preservation of the world's resources to ensure "the habitability of the earth." The attending nations endorsed water and forest protection, the "public ownership of water rights" for hydroelectric sites, and national control over the disposal of minerals to prevent waste.[11] Naturalist William T. Hornaday addressed the delegates; the declaration included a statement on the importance of saving the world's wildlife through "game protection under regulation," with "extensive game Preserves."[12] International conservation meetings had been held earlier, to be sure. The 1900 meeting of European powers seeking to control hunting in Africa had drafted a treaty to stem the decline of wild creatures. The North American Conference was another of these regional or continental gatherings.

TR proposed to go further and hold the first World Congress on Conservation, issuing invitations via the Department of State before leaving office. The Dutch government agreed to host the congress. The proposal stimulated international interest in and knowledge of Roosevelt's conservation program. These interests differed from country to country. Australian interests were in forestry, irrigation, and mineral development. Argentina, India, and Brazil were interested in irrigation; Mexico in forest protection; South Africa in scientific agriculture. For New Zealand, the country's poor coal supplies made energy of greater significance; the Roosevelt administration's stance in favor of government ownership of waterpower sites and its interest in hydroelectric power as a supplement or alternative to fossil fuels all won New Zealand endorsement. As in so many other cases, Roosevelt's ideas on efficient and statesman-like allocation of resources on a sustainable basis appealed especially to the "white" British dominions. In all nineteen countries quickly agreed to come to the proposed Hague meeting; twenty-three signed up by the end of 1909, leading U.S. State Department officials to conclude that positive action could be taken. Ultimately twenty-nine governments expressed a wish to attend.[13]

William Howard Taft, Roosevelt's handpicked successor, procrastinated. He was perturbed about Roosevelt's action in moving outside the remit of congressional legislation and distracted by growing divisions in his own party over conservation. The plan was scuppered in 1911. When the first international conservation conference assembled in Europe two years later, the meeting was a European effort led by Swiss and German conservationists,[14] though the United States was one of seventeen countries sending delegates. The conference mentioned U.S. efforts to protect wildlife, but expressed reservations about the degree of wildlife protection actually offered in American parks.[15] Though the leadership had been seized by other nations, Pinchot intermittently continued the push for TR's international legacy for decades, lobbying Presidents Wilson, Harding, Hoover, and FDR for international conservation conferences along the lines he and Roosevelt had proposed. President Harry S. Truman finally agreed to hold a trimmed down version of the Roosevelt-Pinchot idea.

It would be fair to say that no foreign country blindly followed the lead of Roosevelt. As indicated at the 1913 "Conférence internationale pour la protection de la nature" in Bern, Switzerland, international conservation was the product of the growing awareness of European nations, not just the United States, of the need for programs and laws to protect "nature," whether in the form of farmland, "wild" land, wildlife, or all of these. Roosevelt's achievements should be put in this broader context. He was part of a global movement that sought to come to grips with the extraordinary transformation that occurred in the late nineteenth and early twentieth centuries with the spread of both imperialism and industrialization—trends that strained resources in many countries.

Just as one can look at Roosevelt's international work in terms of its influence and limits, one can also argue that Roosevelt was influenced by his international engagement, particularly in his post-presidency phase. He was an eager and lifelong learner, and his post-presidential trips reinforced his belief that the mistakes of resource depletion in the economic development of the United States during the nineteenth century should not be repeated across the world.

His trips abroad to Africa, Europe, and South America from 1909 to 1914 strengthened his judgment on international interdependency. He tried to fit these experiences to his understanding of the ways the world worked, and to modify his geopolitics as experience dictated. Roosevelt took many opportunities to impress his views of evolution, biology, conservation, and human nature upon his audiences when he traveled through Africa and Europe in 1909–10. In Berlin, especially, he focused on conservation and what would now be called globalization. This came in his address before Kaiser Wilhelm II on "The World Movement," concerning the interdependence of all civilization and its spread across the world with extraordinary rapidity.[16]

He drew the attention of European rulers to the global need for conservation through the "modern scientific development of natural resources." Some of these resources were non-renewable ones that inevitably entailed destruction, Roosevelt warned. He cautioned against exploitation on a "grand scale" of the world's resources because that would be "purchased at the cost of a speedy exhaustion." Fossil fuels loomed large in his concerns about non-renewable world resources, given the "enormous and constantly increasing output of coal and iron." Presciently he predicted that it would be necessary to "invent or develop new sources for the production of heat and use of energy." Roosevelt discussed renewable resources, because "scientific civilization teaches us how to preserve . . . through use." Through efficiencies and scientific investigation, the "best use of field and forest" would make these assets "decade by decade, century by century, more fruitful." This was his utilitarian conservationist message to the world. Roosevelt also drew attention to these matters in the American colonies of Puerto Rico and the Philippine Islands; he worried during his presidency and after about the future exploitation of the tropical world by imperial powers.[17]

His Berlin message was overtly about conservation; likewise, during his overseas hunting and exploration trips, he referred not just to natural history but to the conservation of resources as well. By studying Roosevelt's accounts of these trips, we learn more, not only about what Roosevelt sought to project upon the world, but also how he shaped and adapted his views. Though his African safari has been extensively studied,[18] his trip to South America in 1913–14 also illustrates the way that he saw nature conservation as fitting into the larger patterns of his thought. This trip provides further evidence for how he viewed the relationship between civilization and nature, between development and conservation.

In the wake of his failed bid for a third term as president in 1912, Theodore embarked on a tour less well remembered than the African safari, the Roosevelt-Rondon Scientific Expedition. Roosevelt's party journeyed to the jungles of Brazil to trace an uncharted river, Rio da Dúvida (the "River of Doubt"). There he came close to death by infection of a wound. His party faced torrential rain, rapids, tropical fever, Amerindian arrows, accidents, and a violent murder within the traveling group. Unable to complete the journey on their own, they had to be met by a relief party. The adventure seems at first glance to fit well into ideas of TR as naturalist and advocate of the strenuous life.[19] Like *African Game Trails*, the focus in *Through the Brazilian Wilderness*, his account of his experience, is on the natural world, though not the collection or hunting of animals.

The book asserts Roosevelt's role in authentic, pioneering exploration of the most arduous kind, deemphasizing the scientific purpose of the trip in gathering specimens of flora and fauna.[20] Time and again he hammered home the point that the trip was an original and intrepid exploration of areas not already tracked by earlier explorers—as if to convince himself as much as others of the importance of his trip and its strenuous and dangerous character, suited to a "man of action." Roosevelt had not prepared himself either physically or psychologically for the trip; its outcome called into question his judgment and his capacity for acting out the manly values he held so high. Drawing attention to the extremities of danger made more plausible his failure to complete the mission's original objectives; it was in Roosevelt's eyes no failure provided he had exerted himself to the limit—that he had played the game, as it were, and not shirked danger.

34. Theodore Roosevelt and Cândido Mariano da Silva Rondon pose with a
recent kill during the Roosevelt-Rondon Scientific Expedition, circa 1913–14.
1958 Theodore Roosevelt Centennial Symposium. Dickinson State University.
https://www.theodorerooseveltcenter.org/Research/Digital-Library
/Record?libID=o274861. Theodore Roosevelt Digital Library.
Dickinson State University.

Yet manly action was not all that Roosevelt undertook in his encounters with the natural world abroad. As shown in *African Game Trails*, neither hunting nor scientific collecting, nor exploration, excluded TR's other interests. Altogether, Roosevelt spent seven and a half months in South America, including getting to and from it, of which only two months were on the River of Doubt. He left New York on October 4, 1913, and returned May 19, 1914. For six weeks, different aspects of nature attracted him. He toured Argentina, Uruguay, southern Brazil, Chile, and Argentina, marveling at the landscape of farms, pampas, and the Andes. He visited San Carlos de Bariloche, on Lake Nahuel Huapi, where the American Bailey Willis had only months before been trying to implement a utilitarian conservation plan for the Argentinian government that drew heavily upon the ideas of Roosevelt and Gifford Pinchot. On his trip, TR also found time to give lectures devoted to "American Internationalism," the "Monroe Doctrine," and "Democratic Ideals."[21]

The tensions in Roosevelt's mind between experiencing the wild and wishing to effect a forward and progressive movement of society can be seen in the two books he wrote covering the South American adventure. *Through the Brazilian Wilderness* deals conventionally with the saga of the Amazon, but it should be read with chapters 4 to 6 of his *A Book-Lover's Holidays in the Open* (1916). The purpose of the first was to record the allegedly unique experience of wilderness, while the other was a more conventional survey of the rest of the trip. Nature features in both—the books are not contradictory but complementary.

While *Through the Brazilian Wilderness* deals primarily with the jungle journey, Roosevelt made clear that the *experience* of discovery could not be recovered; it was a unique and transient encounter. The real point of exploration was to build something that was permanent. The relationship of permanence and nature was of high importance to Roosevelt—as president and after. *Through the Brazilian Wilderness* records the justification of exploration as being to open up new territory for others to settle and develop, as in the American West. Even the areas of Brazil that caused him so much hardship during the trip were ultimately valued as experiences because, in his judgment, exploration led to settlement. Roosevelt inserted sections stating that this wild and dangerous area must be developed as a safety valve for the expanding population of the "overcrowded, overpeopled countries of the Old World." The future of the tropics as a site of immigration as well as rational resource development was an important part of Roosevelt's global conservation agenda; he drew heavily on the contemporary geopolitical significance of the global tropics in the context of imperial rivalries. In this necessity of political economy, "fertile land cannot be permitted to remain idle, to be as a tenantless wilderness."[22] Roosevelt envisaged a time when "the very rapids and waterfalls which now make the navigation of the [Rio da Dúvida] so difficult and dangerous would drive electric trolleys up and down its whole length and far out on either side, and run mills and factories, and lighten the labor on farms. With the incoming of settlement and with the steady growth of knowledge how to fight and control tropical diseases, fear of danger to health would vanish." A tropical land like this was "a hard land for the first explorers, and perhaps for their immediate followers, but not for the people who come after them."[23] However fanciful the prediction seems in retrospect, the trip to South America, like the safari in Africa, was an exploration not of the natural world alone, but of its relationship with culture, and with the necessary development of what he saw as civilization.

Apart from his insistence that the wilderness must inevitably be tamed with the help of modern technology, the agent of the civilizing process that he saw as inevitable and necessary was the "settler." Just as in the United States his political agenda reserved a special place for white settlers as farmers in the western landscapes through irrigation and land law changes, he recommended for Brazil that the land laws should be reformed to give "each of these pioneer settlers the land he actually takes up and cultivates, and upon which he makes his home. The small home-maker, who owns the land which he tills with his own hands, is the greatest element of strength in any country."[24] This program drew upon his idealized memories and experience of the American West. But there is a tension in his thought over the role of settlers, given the importance he attached to economic development of the tropics and subtropics through foreign capital.

TR actually seemed happiest when the landscape approximated not simply the past of the American West, but its future as well. His view of the economic trajectory of the West is clearer in comparative perspective. Roosevelt's visit to the Southern Cone of countries was in part an exercise in comparative colonialism: he wished to revisit the issues of colonial development he had raised in his call for the World Conservation Congress and to show that, to perpetuate prosperity, he still intently believed in the efficient and rationally organized conservation of world resources under American global leadership.

In this impromptu survey of settler colonialism, he made a surprising judgment: Argentina, Chile, Uruguay, and Brazil had "far more to teach than to learn from the English-speaking countries which are so proud of their abounding material prosperity and of their wide-spread, but superficial, popular education and intelligence." In part because of "material prosperity," Argentina was the country he found most closely related to his own experience of the American West, but Brazil, too, was "travelling a similar path, although much more slowly." Despite a climate less satisfactory for white settlement, "its natural resources [were] vaster and . . . in the present century" would "undergo an extraordinary development." Much of southern Brazil he described optimistically as potentially like the pampas of Argentina.[25] In addition to material abundance, the Southern Cone of countries met one important condition for progress—an expanding population. Here Roosevelt invoked a favorite topic: race suicide. Argentinians, especially, were producing good-sized families, he averred, unlike their counterparts in the Anglophone countries: "There are no symptoms of that artificially self-produced dwindling of population which is by far the most threatening symptom in the social life of the United States, Canada, and the Australian commonwealths."[26] From these sources of what Progressive conservationists in the United States called "national vitality," the Southern Cone could produce the settler and smaller-scale agriculture required for the development of its vast resources and land.

Abundantly clear in this book, as with *African Game Trails*, is the mixture of nostalgia for the American frontier and its encounter with nature, on the one hand, and the hope that modernization could incorporate frontier values in a way sustaining economic progress and democracy, on the other. In Brazil Roosevelt praised small-scale settlers, but he also favored capitalist agriculture, provided it was forward-looking and efficient in its use of resources. Though he made favorable comments on the big cattle companies in Latin America, he was happiest when he could resolve this tension through a resort to the example of the American West. The case of Murdo Mackenzie is pertinent. Roosevelt traveled through the "open prairie country" to Morungava, less than fifty kilometers from Porto Allegre, to visit the ranch of the Brazil Land, Cattle, and Packing Company (BLCPC). This was the part of Brazil that most resembled the cattle country of Argentina and the American West. The visit illustrated how he prioritized economic development and conservation. Mackenzie is introduced by TR as "an American"—he was indeed that, having moved to the American West in 1885 from Scotland as a thirty-five-year-old. He was one of "the best-known cattleman in our own Western cow country," Roosevelt announced, and an "old friend of mine."[27] Roosevelt appreciated Murdo not because he was a rancher in Colorado and Texas backed by Scottish capital, but because "he was a leader of the far-seeing and enlightened element. He was a most powerful supporter of the government in the fight for the conservation of our natural resources, for the utilization without waste of our forests and pastures, for honest treatment of everybody, and for the shaping of governmental policy primarily in the interest of the small settler, the home-maker."[28] As founding president of the American Stock Growers Association, he had served on the National Conservation Commission in 1908 at Roosevelt's request. In 1912 Mackenzie left the American West to manage the BLCPC, an enterprise backed by French capital. In Brazil he "acquired and stocked ten million acres of land for his employers." That achievement was the context for Roosevelt's renewal of the friendship.[29] As in the American West, Roosevelt was willing to support business interests where they could further his conservation agenda. Murdo Mackenzie was a reminder of business allies and, at the same time, of TR's fondness for self-made settlers. Mackenzie did not signify to him an American dominance, but the role of Anglo-Saxon stock in global development. The warm response to Mackenzie mirrored his bonding with similar figures in British Kenya such as Leslie Tarlton, the Australian immigrant to Africa with whom he hunted in 1909.[30] For Roosevelt, these were the resourceful white settler colonists of Canada, New Zealand, Australia, and British South and East Africa who, along with Americans, would best guide the worldwide development of civilization without waste of resources by utilizing their strength of personality forged in frontier circumstances.

However, Roosevelt concluded that settlers in the Southern Cone could not, for the most part, be purely white, even in Argentina and certainly not in Brazil. He repeatedly drew attention to racial mixture on his trip, especially during the travail of the River of Doubt. At times his narrative of that journey reveals unease at this mixture, but in the end he accepted that the strenuous life could overcome supposed biological limitations and that the men who went with him on his trip could be judged by the moral and practical standards of the strenuous life. That is to say, he viewed his visit to South America in part as a study of the experiment in racial as well as economic development, recognizing that the white "race" could not demographically dominate in Latin America, especially in its tropical and subtropical zones. Given that conclusion, he believed it necessary for small-scale settlement to be based on racial mixture, just as he noted the mixture of ethnic groups on the American frontier. The question for Roosevelt was not how to preserve the purity of blood lines; rather he advocated an evolutionary adaptation of the race in the struggle for survival that human civilization—as much as "nature"—required.

Conservation was something that Roosevelt always saw as a product of human struggle with and through nature, not as a discrete aspect of life. Every experience, whether in the American West or abroad, was made part of this encounter between nature and civilization. An evolutionary and yet activist and interventionist stance was the prism through which Roosevelt viewed the environmental challenges of his times, in order to speak forcefully about ending waste and promoting a more conservation-oriented economic and social development globally. A globally oriented thinker, Roosevelt naturally looked abroad, just as many people abroad took a particular interest in Roosevelt's conservation initiatives at home.

Notes

1. Kathleen Dalton, *Theodore Roosevelt: A Strenuous Life* (New York: Alfred A. Knopf, 2002), 430; Theodore Roosevelt, "Buenos Aires: A Fine Modern Capital," *Outlook*, March 28, 1914, 696–713.

2. "US 'Great White Fleet' arrives in Auckland, 9 August 1908," New Zealand History, https://nzhistory.govt.nz/the-us-great-white-fleet-arrives-in-auckland; "American Fleet Number: President Roosevelt," *Sydney Mail and New South Wales Advertiser*, August 19, 1908, 475.

3. "America's Strong Man," *Oamaru Mail* (NZ), October 10, 1910.

4. "A Man of Action," *Daily Mail* (London), March 4, 1909, 6. See also the editorial, "A Notable Exit," *Daily Mail* (London), March 4, 1909, 6.

5. "Man of Action," *Star* (Christchurch, NZ), May 3, 1909, 2; Serge Ricard, "A Hero's Welcome: Theodore Roosevelt's Triumphant Tour of Europe in 1910," in *America's Transatlantic Turn: Theodore Roosevelt and the "Discovery" of Europe*, ed. Hans Krabbendam and John M. Thompson (New York: Palgrave Macmillan, 2012), 143–58.

6. "A Man of Action," *Times of India*, March 26, 1909, 7.

7. "Mr. Roosevelt's Progress: Five Lions Bagged," *Kalgoorlie Miner*, July 19, 1909, 3; *Bush Advocate* (NZ), May 7, 1910, 5.

8. *Geelong Advertiser*, November 5, 1910, 8.

9. Theodore Roosevelt, "Extract from Message from the Hon. Theodore Roosevelt, President of the United States," *Journal of the Society for the Preservation of the Wild Fauna of the Empire* 4 (1908): 8.

10. Samuel P. Hays, *Conservation and the Gospel of Efficiency* (Cambridge MA: Harvard University Press, 1959).

11. Treadwell Cleveland Jr., "The North American Conservation Conference," *Conservation* 15 (March 1909): 159–68, at 165, 168 (quotes); "Conservators End Work," *Washington Post*, February 25, 1909, 14.

12. "Saving of America," *Washington Post*, February 19, 1909, 1; Roosevelt to William T. Hornaday, December 29, 1908, series 2, reel 353, Roosevelt Papers, Library of Congress; Cleveland, "North American Conservation Conference," 167, 168 (quotes).

13. "The World's Resources," *Poverty Bay Herald* (Gisborne, NZ), October 21, 1909. For Australia, see especially file A 6661 Governor-General's Office, Correspondence 1172, Proposed International Conference for the Preservation of Natural Resources (at The Hague), Australian Archives, Canberra.

14. Hugo Conwentz, "On National and International Protection of Nature," *Journal of Ecology* 2 (June 1914): 109–22.

15. *Conférence internationale pour la protection de la nature: Recueil de procès-verbaux* (Berne: K. J. Wyss, 1914), 6; "Exposé introductif de M. Paul Sarasin," in *Conférence internationale pour la protection de la nature*, 24–56, 49–51, 58.

16. Theodore Roosevelt, "The World Movement," *Outlook*, May 14, 1910, 63–73; Theodore Roosevelt, *African and European Addresses* (New York: G. P. Putnam's Sons, 1910), 122.

17. Roosevelt, "The World Movement"; Roosevelt, *African and European Addresses*, 122; Ian Tyrrell, *Crisis of the Wasteful Nation: Empire and Conservation in Theodore Roosevelt's America* (Chicago: University of Chicago Press, 2015), chapters 4, 10.

18. Tyrrell, *Crisis of the Wasteful Nation*, chapter 10.

19. On the trip, see Edmund Morris, *Colonel Roosevelt* (New York: Random House, 2010), 313–47; Michael R. Canfield, *Theodore Roosevelt in the Field* (Chicago: University of Chicago Press, 2015), chapter 11; Candice Millard, *The River of Doubt: Theodore Roosevelt's Darkest Journey* (New York: Doubleday, 2005); Patricia O'Toole, *When Trumpets Call: Theodore Roosevelt after the White House* (New York: Simon and Schuster, 2005), 249–57.

20. Canfield, *Theodore Roosevelt in the Field*, 352, 355.

21. E.g., *American Ideals. Speeches of the president of the "Museo social argentino" Dr. Emilio Frers and of Col. Theodore Roosevelt at the banquet given in the Colón theatre, Buenos Aires, November 12, 1913* (n.p., n.d.); John A. Zahm, *Through South America's Southland* (New York: D. Appleton and Co., 1916), 142–44; Theodore Roosevelt, "South America and the Monroe Doctrine," *Outlook*, March 14, 1914, 582–89. Morris, *Colonel Roosevelt*, does not mention the political aspect; Dalton, *Theodore Roosevelt*, 430, gives the trip a page; and Canfield, *Theodore Roosevelt in the Field*, 332, gives it a sentence. For better coverage, see Millard, *River of Doubt*, 65–69; O'Toole, *When Trumpets Call*, 249–51.

22. Theodore Roosevelt, *Through the Brazilian Wilderness* (1914; repr., New York: Charles Scribner's Sons, 1919), 299.

23. Roosevelt, *Through the Brazilian Wilderness*, 299.

24. Roosevelt, *Through the Brazilian Wilderness*, 332.

25. Theodore Roosevelt, *A Book-Lover's Holidays in the Open* (New York: Charles Scribner's Sons, 1916), 107.

26. Roosevelt, *Holidays*, 103.

27. Roosevelt, *Holidays*, 112, 113. For the context, see W. G. Kerr, *Scottish Capital on the American Credit Frontier* (Austin: Texas State Historical Association, 1976).

28. Roosevelt, *Holidays*, 113.

29. Delmar J. Hayter, "MacKenzie, Murdo," *Handbook of Texas Online*, updated June 15, 2010, http://www.tshaonline.org/handbook/online/articles/fmabf.

30. Theodore Roosevelt, *African Game Trails: An Account of the African Wanderings of an American Hunter-Naturalist* (London: John Murray, 1910), 4.

II

Memorializing Theodore Roosevelt

Si Monumentum Requiris, Circumspice

CLAY S. JENKINSON

His legacy can be seen in Devils Tower National Monument and in the Grand Canyon and Crater Lake national parks, which began as Roosevelt-designated national monuments. Roosevelt designated five new national parks and the first eighteen national monuments during his seven years and 171 days as president of the United States. His legacy may be found in 150 million acres of national forest; the splendid National Wildlife Refuge System, which began in a boyish executive order ("I do declare it!") in 1903; the saving of the buffalo from extinction, a cooperative effort by Roosevelt, Grinnell, Hornaday, and others; and the nation's first conservation organization, the Boone and Crockett Club, co-founded by Roosevelt and Grinnell in 1887. But we find his legacy also in the Roosevelt Elk (*Cervus canadensis roosevelti*), named for him by his friend C. Hart Merriam partly in tribute, partly in irony, to "settle" a taxonomical dispute. His legacy is found in Roosevelt schools, Roosevelt highways, Roosevelt forests, Roosevelt mountains, and Theodore Roosevelt National Park, in his beloved North Dakota badlands. Few individuals have left as large a footprint on the American landscape. It all began on lower Broadway in New York, when a fragile, earnest, and intense young naturalist happened upon a dead seal at a grocer's stall. Given all this, the search for a single physical monument to Theodore Roosevelt is less urgent than it would be for any other great president of the United States.

Then there is Roosevelt Island, set within the Potomac River,

35. William Henry Jackson took this photograph of Devils Tower (also known as Bear Lodge Butte) in 1892; President Theodore Roosevelt designated it a national monument in 1906, the first of eighteen he created under the auspices of the Antiquities Act. Library of Congress Prints and Photographs Division.

dedicated to a president of the United States who intended, when he matriculated at Harvard in 1876, to become a professional naturalist; to the individual who among our forty-five presidents spent the most time in nature, particularly in the American West; to the president who wrote a book, one of about forty, called *A Book Lovers Holidays in the Open*; the president who used the District of Columbia—Rock Creek Park, the Potomac shore, the C&O Canal, even the Potomac River itself—as a natural playground (climbing, hiking, scrambling, swimming, horseback riding, and point-to-point with French ambassador Jules Jusserand); the only president who got some of his deepest satisfactions in the American wilderness. These are some of the reasons why H. W. Brands has called TR "the most visibly sporting president in the nation's history."[1]

No American should visit our nation's capital without having an encounter with Theodore Roosevelt. In every poll of professional historians, Roosevelt ranks in the top ten American presidents; in polls of the American people, Roosevelt generally ranks in the top five. He is one of the Rushmore Four—the only one who actually set foot in the state of South Dakota—and he is without question one of the most consequential presidents in American history, in many respects the inventor of the modern presidency as we know it.

The question that has been asked repeatedly in the century since Roosevelt's death, and even during his hectic, often heroic life, is what constitutes a fitting and proportionally appropriate monument or memorial to a man of Roosevelt's dynamism, ambition, consequence, and achievement. It should not surprise us that Roosevelt had thoughts about this question, though just what those thoughts were may indeed surprise you.

When Theodore Roosevelt died on Monday January 6, 1919, President Woodrow Wilson issued a proclamation from Paris, directing government offices to fly flags at half-mast for a month. Both houses of Congress adjourned; for the first time in its history, the United States Supreme Court adjourned without doing any legal business. Army, marine, and naval posts around the world were directed to fire salutes at sunrise on the day of Roosevelt's obsequies. Secretary of War Newton D. Baker offered to send a full military honor guard to Oyster Bay for the funeral. The Roosevelt family declined. The family chose to bury "the old Lion," as Archie called him, in a modest private ceremony at Youngs Memorial Cemetery on Long Island. Only 350 seats would be available.

To those who pushed for something bigger, Archie wrote: "It was my father's wish that he would be buried among the people of Oyster Bay, and that the funeral service would be conducted entirely by those friends among whom he had lived so long and happily."[2] TR's biographer Edmund Morris says, "The service was almost cruelly short and Spartan."[3]

The modesty of Roosevelt's funeral feels a little odd and anticlimactic, given the place of Roosevelt in American life. Roosevelt was the best loved, best known American of his time, and he was almost certainly the most famous person in the world. In view of Roosevelt's outsized personality—one visitor said: "You go to the White House, you shake hands with Roosevelt and hear him talk—and then go home to wring the personality out of your clothes"[4]—we might have expected Roosevelt to have one of the grandest presidential funerals in American history. His inauguration in 1905 was spectacular: the inaugural parade appeared more like a Roman triumph of Pompey or Julius Caesar than anything the American people had experienced before. Cowboys, Indians, coal miners, soldiers, Civil War veterans, and of course Rough Riders paraded past the triumphant president. Just as Caesar in his triumph had Vercingetorix march through the streets of Rome following the Gallic Wars, so Roosevelt watched the leaders of vanquished Indian tribes pass before his viewing stand: Quanah Parker of the Comanche, Buckskin Charlie of the Ute, Hollow Horn Bear and American Horse of the Sioux, Little Plume of the Blackfeet, and the notorious Apache warrior Geronimo, who had been defeated for the last time in 1886 by Roosevelt's friend Leonard Wood.

We know that Roosevelt thought more about his legacy than perhaps he was willing to acknowledge. He wrote more than 150,000 letters in his lifetime, from short, delightfully illustrated letters to his children to detailed policy memos of a dozen or twenty pages. In August 1903 he wrote a ten-thousand-word narrative to his secretary of state John Hay that had nothing to do with foreign policy. TR wrote the massive letter to tell stories about his fourteen-thousand-mile, twenty-five-state train trip through the American heartland, with two weeks in Yellowstone National Park, his first encounter with the Grand Canyon and California's great redwood trees, his three-day camping trip with John Muir in Yosemite National Park, and a return to the Dakota badlands, where the romance of his life began. Members of TR's family could instantly discern when he was writing through them to speak to his future place in American history. They called these Theodore's "posterity letters." Nor did TR lack confidence in his status as America's most consequential individual. When he was wrestling with the idea of running again for president in 1916, he wrote a friend, "It would be a mistake to nominate me unless the country has in its mood something of the heroic."[5] That sounds more like our Roosevelt.

Theodore Roosevelt spent a quarter of his life in Washington DC. Six years as U.S. civil service commissioner, a year as the assistant secretary of the U.S. Navy, six months as vice president, and seven years and 171 days as the twenty-sixth president of the United States. That's fifteen years altogether, not to mention all the time he spent thinking about being president before and after his two terms in that office.

Roosevelt was not particularly in favor of statues being erected in his honor; after his death, his family was lukewarm, sometimes outright negative, about commemorative statues. When North Dakota governor Louis B. Hanna wrote to Roosevelt in 1910 to inform him that grateful North Dakotans were raising funds to erect a statue in his honor, TR announced his "firm belief that no man should ever have a statue until he has been dead some little time."[6] Roosevelt insisted that a statue of a hardy pioneer or pioneer family, perhaps a cowboy, would be much more appropriate, a greater tribute to the frontier dynamics that brought North Dakota into the union in 1889.

Roosevelt had strong and surprisingly humble convictions about his place in history. In a letter about history and fame written in 1906, Roosevelt wrote:

> I am not in the least concerned as to whether I will have any place in history, and, indeed, I do not remember ever thinking about it.... I want to be a straight and decent man and do good service... While I live it will be a great satisfaction if I can feel this, and I should like my descendants to know it; and I should like to feel that those who know me and care for me, and whom I value, will also feel it. But aside from this it does not seem to me that after a man is dead it matters very much whether it is a little longer or a little shorter before the inevitable oblivion, steadily flooding the sands of time, effaces the scratches on the sand which we call history. As the ages roll by in the life of this globe, small indeed does the difference seem between the few weeks' remembrance of the average hard-working, clean-living citizen, and the few years, or few hundreds of years, or few thousands of years, before the memory of the mighty fades into the dim gray of time and then vanishes into the blackness of eternity.[7]

This could only have been written by a man who practiced the active and the contemplative life. Roosevelt, perhaps the intellectually best prepared individual who ever served as president of the United States—and that includes Thomas Jefferson and John Adams—had read (and written) enough history to know that most individuals, even temporarily important ones, are swallowed up by time and oblivion. Roosevelt was a Darwinian. He had a realistic, at times pessimistic, view of how long any man's memory lingered after he left the arena. "Nature," he wrote, is "ruthless, and where her sway is uncontested there is no peace save the peace of death; and the fecund stream of life, especially of life on the lower levels, flows like an immense torrent out of non-existence for but the briefest moment before the enormous majority of the beings composing it are engulfed in the jaws of death, and again go out into the shadow."[8]

When John Hay died in office as Roosevelt's secretary of state in July 1905, the president wrote to his friend Cecil Spring-Rice, "It is a good thing to die in the harness at the zenith of one's fame, with the consciousness of having lived a long, honorable, and useful life. After we are dead, it will make not the slightest difference whether men speak well or ill of us. But in the days and hours before dying it must be pleasant to feel that you have done your part as a man and have not yet been thrown aside as useless, and that your children and children's children, in short all those that are dearest to you, have just cause for pride in your actions."[9]

He was constantly explaining in letters to his children and his friends that even he could not hold the public's attention very long, not even in his own lifetime; that electors and whole populations move on quickly and capriciously to the next strong leader or the next wave of social ideas. When TR wrote that "the average, hardworking citizen" can expect to be remembered after his death only a few weeks or years, before adding, for public figures like himself, perhaps a few hundred years, and then, perhaps dreaming hopefully about his own place in history, possibly even a few thousand years, we are offered an insightful, earnest, and slightly comic glimpse into the soul of the great but ultimately realistic man. This letter was written by a man who had read Shelley's "Ozymandias":

> My name is Ozymandias, King of Kings;
> Look on my Works, ye Mighty, and despair!
> Nothing beside remains. Round the decay
> Of that colossal Wreck, boundless and bare
> The lone and level sands stretch far away.

In a December 1904 letter to Oliver Wendell Holmes, Roosevelt wrote: "What does the fact amount to that here and there a man escapes oblivion longer than his fellows? Ozymandias in the Desert— when a like interval has gone by who will know more of any man of the present day than Shelley knew of him?" This is a slight misreading of Shelley's sonnet, but it nevertheless illustrates how deeply Roosevelt's understanding of history, memory, and oblivion was grounded in his incessant reading, including of English poetry. In his letter to Holmes, TR also observed: "It makes small odds to any of us after we are dead whether the next generation forgets us, or whether a number of generations pass before our memory, steadily growing more and more dim, at last fades into nothing. On this point it seems to me that the only important thing is to be able to feel, when our time comes to go out into the blackness, that those survivors who care for us and to whom it will be pleasure to think well of us when we are gone, shall have that pleasure."[10]

Roosevelt's fullest pronouncement about the best way to memorialize great ones came on May 18, 1916, in a letter to Dr. H. Holbrook Curtis, a voice therapist and ear, nose, and throat physician whose ideas about monuments and philanthropy were similar to his own:

> I wish to back you as strongly as I know how in your effort to build a hospital as a protest against the erection of meaningless mausoleums and monuments to the dead. There is an occasional great public servant to whom it is well to raise a monument; really not for the man himself, but for what he typified. A monument to Lincoln or Farragut is really a great symbolic statue to commemorate such qualities as valor and patriotism and love of mankind, and a willingness to sacrifice everything for the right. There are very very few men in a generation who have the character or widespread reputation which makes a monument to them symbolize all these things. As for the rest of us, with failures and shortcomings, but according to our lights, have striven to lead decent lives, if any friends of ours wish to commemorate us after death the way to do it is by some expression of good deeds to those who are still living. Surely a dead man or woman, who is a good man or woman, would wish to feel that his or her taking away had become an occasion for real service for the betterment of mankind, rather than to feel that a meaningless pile of stone, no matter how beautiful, had been erected with his or her name upon it in an enclosure crowded with similar piles of stone—for such a tomb or mausoleum often bears chief reference not to the worth, but to the wealth of the one who is dead.[11]

Roosevelt's modest, sometimes stark attitude about death, history, and memory is also seen in his insistence that members of his family be buried where they died, even if those deaths occurred far from the family compound on Long Island. Thus Quentin was buried in France where his plane was shot down in July 1918. Almost the first thing Edith Roosevelt did after TR died was go to France to visit the grave of her youngest son. Kermit Roosevelt was buried in Alaska, where he died in 1943. Ted, too, was buried where he fell. On July 12, 1944, while serving as military governor of Cherbourg, he died of a heart attack. He was fifty-six years old. He was buried at Normandy. After the war, his Edith had Quentin's body moved to the same cemetery to lie near his brother's grave. Had TR been permitted to lead a second group of Rough Riders to France in 1917–18, he might well be the only U.S. president buried on foreign soil.

I am not suggesting that Roosevelt would be opposed to Roosevelt Island or any of the other public memorials that have been fashioned to commemorate his life and achievement. What I am attempting to illustrate is that, however counter to the usual Roosevelt mythology it might seem, TR was less interested in achieving lasting fame for himself than for the things he did for American civilization. Here's an example. Roosevelt traveled to Arizona Territory for the dedication of Roosevelt Dam on the Salt River in 1911, two years after he left the presidency. The Salt River project was one of the first fruits of the Newlands Reclamation Act, signed by Roosevelt in the summer of 1902. At the dedication ceremony, on March 18, 1911, Roosevelt declared that the two greatest achievements of his presidency were the passing of the Reclamation Act and the authorization and construction of the Panama Canal. To the assemblage of a thousand citizens who gathered at the top of the dam, then the largest in the world, Roosevelt said: "If there could be any monument which would appeal to any man, surely this is it. You could not have done anything which would have pleased and touched me more than to name this great dam, this reservoir site, after me. And I thank you, from my heart, for having done so."[12]

The unmistakable sense one gets from reading Roosevelt on this subject is that he wanted his historical memory to be tied to civic, even civilizational achievement, and that the giant cyclopean dam in the Arizona desert—named in his honor for his vision, his Americanism, his legislative mastery, and his love of the American West—appealed to him as the right way to pay tribute to his life and work.

Even if Roosevelt had wholeheartedly supported the idea of a grand monument in his honor, it would be hard to know quite how to reduce his hyperactive, hyperkinetic life to a thing of water, concrete, and bronze. When the Roosevelt Memorial Association began planning a District of Columbia monument to TR in the years following his death, Hermann Hagedorn, Elihu Root, and others struggled to determine what would capture the essence of a man of such wide, varied, and outsized achievement. The fundamental paradox was that they would be creating an immobile monument to a man whose life was synonymous with action. Roosevelt said he felt only "horror of words that are not translated into deeds, of speech that does not result in action."[13] Gamaliel Bradford said "he killed mosquitoes as if they were lions, and lions as if they were mosquitoes."[14] When Roosevelt died in his sleep, Vice President Thomas Marshall declared: "Death had to take him sleeping, for if Roosevelt had been awake there would have been a fight."[15] TR cartoons frequently depict him outdistancing, outlasting, and exhausting everyone around him, and doing more before breakfast than most others do in a day or a week. The historian and medievalist Henry Adams perhaps said it best: "Roosevelt, more than any other man living within the range of notoriety, showed the singular primitive quality that belongs to ultimate matter—the quality that mediaeval theology assigned to God—he was pure Act."[16]

In the course of his life Roosevelt ran many variations on his "man in the arena speech." In 1894 he wrote, "It is the doer of deeds who actually counts in the battle for life, and not the man who looks on and says how the fight ought to be fought, without himself sharing the stress and the danger."[17] The list of his deeds is virtually endless. Roosevelt climbed the Matterhorn on his honeymoon. Out west, in 1886, Roosevelt, without daring to doze off for a single moment, marched Red Headed Mike Finnegan and the two other boat thieves more than forty miles in three days over gumbo mud in freezing temperatures to the sheriff in Dickinson, Dakota Territory. The local doctor who attended to his blistered feet said he was covered with mud from head to toe, but as happy as a boy and "all teeth and eyes." On a vice presidential visit to Colorado in 1901, TR waded into a circle of snarling, slathering dogs and killed a mountain lion with a Bowie knife. Afterward he wrote a cheerful letter about it to his children. On January 13, 1909, President Roosevelt undertook a 104-mile horseback ride to Warrington, Virginia, and back, to counter criticism that he was demanding too much strenuosity of the men in America's armed services. It was cold, icy, and the visibility was increasingly poor. The only provision carried by the riding party was a flask of cold tea brought by TR's aide-de-camp Archie Butt. On another occasion he had himself lowered on a rope over a remote waterfall in Idaho so that he could take a photograph and, when his companions were unable to haul him back up, he eventually cut the rope and plummeted into the river below. Even TR said he was grievously hurt in the incident.

The question is, how capture such a mighty spirit in bronze? The problem with a statue is that it is static. It freezes its subject in time. However much it attempts to get at the deeper essence of the individual, it has to lock him into a certain moment of his life. But how do you lock up Theodore Roosevelt, who was at once cowboy, rancher, soldier, big-game hunter, explorer, man of letters, family patriarch, politician, progressive reformer, perennial youth, and—oh yes—the twenty-sixth president of the United States? Which hat does he wear—that of New York state assemblyman, civil service commissioner, New York City police commissioner, lieutenant colonel of the 1st U.S. Volunteer Cavalry, governor of New York, vice president, or president of the United States?

Perhaps TR's antipathy to statues was based on their inability to move, to act, to fight, climb, shoot, and gesticulate. A Roosevelt statue would require animatronics to begin to get close to his dynamism.

There are those who believe that Roosevelt deserved a more prominent location in the District of Columbia for his monument. Not long after his death the possibility arose that TR's monument would be built in the Tidal Basin, the last major remaining space

36. Cartoonist Jay Ding Darling created this elegiac cartoon following news of Theodore Roosevelt's death on January 6, 1919. 1958 Theodore Roosevelt Centennial Symposium. Dickinson State University. https://www .theodorerooseveltcenter.org/Research/Digital-Library/Record?libID= 0274873. Theodore Roosevelt Digital Library. Dickinson State University.

in Pierre Charles L'Enfant's axis: the Capitol, the White House, the site of the Lincoln Memorial, and the Tidal Basin. That plan miscarried for a range of reasons. Perhaps the principal reason was that it was then too soon to designate so important a piece of District real estate for a president so recently deceased. It failed to meet the "some little time" criterion that TR noted in his letter to North Dakota's Louis Hanna. The Tidal Basin would have been a superb site for a TR memorial. And there is a kind of strange irony in that one of the factors that scotched the Tidal Basin memorial was the death of Woodrow Wilson in 1921—public memory of the tension between these two mighty titans was still fresh, and political scars, some dating back to the Bull Moose apostasy in 1912, still ran pretty deep. It is perhaps even more ironic that the Tidal Basin eventually became the site of the Jefferson Memorial, devoted to the memory of one of Roosevelt's least favorite presidents, a man TR believed tended to slip away from the arena whenever the going got tough.

After exhausting other options, the Roosevelt Memorial Association purchased an island in the Potomac near the Lincoln Memorial in 1931. The Depression and World War II prevented the development of a suitable memorial. It was not until 1967 that Eric Gugler and Paul Manship's monument was completed. By then TR had been dead for forty-eight years. Although the Roosevelt Island Memorial has many admirers and defenders, most visitors come away with the sense that TR's national memorial is a poor relation to other monuments in the District of Columbia, including the one to his fifth cousin Franklin.

Roosevelt may not have one central, uncontested, world-class memorial in the nation's capital or anywhere else, but he has been really well served by monuments and memorials throughout the United States. It is fair to say that Roosevelt is the best memorialized president in American history, and that includes FDR, Lincoln, and Thomas Jefferson. The list of what might be called Roosevelt shrines in America is very long and very impressive. It includes the Theodore Roosevelt Island Memorial; his home at Sagamore Hill on Long Island, which ranks with Mount Vernon and Monticello as one of the handful of truly extraordinary presidential home sites; TR's birthplace on East 20th Street in New York City; the Theodore Roosevelt Inaugural National Historic Site in Buffalo; the rural retreat Edith found for them at Pine Knot in Virginia; Mount Rushmore in the Black Hills of South Dakota; Theodore Roosevelt National Park in the Little Missouri River badlands of North Dakota, the only national park named for an American president, and which the *New York Times* listed as one of the year's top five destinations in the United States; the Nimitz-class aircraft carrier, the uss *Theodore Roosevelt*, launched during the Reagan administration in 1984; the Panama Canal, one of the greatest engineering feats of the twentieth century, indeed in world history; TR's Maltese Cross Cabin in Medora, North Dakota; the greater Elkhorn Ranch site thirty-five miles north of Medora, North Dakota, preserved in the last decade thanks to the work of a number of organizations and individuals, including Lowell Baier, who called the Elkhorn Ranch "the cradle of American conservation"; the Mount Theodore Roosevelt Monument at Deadwood, South Dakota, created by TR friend and admirer Seth Bullock; the Theodore Roosevelt Dam on the Salt River in Arizona, which enabled the phenomenal growth of Phoenix, Scottsdale, and Tempe in a place that was a desert territory before the presidency of Theodore Roosevelt; and the forthcoming Theodore Roosevelt National Presidential Library in western North Dakota.

The fact that there are so many outstanding monuments and memorials to Roosevelt in so many zip codes takes a little of the pressure off of the Potomac River island sanctuary. There is a larger memorial still: the 230 million acres of the public domain that, as president, TR set aside for permanent conservation purposes. Any time you visit his five national parks, eighteen national monuments, fifty-one national wildlife refuges, four national game preserves, twenty-four national reclamation projects, or one hundred and fifty national forests, you are encountering a monument to the greatest conservationist in American history. When you visit America's first national park, Yellowstone, created by an act of Congress in 1872, when TR was only thirteen years old, you enter a conservation sanctuary saved by the Boone and Crockett Club from poaching, railroad and industrial development, mining, and the threat of being turned into an exclusive playground for the rich and privileged. Theodore Roosevelt, George Bird Grinnell, John Lacey, William Hornaday, and their conservationist friends not only saved Yellowstone National Park, but they forged the ethos that came to characterize the mission of the entire National Park System, subsequently embodied in its Organic Act of 1916.

My point is that Theodore Roosevelt's monumental footprint can be found in nearly every state in America and that, while some of it is appropriately visible, as at Theodore Roosevelt Island, still more is quietly enshrined in the U.S. Navy, in the National Park Service, in the modern identity of the American presidency, and in countless landscapes, parks, and forests across the western hemisphere. No other president has such a legacy. No other president even comes close.

After the Great Fire of London in 1666, the architect Christopher Wren helped to rebuild the city. He designed and built fifty-one parish churches (most of which are still standing) and topped it off with his magnum opus, St. Paul's Cathedral, one of the world's greatest buildings. It took thirty-five years to complete. When Wren died in 1723 he was entombed in the center of the cathedral directly below the apex of the dome. His son saw to it that his father's crypt was circumscribed with the Latin inscription: *Si Monumentum Requiris, Circumspice.* If you are looking for his monument, just look around you. So, too, if you want to see Theodore Roosevelt's monument, just look around you. Perhaps it will come when horseback riding in Theodore Roosevelt National Park, scrambling among the shattered rock pillars at the base of Devil's Tower, or hiking down to Phantom Ranch in the Grand Canyon. Or at Rock Creek Park or Roosevelt Island in the nation's capital. President Lyndon Johnson recognized the latter site's significance when at its dedication ceremony he declared that if "Theodore Roosevelt had wanted any memorial at all, he would have wanted it here—in this wild little island in the center of a historic river—where his statue is sheltered in the trees."[18]

Notes

1. H. W. Brands, *T.R.: The Last Romantic* (New York: Basic Books, 1997). I want to thank Melanie Choukas-Bradley for leading me on a nature tour of Theodore Roosevelt Island, and for teaching me to see the island as a nature sanctuary. See her chapter in this volume, drawn from her forthcoming book, *A Year at Theodore Roosevelt Island*.

2. Edmund Morris, *Colonel Roosevelt* (New York: Random House, 2010), 554.

3. Morris, *Colonel Roosevelt*, 557.

4. Edward Wagenknecht, *The Seven Worlds of Theodore Roosevelt* (New York: Longmans, Green & Co., 1958), 108.

5. Theodore Roosevelt in a statement given to the press in Port of Spain, Trinidad, March 9, 1916 (this statement appeared in numerous newspapers, including the *New York Times*, March 10, 1916).

6. Letter from Theodore Roosevelt to Louis B. Hanna, May 6, 1910, Theodore Roosevelt Papers, Library of Congress Manuscript Division, https://www.theodorerooseveltcenter .org/Research/Digital-Library/Record?libID=o214322, Theodore Roosevelt Digital Library, Dickinson State University.

7. Letter from Theodore Roosevelt to William Allen White, November 28, 1906, Theodore Roosevelt Papers, Library of Congress Manuscript Division, https://www .theodorerooseveltcenter.org/Research/Digital-Library/Record?libID=o197384, Theodore Roosevelt Digital Library, Dickinson State University.

8. Theodore Roosevelt, *A Book-Lover's Holidays in the Open* (New York: Charles Scribner's Sons, 1919), 288.

9. Letter from Theodore Roosevelt to Cecil Spring Rice, July 24, 1905, Theodore Roosevelt Papers, Library of Congress Manuscript Division, https://www.theodorerooseveltcenter .org/Research/Digital-Library/Record?libID=o192242, Theodore Roosevelt Digital Library, Dickinson State University.

10. Letter from Theodore Roosevelt to Oliver Wendell Holmes, December 5, 1904, Theodore Roosevelt Papers, Library of Congress Manuscript Division, https://www .theodorerooseveltcenter.org/Research/Digital-Library/Record?libID=o190325, Theodore Roosevelt Digital Library, Dickinson State University.

11. Letter from Theodore Roosevelt to H. Holbrook Curtis, May 18, 1916, Theodore Roosevelt Papers, Library of Congress Manuscript Division, https://www .theodorerooseveltcenter.org/Research/Digital-Library/Record?libID=o290388, Theodore Roosevelt Digital Library, Dickinson State University.

12. Speech at Roosevelt, Arizona (dedication of Roosevelt Dam), March 18, 1911, Theodore Roosevelt Papers, Library of Congress Manuscript Division, https://www .theodorerooseveltcenter.org/Research/Digital-Library/Record?libID=o269233, Theodore Roosevelt Digital Library, Dickinson State University.

13. Theodore Roosevelt, *Autobiography* (New York: Macmillan, 1913), 187.

14. Gamaliel Bradford, *The Quick and the Dead* (New York: Houghton Mifflin Company, 1931), 24. Bradford's quip is a clever retelling of an account of Roosevelt killing a mosquito that John Burroughs related in *Under the Maples* (New York: Houghton Mifflin, 1921), 106.

15. William Roscoe Thayer, *Theodore Roosevelt: An Intimate Biography* (New York: Houghton Mifflin Company 1919), 450.

16. Henry Adams and Henry Cabot Lodge, *The Education of Henry Adams: An Autobiography* (Boston: Houghton Mifflin Company 1918), 417.

17. Theodore Roosevelt, "The College Graduate and Public Life," *Atlantic Monthly*, August 1894; reprinted in Theodore Roosevelt, *American Ideals and Other Essays, Social and Political* (New York: Charles Scribner's Sons, 1906), 55.

18. Lyndon Johnson, "Remarks on the Dedication of the Theodore Roosevelt Memorial in Washington," October 27, 1967, http://www.presidency.ucsb.edu/ws/index.php?pid=28506.

Contributors

Thomas C. Bailey is Emeritus Professor of English Literature and Environmental Studies at Western Michigan University. With Katherine Joslin, he is the author of *Theodore Roosevelt: A Literary Life*.

Melanie Choukas-Bradley is the author of several natural history books, including *City of Trees* and *A Year in Rock Creek Park*, winner of a 2015 IPPY award. She is currently working on her fifth book, *A Year at Theodore Roosevelt Island*.

Clay S. Jenkinson is the Theodore Roosevelt Humanities Scholar at Bismarck State College and the Theodore Roosevelt Center, and author of *Theodore Roosevelt in the Badlands: A Historical Guide* and *The Character of Meriwether Lewis*, among other books.

Katherine Joslin is a professor of American literature and culture at Western Michigan University. Her books include *Jane Addams, A Writer's Life* and *Edith Wharton and the Making of Fashion*. With Thomas Bailey, she is the author of *Theodore Roosevelt: A Literary Life*.

Duane G. Jundt taught American and European history for twenty years, most recently at Northwestern College in Iowa. He has authored numerous articles, review essays, and papers on Roosevelt and currently serves on the advisory board of the Theodore Roosevelt Association.

Darrin Lunde, a Supervisory Museum Specialist in the Division of Mammals at the Smithsonian's National Museum of Natural History, is author of *The Naturalist: Theodore Roosevelt, A Lifetime of Exploration* and the *Triumph of American Natural History*.

Char Miller is the W. M. Keck Professor of Environmental Analysis and History at Pomona College. His recent books include *America's Great National Forests, Wildernesses, and Grasslands, Seeking the Greatest Good: The Conservation Legacy of Gifford Pinchot*, and *Gifford Pinchot: Selected Writings*.

John F. Reiger, Professor Emeritus at Ohio University, is author of *American Sportsmen and the Origins of Conservation, Escaping Into Nature: The Making of a Sportsman-Conservationist and Environmental Historian*, and editor of *The Passing of the Great West: Selected Papers of George Bird Grinnell*.

Barb Rosenstock is the author of narrative nonfiction and historical fiction picture books for children, including *The Camping Trip that Changed America: Theodore Roosevelt, John Muir, and Our National Parks*, winner of the California Library Association's Beatty Award.

Ian Tyrrell is Emeritus Professor of History at the University of New South Wales. Among his many books are *Transnational Nation: United States History in Global Perspective since 1789* and *Crisis of the Wasteful Nation: Empire and Conservation in Theodore Roosevelt's America*.

Elliott West, Alumni Distinguished Professor of History at the University of Arkansas, is author of *The Way to the West: Essays on the Central Plains, The Contested Plains: Indians, Goldseekers and the Rush to Colorado*, and *The Essential West: Collected Essays*.

Index

CPSIA information can be obtained
at www.ICGtesting.com
Printed in the USA
LVHW030916130320
649972LV00002B/260